Bobbie, G

A Novel

Olive Higgins Prouty

Alpha Editions

This edition published in 2021

ISBN : 9789355341204

Design and Setting By
Alpha Editions
www.alphaedis.com
Email - info@alphaedis.com

As per information held with us this book is in Public Domain.
This book is a reproduction of an important historical work. Alpha Editions uses the best technology to reproduce historical work in the same manner it was first published to preserve its original nature. Any marks or number seen are left intentionally to preserve its true form.

Contents

CHAPTER I	- 1 -
CHAPTER II	- 6 -
CHAPTER III	- 14 -
CHAPTER IV	- 21 -
CHAPTER V	- 29 -
CHAPTER VI	- 38 -
CHAPTER VII	- 49 -
CHAPTER VIII	- 57 -
CHAPTER IX	- 65 -
CHAPTER X	- 75 -
CHAPTER XI	- 82 -
CHAPTER XII	- 92 -
CHAPTER XIII	- 98 -
CHAPTER XIV	- 107 -
CHAPTER XV	- 115 -
CHAPTER XVI	- 121 -
CHAPTER XVII	- 129 -
CHAPTER XVIII	- 140 -
CHAPTER XIX	- 149 -

CHAPTER XX	- 158 -
CHAPTER XXI	- 168 -
CHAPTER XXII	- 176 -
CHAPTER XXIII	- 186 -
CHAPTER XXIV	- 196 -
CHAPTER XXV	- 207 -

CHAPTER I

I AM a junior in the H.C.H.S., which stands for Hilton Classical High School, and am sixteen years old. I live in a big brown house at number 240 Main Street, and my father is a state senator in Boston. I am a member of the First Congregational Church, which I joined when I was thirteen, and am captain of the basket-ball team at the high school. I have travelled as far east as Revere Beach, as far west as the Hoosac Tunnel, on my way to Aunt Ella's funeral in Adams, and as far south as New London, Connecticut, where I watched my oldest brother Tom row in a perfectly stunning eight-oared boat-race on the Thames. I haven't been north at all. I have had six diseases, including scarlet fever and typhoid, with which I almost died last year, and as a result of which am now wearing my hair as short as a child with a Dutch-cut.

I am not pretty, nor a bit popular with the boys. I can't play the piano, and I never went to dancing-school in my life. Most of my clothes are as ugly as mud, for I haven't any mother; and my hair has always been as straight as a stick. They say that the kink that has appeared in it since the typhoid won't last but a little while, so it isn't much comfort. In fact, the only real consolation that I have is a secret conviction which I keep well concealed in the innermost compartment of my heart. No one knows of its existence except myself, and I wouldn't be the one to tell of it for anything in the world. It is on account of it, however, that I am writing the experiences of my early life. I often think how valuable it would have been if William Shakespeare had told us about his school-days or Julius Caesar had described his family and what they used to do when he was a boy of fifteen. Of course I may not be a genius; but facts point that way. I hate mathematics, my imagination is vivid, my life is difficult and full of obstacles, and my handwriting illegible. My Themes are generally read out loud in English, and my quarterly deportment mark is frightfully low. Moreover, if I am not a genius I shall be awfully disappointed. Why, I think I should rather be a genius than to go to a College Prom. It makes everything so bearable, from a flunk in geometry, to not being invited to Bessie Jaynes' birthday-party last week.

My life has not been an easy one. Ever since I can remember I have been the mother of five children—two of them older and three younger than myself. They all call me Bobbie for short, but my real name is Lucy Chenery Vars.

Our house is a big ugly brown affair which Father built when we were all babies and the business was prosperous. The house has twenty rooms in it, and on the top an octagon cupola, which I have fixed up with a fish-net and some old tennis rackets, and call my study. I have a plaster cast of a skull up here, and a "No Trespassing" sign which Juliet Adams and I stole out of old Silas Morton's blueberry-pasture. It looks exactly like a college man's room now and I intend to do all my writing up here. It is a perfectly lovely place for inspirations! From my eight little windows I can see all over New England, and at night every star that shines. It is simply glorious up here in a thunder-storm, and when I have the trap-door once closed behind me, with all my cares and troubles shut safely away down below, I feel as if I could fly with the birds. I ought to write something wonderful.

In the first place I had better state that I haven't anything distinguishing about me except my experience. I am middling tall—five feet five inches, to be precise; middling heavy—112 pounds; and am one of six children—four boys and two girls—without the honour of being either the oldest or youngest. With Father there are seven of us; with Nellie and the cook (when we have one) and poor little Dixie, the horse, there are ten.

Father is a big, quiet, solemn man and is sixty-eight years old. He is president of the Vars & Company Woollen Mills, has perfectly white hair, and wears grey and white seersucker coats in the summer. Tom is the oldest and is in business out West. We're all awfully proud of Tom. He was a perfect star in college, and is making money hand over fist with his lumber camps in Michigan. Alec, the next to oldest, is struggling along in business with Father. Then I come, and next to me the twins—Oliver and Malcolm, aged fifteen and perfect terrors. Last is Ruthie; and after her, mother died and so there weren't any more. *I* was the mother then, and I was only a little over five. Father says he used to put me on the dictionary in mother's chair at the table when I was so little that Nellie had to help lift the big silver pot while I poured the coffee. Well, I've sat there ever since, pushed the bell, scowled at the twins and performed a mother's duty generally, as well as I knew how.

It hasn't been easy. Ruthie isn't the kind of little sister who likes to be petted or cuddled. The twins scorn everything I do or say. The house is a perfect elephant to run (there are thirty-three steps between the refrigerator and the kitchen sink) and our washings are something frightful. Alec says we simply can*not* afford a laundress, and the result is that I spend most of my Saturday mornings in intelligence-offices hunting cooks. Intelligence-offices are dreadful on inspirations.

Ever since I can remember, the house has been out of repair—certain doors that won't close, certain windows that have no shades, certain ceilings that are stained and smoked. It's hard to give the rooms the proper look when there are paths worn all over the Brussels carpet, exactly like cow-paths in a pasture, and the stuffed arms of the furniture in the parlour are worn as bare as the back of a little baby's head I once saw.

When Tom wrote that he was going to bring Elise, his young bride, whom we had never laid eyes on, to Hilton on their wedding trip, I nearly had a Conniption Fit. I thought Tom must have lost his mind. Any one ought to know what a shock our house would be to the kind of girl Tom would choose to marry. The concrete walk that leads up to the front door was dreadfully cracked, and the crevices were filled with a healthy growth of green grass. The iron fountain in the centre of the walk was as dry as a desert, and the four iron urns on the square porch as empty as shells. The ninety feet of elaborate iron fence that runs in front of the house needed a new coat of paint, and the little filigree iron edging, standing up like stiffly starched Hamburg embroidery around the top of the cupola, had a piece knocked out in front. But Tom *would* come, so I buckled down and made preparations.

I must explain a little about Tom. It isn't simply because he is the oldest son that we all look up to him so much. Every one in Hilton admires Tom. The *Weekly Messenger* refers to his "brilliant career," and the minister at our church calls him "an exceptional young man." He isn't a genius—he's too successful and everybody likes him too much for a genius—but he's different from the other young men in Hilton. When Father picked out some little technical school or other for Tom to go to, Tom announced that he was awfully sorry but that he had made up his mind to graduate from the biggest university in the country. And once there, Tom had a perfectly elegant time! Every one adored him. I saw him carried off once on the shoulders of a lot of shouting young men, who were singing his name. Why, I was proud to be Tom Vars' sister! He was captain of the crew, president of his class, a member of a whole lot of societies, and when he graduated his name was printed under the *magna cum laude* list on the programme (I can show it to you in my Souvenir Book) which meant that he was a perfect wizard in his lessons.

Tom graduated the year that Father's business began to look a little wobbly. Just when Father was looking forward, with a good deal of hope, to his oldest son's help and coöperation, Tom ran up home for over Sunday one day in May, and broke the news that after Commencement he had decided to accept a position from his room-mate's rich uncle in some wild and woolly lumber camps in Michigan. It just about broke poor Father's heart. He couldn't enjoy the honours of Tom's Commencement. But Tom went out West just the same—for Tom always carries out his plans—he went, smiling and confident, with never a single reference to Father's silence, ignoring absolutely the sad look in Father's eyes. He went just as if he were carrying out Father's dearest hope; and the funny part is, that inside of three years Tom had made Father so proud of his hard work and steady success that the poor dear man's disappointment faded away like mist before the sun, as they say in Shakespeare or the Bible—I forget which. The whole scheme worked like a charm, as Tom's schemes always do. There was faithful Alec to help

Father; and the rich uncle, who had no son of his own, was simply aching to get hold of a fine, smart, clean young man like Tom Chenery Vars to boost up to success.

Whenever Tom had a holiday, except Christmas when he came home, he spent it in Chicago with his room-mate or the uncle. That is how he happened to fall in with such a lot of fashionable people—not that Tom ever boasted that his friends were fashionable, for Tom never blows his own horn—but I knew they were, just the same. He used to send stunning monograms to Ruthie and me for our collections, torn off from the notes which his wealthy young-lady friends wrote to him; besides, when he came home for Christmas he always had a pocketful of kodak pictures to show us of his life in the West. They weren't *all* taken in the lumber camps. Some were snapshots of house-parties, which he'd been on, and I assure *you*, I always took in the expensive background of these pictures—carved stone doorways, perfectly elegant houses, lawns kept like a park, and automobiles with chauffeurs sitting up as stiff as ramrods. I hadn't much doubt, when Tom wrote that he was engaged to be married to Miss Elise Hildegarde Parmenter, but that she was an inmate of one of these millionaire mansions, and I was absolutely convinced of it when I laid eyes on her photograph— one of those brown carbons a foot square—and counted the six magnificent plumes on her big drooping picture-hat. I knew that 240 Main Street, Hilton, Mass., would look pretty worn and dingy alongside Sunny-lawn-by-the-Lake, which was engraved in gold letters and hyphens at the top of Miss Parmenter's heavy grey note-paper.

The minute Tom wrote that he was going to bring his elegant bride to Hilton I button-holed Father and Alec one day after dinner, and told those two men that the house had simply *got* to be done over. It was disgraceful as it was; it hadn't been painted since I could remember; it was unworthy of our name. Father reminded me that the reason none of us went to the wedding (Tom was married in California, on Elise's father's orange ranch) was to save expense, as I already knew, and merely to paint the house would cost the price of a ticket or two.

"Let us be ourselves, Lucy," said Father to me, "*ourselves*, child. If Tom's wife is the right kind of woman, she will look within, *within*, Lucy."

"Oh," I said, "but the inside is worse than the out, Father. The wall-paper in the guest-room—"

Father interrupted me gently.

"Within our hearts," he corrected, touching his heavy gold watch-chain across his chest. "Within our hearts, Lucy."

Father is a perfectly splendid man, but I knew that spotless hearts wouldn't excuse smoked ceilings; and when, the next day being Sunday, I saw Father drop his little white sealed envelope, which I knew contained five perfectly good dollars, into the contribution box, I didn't believe any heathen girl needed that money more than I.

I am going to tell about that first appearance of Elise's in detail. But it's got to be after dinner, for fifteen minutes ago the big whistle on Father's factory spurted out its puff of white steam (I could see it from my north window before I heard the blast) and Father and Alec will soon be driving up the hill in the phaeton, with the top down and the reins slack over faithful Dixie's back. I must be within calling-distance when Father strikes the Chinese gong at the foot of the stairs. It's the first thing he always does when he enters the house at noon. We all recognise his two strokes on each one of the three notes as surely as his voice or step. Why, that ring of Father's simply speaks! It is as full of impatience as a motorman ringing for a truck to get off the track.

Father hates to wait for dinner. By the time he has taken off his overcoat, and scrubbed up in the wash-room off the hall, he likes us all to be seated at the table when he comes into the dining-room. "Hello, chicken," he says to me. "Hello, baby," to Ruth. (He calls Dixie "baby" too.) "Hello, boys," to the twins. Then he sits down at the head of the table, opposite me, clears his throat as a signal, and asks the blessing.

Father's blessing is always the same except when we have company. I can tell how important the company is by the length of Father's prayer. When Juliet Adams, my best friend, drops in for supper, she is served the regular everyday family blessing, but when we have company important enough to put on the best dishes, or at the first meal that Tom is with us, Father keeps at it so long that the twins get to fooling with each other under cover of the tablecloth. I wished Father would omit the blessing entirely when Elise came, and family prayers too. They're so old-fashioned nowadays; but I knew better than to suggest such a preposterous thing. Father is a member of the Standing Committee at our church, and has a lot of principles.

There he is coming now! I wish he could afford a new carriage. I'm simply dying for one of those sporty little red-wheeled runabouts!

CHAPTER II

AMONG the first things I did in preparation for Elise's visit was to set the twins to work on the lawn, and Ruthie to clearing up a rubbishly-looking place back of the barn where there was a pile of old boxes and barrel hoops.

I myself harnessed up Dixie, made a trip to the country, and brought back three bushel-baskets full of rock ferns from the woods. Juliet Adams helped me fill the iron urns the next day. I know very well that red geraniums, hanging vines, and a little palm in the centre are the correct plants for urns (there's a painting of one on the garden scenery at our theatre here in Hilton) but as geraniums are a dollar and a quarter a dozen, and the urns are perfectly enormous, I knew that such luxuries could not be afforded. I also knew that it was out of the question to work the fountain. I cleared out its collection of leaves, soused it well with the hose, and was obliged to leave it in the middle of the walk, out of commission, but at least clean. The tennis-court, which hadn't been used for tennis for ten years, had now passed even the potato-patch era and was a perfect mass of weeds. I paid the twins five cents each for mowing it twice, and then set out the croquet set with a string. I put a fresh coat of white paint on the wickets, and though the ground was far too uneven for any practical use, the general effect at a distance was not bad at all.

I spent two solid afternoons in the stable sweeping and cleaning as if my life depended on it. We don't keep a man now. Dixie is the only horse we own, and Alec does all the feeding and rubbing-down that Dixie gets. Poor little Dixie, rattling around in one of the big box stalls, can't give the place the proper air. It's a stunning stable—stalls for eight horses and a big room filled with all sorts of carriages. They are dreadfully out of style now (I used to play house in them when I was ten and they had begun their dust gathering even then), but Father says they were the best that could be bought in their day. I pinned the white sheets that cover them down around their bodies as closely as I could, so that Miss Parmenter couldn't see how out-of-date the dear old arks were. I cleaned up all the harnesses and hung them up, black and shining, on the wooden pegs. In an old sleigh upstairs I discovered a girl's saddle, which I dusted and hung up in plain view by the whip-rack; there's something so sporty about horseback riding! I was bound to have Miss Parmenter know that at one time we were prosperous.

But most of my efforts of course went into the house. It was terribly discouraging. We own loads of black walnut, and though I begged and begged for a brass bed for the guest-room, Father was adamant. He had allowed me to have the room repapered and *that*, he said, was all that I must ask for. The new paper really was lovely. I picked it out myself, pink roses on a light blue ground and a plate-rail half-way up.

I spent a lot of pains on the guest-room, carrying out the pink and blue colour-scheme in every possible detail. I took the light blue rose bowl off the mantel in the sitting-room and put it on the bureau, for hatpins. I rehung my "Yard of Pink Roses" over the guest-room mantel. My blue kimono I had freshly laundered and hung it up in the closet. A pair of pink bedroom slippers were carefully placed beneath. I found a book in the library bound in pink, entitled "Baby Thoughts," and put it on the marble-topped guest-room table alongside a magazine and my work-basket on which I had sewed a huge blue bow and inside of which I had placed my solid gold thimble. I also tied a smashing pink and blue rosette on the waste-basket; and the half-dozen coat-hangers which I was able to scare up out of Alec's and Father's closets Ruthie wound with pink and blue ribbons. I didn't neglect the more necessary details either. I paid thirty-five cents for a cake of pink French soap; and the only embroidered towels we own I strung along in a showy row on the back of the commode. In the tooth-brush holder I placed a sealed Prophylactic tooth-brush, which I read in the *Perfect Housekeeper* should be found in every nicely appointed guest-room; nor did I overlook the Bible, and candle and matches by the bed. The *Perfect Housekeeper* says that it is the little touches in your home, such as a fresh bunch of flowers on the shelf in your guest-room, or in cold weather a hot-water bag between the sheets, that count with a guest. I was dreadfully sorry that it was too warm for hot-water bottles.

I was in perfect despair about Nellie. Nellie is our second-girl and has been with us for years. Nellie doesn't look a bit like a servant. She has grey hair and wears glasses. People are always mistaking her for an aunt. I wrote out a set of rules for Nellie, tacked them up over the sink in the butler's pantry, and told her to study them during the week before Tom and Elise were due to arrive. Here's a copy of them:

- *Rule 1* When a meal is ready don't stand at the foot of the stairs and holler "Dinner!" Come to me and say in a low, well modulated voice, "Dinner is served, Miss Lucy."

- *Rule 2* Be sure and call me *Miss* Lucy, and Tom, *Mister* Tom. Never plain Tom or plain Lucy. And so on through the family.

- *Rule 3* When I ring the bell during a meal, don't just stick your head in through the swinging-door but enter all-over and find out what is wanted.

- *Rule 4* Don't offer a last biscuit or piece of cake and say, "There's more in the kitchen."

- *Rule 5* If any member of the family asks for any other member of the family, don't say, "They're in the barn, or down-cellar, or upstairs," but go quietly and find them yourself.
- *Rule 6* Be sure and put ice-water every night into Mrs. Vars' bedroom when you turn down the bed.
- *Rule 7* If you get the hiccups when waiting on the table, withdraw to the kitchen immediately and take ten swallows of water.

Nellie is a good-natured old soul. I can manage her beautifully, but it took a head to do anything with Delia. Delia was the cook. I was in the butler's pantry the day before Tom and Elise arrived, putting away the family napkin-rings (for of course I know napkin-rings are tabooed) when it occurred to me that we had got to have clean napkins for every meal as long as Elise stayed. If she was with us a week that would make a hundred and sixty-eight napkins in all, counting three meals a day and eight people at the table. We owned just four dozen napkins and that meant—I figured it all out on a piece of paper—that the whole four dozen would have to be washed every other day. I went out into the kitchen and explained it to Delia just as nicely and sweetly as I could. She went off on a regular tangent. It was enough, she said, all the extra style I was planning on, without piling on a week's washing for every other day. She said she'd never heard of such tommyrot, and if a napkin was clean enough for Tom and Tom's family, she guessed it was clean enough for Tom's wife, whoever she was. I was simply incensed!

"We won't discuss it," I said with much dignity. "Not another word, please, Delia," and I left the kitchen.

I heard her slam a kettle into the iron sink, and mutter something about "another place," so I thought it better policy not to press my point. I hate being imposed upon—there isn't a teacher at the high school who can talk Lucy Vars into a hole—but I wasn't going to cut off my own nose. So I went straight to the telephone, called up a dry goods store and ordered ten dozen medium-priced napkins to be sent up special. All the rest of the afternoon I sat at the sewing-machine hemming like mad, and Nellie folded the things so that the machine stitches wouldn't show. I knew that napkins should be hemmed by hand.

Tom and Elise were due at eight o'clock on a Wednesday night. I had it planned that Father and Alec would meet them at the station and I would remain at the house to greet them as they came in. I wished awfully that we had a coachman and some decent horses, but I begged Father to hire a carriage and he promised that he would. The suspense while I waited for them to drive up over the hill was as awful as when I've been sent for by the principal at the high school—kind of thrilly inside and as nervous as a cat. I walked from room to room like a caged animal, trying to imagine how the old house would look to a person who hadn't lived in it forever. I lit the open fire in the hall, arranged the books on the sitting-room table for the hundredth time, and watched the piano-lamp like a hawk. It smokes the ceilings if you leave it alone.

The twins, Oliver and Malcolm, stationed themselves in the parlour to keep watch of the road. About half-past eight Oliver hollered out, "They're coming, Bobbie!" and I went out into the hall and opened the door. I saw the big bulky old depot carriage draw up to the curbing out beyond the iron fountain, and I whispered to the twins, "Go down and help with their bags!" They pushed by me; and a minute after, everybody was in a confused bunch in the vestibule—Oliver and Malcolm with the suitcases, Father and Alec, Ruthie hanging on to my skirt, and finally Tom, big and handsome and natural!

"Hello, Bobbie, old girl," he said. "Hello, little Ruthiemus!" And suddenly behind him Elise appeared—tall, pale as a lily, quiet, and very calm. "Well, here they all are, Elise," Tom went on lustily, "Malcolm and Oliver, and Bobbie who is the mother of us, and Ruthiemus the baby."

Elise came forward, shook hands with the boys, and when she came to me she kissed me. I'd never been so near such a perfectly gorgeous Irish-lace jabot in my life. After she had leaned down and kissed Ruth she said in the quietest, lowest voice I ever heard, while we all stared, "I know you all, already, for Chenery has told me all about you."

Chenery! How perfectly absurd! No one ever calls Tom anything but just plain Tom. We all have Chenery for a middle name—it was mother's before she was married—but it is only to sign. After that remark about Chenery the silence was simply deathly, but Alec, who always comes to the rescue, exclaimed, "Don't you people intend to stop with us to-night? Usher us in, Bobbie."

There was none of the Vars hail-fellow-well-met, slap-you-on-the-back spirit about that evening. We all distributed ourselves in a circle about the sitting-room, exactly like a Bible-class at church, and talked in the stiffest, most formal way imaginable. I don't know why we couldn't be natural; but Elise, sitting there so perfectly at ease, smiling and talking so gracefully made us feel like country bumpkins before a princess. I was furious at her for making us appear in such a light. Why couldn't Tom have married somebody like ourselves, some jolly good sport who wouldn't be afraid to hurt her clothes? I knew Elise Hildegarde Parmenter's style. She wore some of those high-heeled shoes, like undressed kid gloves, and her feet were regular pocket editions. If we had acted as we usually do when Tom comes home, all talking and laughing at once, we'd have shocked this delicate little piece of china into a thousand bits.

I was dreadfully surprised at Tom when he said, as if Elise was not there, "Come on, Bobbie, bring in the apples."

You see it is one of our customs, the first night that Tom comes home, to sit up awfully late and eat apples, Father paring them with an old kitchen knife. But of course I wasn't going to have apples to-night, of all times, passed around in quarters on the end of a knife. So I said to Tom as quietly as possible, for really I was catching Elise's manner, "Not apples to-night, Tom. I ordered a little chocolate. I'll speak to Nellie." I had gotten out our best hand-painted violet chocolate cups, told Delia to make some cocoa and whip some cream, and had opened a fresh package of champagne wafers. Everything was all ready on a tray in the dining-room, so I went out and told Nellie to bring it in. When she appeared holding the big tray out before her I had to bite my tongue to keep from laughing. Nellie had never worn a cap before and it didn't seem to go with her style. It was sticking straight up on the top of her grey pug of hair like a bird on the tip end of a flag pole. I saw Malcolm and Oliver begin to giggle. I squelched them with a look and began stirring my chocolate hard.

"Hello, Nellie," said Tom, when the tray reached him, and though I'd cautioned Nellie a hundred times to address Tom as *Mister* Tom, she got it mixed up in some stupid fashion, and replied, "How do you do, Mister Vars," and Father who heard her come out with his name asked, "Did you speak to me, Nellie?" Nellie replied, "No, I didn't. I was speaking to Tom."

Late that first night, as I was turning out my light, and after I had set my alarm-clock for quarter of six (for I thought I'd better get up early and see how things were running) Malcolm and Oliver pushed open my door and came in. Behind them was Alec on his way to bed.

"Hello, Bobbie," they said, grinning.

"Close the door," I whispered, and then I wrapped myself up in a down comforter and crawled up on the bed. My brothers came over and all sat down around me.

"Well," I said, "what do you think of her?"

"Did you see the diamond pendant?" Malcolm began. "It was a ripper!"

"Tom gave her that for a wedding-present," Oliver explained.

"He did!" I was amazed. "Plain Tom slinging around diamond pendants like that!"

"He'll have to, to live up to being called Chenery. Did you get on to that?"

"Did I? Isn't it too silly? I hate such airs! We stand for good plain things and why couldn't Tom get something plain?"

"Oh, she's a blue-blood," said Oliver. "We're regular Indians beside her."

"No, we're not, Oliver Vars," I flared back. "Don't you say that. I shan't eat humble-pie for any one. We're just as good as she is. It's brains that count."

"I bet a dollar she couldn't throw a ball straight; and she looks as if she'd be afraid of the dark," said Malcolm.

"Oh, come ahead, you young knockers," interrupted Alec, who hadn't said a word till now—Alec never says much and when he does it's always nice—"Come along to bed, and let the General-manager here get a little rest. Good-night, Bobbie," he said, coming up to me and giving me a little good-natured shove, so that I toppled over on the bed. Oliver and Malcolm each grabbed a pillow.

"Good-night, angel," they sang out as they lammed them at me hard. I heard them dash out of the room and slam the door with a bang. Nice old brothers! We Vars never waste much time in kissing, but we understand all right.

The next morning I was down in the kitchen before Delia had her fire made. About eight o'clock when we were all flaxing around as fast as we could there suddenly broke out upon us a very queer noise. It sounded like a cat trying to meow when it had a dreadful cold. It startled me awfully and Delia gave a terrible jump.

"For the love of Mike, what's that?" said she.

I investigated, and after a little, I discovered the cause. Years ago we had some sort of a bell system that connected with all the rooms, with an indicator in the kitchen. We hadn't used it for a long time and I supposed the whole system was as dilapidated as the stable. Whenever we wanted Nellie for anything we found it easier to go to the back stairs and holler. It occurred to me that the electrician who had put in some new batteries the week before, for the front door bell, which before Elise came was dreadfully unreliable, must have monkeyed with the other bells too.

"Elise has rung for you," I said to Nellie, thankful with all my heart that the old thing had worked. I knew that Tom was already downstairs, so of course wasn't there to tell her that the old push-button didn't mean a thing, and I was glad of that. Heaven knew there was enough else to apologise for.

When Nellie came back I asked, "What did she want?"

"She wanted me to button up her waist and also to give me her laundry."

"Laundry!" gasped Delia. I never could understand why cooks hate washing so.

"Yes," I said, turning to her, "laundry! I told Mrs. Vars," I went on with much authority, "to put any soiled clothing she might have in a pink and blue bag which I made to match the guest-room, for this express purpose—for her to put her laundry in. That's only hospitality." I crossed the room. "And now you may put breakfast on, Delia," I finished, and went out.

After breakfast Nellie came to me and said, "Delia wishes to speak to you in the kitchen."

My heart sank. I left Elise in the sitting-room talking in her lovely soft way to Father and Alec. Delia was in the laundry standing by a regular haystack of lacy lingerie. She was holding up the most superb lace skirt I ever saw, rows upon rows of insertion and if you'll believe me made every inch by hand.

"I just wanted to say," she began, "that I don't stay if I have to wash these. They aren't dirty, in the first place, and what's more I'm not hired to wash company's clothes, and what's more I won't. And what's more still, I think you better hunt for another girl."

I couldn't have received more depressing news. I hated being ruled by a cook, and I hated to let her go. I didn't have a soul to ask about it. I didn't know what to do. I flared right up.

"The washing must be done," I said sternly. "*That's* settled."

Delia dropped the skirt.

"All right. I'll do the washing to-day," she announced, "and I'll leave to-morrow."

I just wanted to sit down and cry and cry and say, "O please be nice about it and help us out. Please stay! O please, please, *please!*" But I did no such thing. I bit my lip hard and replied, "Very well," and when I joined the others in the sitting-room, I was apparently as undisturbed as a summer's breeze.

Things got no better as time went on. Elise didn't fit into our family a bit. None of us was natural. Father didn't ring the gong when he came in at noon and call up to me, "Slippers, chicken"; the twins didn't fool under the tablecloth and call me "Snodgrass," "Angel" or "Trolley" (because of my shape); Alec didn't tilt back on the hind legs of his chair after dessert, with his hands shoved down in his pockets; Ruthie didn't practice a note on the piano; even Tom was different. At first he tried to whoop things up in the old Vars fashion, but he gave it up after an attempt or two. We wouldn't respond. We balked like stubborn horses, while all the time Elise kept right on being very sweet and charming, but, oh my, cold and far away.

Her tact got on my nerves. I realised that she was trying to be nice, but her appreciation of everything made me tired. Of course she had seen grander houses than ours and yet she pretended to enthuse over our old-fashioned mantels. "What fine woodwork in them," she'd say to Father, "and what beautiful mahogany in those sliding-doors!" or, as she gazed at our ornate black walnut bookcase, she would remark, "Black walnut is becoming so popular!" Once she exclaimed, "How many books you have!" and her eyes were resting on a row of black-bound town records Father insists on keeping. When she and I attempted a miserable game of croquet she remarked, "I think it is more fun having the ground a little uneven." Heavens, I would have loved her if she had blurted out, "Say, this is rotten! Let's not play." I despise insincerity.

CHAPTER III

ONE day at dinner (I've forgotten whether it was the first or second day of Elise's visit, but anyhow it was before the ice was broken) Father suggested that Tom take the new member of our family for a drive in the afternoon with Dixie (he and Alec, could go out to the factory by electrics), so as soon as Elise went upstairs to rest, as she always did after dinner, I escaped to the barn, to hitch up. Alec doesn't have much time to devote to Dixie and I gave that poor little animal such a currying as he had never had before in his life. Then I drew up the check two holes higher, dusted out the phaeton, and put in the best yellow plush robe and lash whip.

Elise and Tom got back about half-past six. I was in the sitting-room when Elise came into the house.

"Chenery has been showing me all the sights," she said. "I think Hilton is lovely. I told Chenery we were staying too long. I'm afraid we're late for dinner. But I'll hurry. It won't take me ten minutes to dress."

Dinner indeed! I wondered if she called the layout we had at noon just lunch. We've always had supper at night and I hadn't intended changing for Elise. But if she'd gone upstairs to dress for it, I'd got to prepare something besides tea, sliced meat and toast, for all the trouble she was taking. I flew to the kitchen. We had a can of beef-extract, and I told Delia to make soup out of that. Then I sent Ruth for some beefsteak, hauled down a can of peas for a vegetable, and the sliced oranges which were already prepared would have to do for dessert. I rushed to my room, put on my best light blue cashmere and laid out Ruth's white muslin.

It was, after all, on the first day of Elise's visit that she took that drive with Dixie, for *this*, I remember now, was the first evening meal that she had had with us. An awful catastrophe took place during the ordeal too. In the first place, having dinner at night added to the strain the family were all under, and it may have been due to the general atmosphere of uneasiness that made Nellie so stupid and careless. I don't know how it happened, but when she was passing the crackers to Elise, during the soup course, her cap got loose somehow and fell cafluke on Elise's bread-and-butter plate. There was an instant of dead quiet, and then Oliver, who just at that moment happened to have his mouth full of soup, exploded like a rubber ball with water in it. He shoved back his chair with a jerk, and coughing and choking into his napkin, got up and left the room. Of course that sent Malcolm off into a regular spasm, and little Ruth began to giggle too. I could feel myself growing as red as a beet, but I didn't laugh. No one laughed outright.

Elise was the first one to break the pause, and this is what she said:

"I've had the loveliest drive this afternoon," and then as no one replied she went on, "Chenery took me around the reservoir. How old are the ruins of that old mill at the upper end?"

Perhaps you think that that was a very graceful way of treating the situation, but I didn't. We were all simply dying to laugh. We couldn't think of old mills with that cap sticking on Elise's butter. However, I heard Father at the other end of the table making some sort of an answer to Elise, and all of us managed to control themselves somehow or other. Nellie, red in the face, carried the bread-and-butter plate away; Oliver sneaked back into his place; and I slowly began to cool off. But of course it spoiled the meal for me.

As soon after the horrible occurrence as possible, I escaped up here to my cupola, and Tom found me here before he went to bed. I knew he must be disappointed at the way I was running things. I hadn't been alone with him before, and when his head pushed up through the trap door and he asked, "You here?" I didn't answer. I was sitting in the pitch dark on the window-seat, but Tom must have seen my shadow for he came up and stood beside me. He remained perfectly silent for a minute then he said, "Aren't there a lot of stars out to-night!"

"Oh, Tom," I burst out, "I'm so sorry! Wasn't it awful? Everything's going all wrong."

He sat down.

"It's all right, Bobbie," he said quietly. "Only I wish Elise might see us as we really are. *Then*," he added, "you would see Elise as *she* really is."

Tom didn't ask me how I liked her (he knew better than to do that), and suddenly I felt sorry for my brother. I could have almost cried, not because of the accident at dinner, not because of my failure, but because Elise hadn't made us like her. I did so want Tom's wife to be the same bully sort of person Tom was.

The crisis came the next day. At eleven o'clock in the morning, I found Delia putting on her coat and hat, actually preparing to go.

"What does this mean?" I exclaimed.

"Can't you see?" she asked very saucily.

"But the washing. Have you—"

"No, I haven't, and what's more I'm not going to." She was spitting mad.

I stood there, just helpless before her.

"I have telephoned to all the intelligence offices," I said, "and I can't get anyone to come until Saturday night. I thought, to accommodate us, you might be willing—"

She cut me right off:

"Well, I'm not! No one accommodates me here, and I'm not used to being treated like this. Two dinners a day and up until all hours!"

It didn't seem to me as if she had half so much to stand as I did. I wished I could up and clear out too. I thought she was very disagreeable to leave me in the lurch that way. But I didn't have any words with her. I told her she might go as soon as she pleased. I hated the sight of her standing there in the kitchen, which she had left all spick and span, not as a kitchen should look at eleven in the morning with half a dozen full-grown mouths to be fed at one o'clock.

I was on my way upstairs to break the news to Nellie when Elise called to me from the sitting-room.

"Oh, Lucy," she said in her musical voice, "will there be time for me to run over to the postoffice with some letters before lunch?"

I stalked into the sitting-room. She was sitting at the desk in her graceful easy way, with a beautiful French hand-embroidered lingerie waist on, that I'd be glad to own for very best. There were gold beads about her neck, and her hair, even in the morning, was soft and fluffy and wavy. She had her feet crossed and I took in the silk stockings and the low dull-leather pumps.

I had a sudden desire to tear down all her beautiful appearance of ease and grace.

"We don't have lunch at noon," I said bluntly. "We have dinner, just dinner. We've always had dinner."

"Yes, I know," she began in her persistently pleasant way; "people do very often, in New England."

I couldn't bear her unruffled composure.

"Oh," I said, bound to shock her, "it isn't because we're New England. It's because we're plain, plain people. The rich families in New England as well as anywhere, have dinner at night. But *we*," I said, glorying in every word, "are *not* one of the rich families. We have doughnuts for breakfast, baked beans and brown bread Saturday nights, and Saturday noons a boiled dinner. We love pie. We all just *love it*. Father came from a farm in Vermont. He didn't have any money at all when he started in. You see we're common people. And so's Tom. Tom comes from just a common, common, *common* family," I said, loving to repeat the word.

She was sitting with her arm thrown carelessly over the back of the chair, and her gaze way out of the west window. When I stopped to see what effect my words had had she just laughed—a quiet pleased laugh—and mixed up with it I heard her say, "Why, Chenery is the most uncommon man I ever met." And she blushed like eighteen.

I went right on.

"We don't call him Chenery, either," I said. "We cut off all such fringes. He's plain Tom to us. I know how the plain way we live must impress *you*. I know you've been used to French maids, and push-a-button for everything you want. I'm sorry for the shock you must have got coming here. But you might as well wake up to the truth. You see what a mess the house is in, and how Nellie won't call us Mister and Miss, and how if she is on the third floor and she wants me she just yells. And," I said, pointing out of the window, "there goes Delia now. And there isn't a sign of a cook left in the house."

Elise sat up straight.

"Is she leaving without notice?" she exclaimed.

"Naturally," I laughed.

"How dreadfully unkind of her!"

"That's what I think, but Delia doesn't care if I do."

"Haven't you some one to help you out? What will you do?" Elise was really excited.

"Do?" I replied grimly. "Oh, I'll duff in and cook myself, I suppose."

Elise put down her pen.

"I can make delicious desserts," she said. "Can't you telephone to the family not to come home this noon? We can be ready for them by to-night. I know how to make the best cake you ever tasted in your life."

That's the way it came about. I took her out into the kitchen and didn't try to cover up a thing. She could see everything exactly as it was—smoked kitchen ceiling, uneven kitchen floor, paintless pantry shelves. She could go to the bottom of the flour barrel if she wanted to; and she did. Covered with an old apron and her sleeves rolled up, she was first in the kitchen pantry looking into every cupboard, drawer or bucket for powdered sugar; next in the fruit-closet feeling all the paper bags, in search of a lemon; then calling to me in her musical voice to come here and taste some dough to see if it needed anything else; in the butler's pantry choosing just the plate she wanted for her cookies; and actually underneath the sink, pulling out a greasy spider for panouchie, which she was going to make out of some lumpy brown sugar she discovered in a wooden bucket. I took grim pleasure in having her see the worst there was. I wondered if she could stand the fact that we didn't own an ice-cream freezer, when she suggested ice-cream for dessert, nor possess a drop of olive oil for her mayonnaise. I didn't care. I liked telling her the things we didn't have. When I heard her burst into laughter in the butler's pantry, and pushing open the swinging-door, saw her gazing at my set of rules tacked up over the sink for Nellie, I made no explanation whatsoever. I was delighted to have her read them. At sight of me she went off into regular peals.

Finally she gasped, with her finger on Rule 6, "She put—the ice—in a hunk, in the big pitcher in the wash-bowl!" and the tears ran down her cheeks.

I laughed a little then in spite of myself.

"Nellie's an old fool," I said and went back to my work.

It happened that Father and Alec had gone to Boston for the day on business, and the last minute Tom had joined them, so the men wouldn't be home until night anyhow. I called up the twins, just before their fifth-hour period (I had cut school myself) and told them to get a bite to eat at the high school lunch-counter. "I'll pay for it," I assured them, for I knew the twins would jump at the chance of a free spread, and as they had manual-training that afternoon, Elise and I were safe from any interruption from the male section.

We had supper at half-past six as usual. It was very queer about that meal. The awful strain we had all felt the same day at breakfast had suddenly disappeared. Elise had suggested that we shouldn't tell any one of Delia's departure, and on the outside everything was just as it was in the morning, even to Nellie's ridiculous cap.

"These biscuits are good, Lucy," Father said suddenly, as he reached for the plate. Father usually speaks of the food, but he hadn't done so once since Elise had come.

"There's more in the kitchen," announced Nellie blandly.

"There's a whole panful," added Elise. "I'm awfully glad you like them!" she exclaimed and then stopped short.

"There," I said, "I knew you'd let the cat out. Elise made them!" I announced.

"Delia's left—" Elise hurried to say.

"And we—" I put in.

"We got supper!" she finished proudly.

"*You* and Bobbie?" exclaimed Alec.

"Bobbie and *you*?" gasped Tom.

"Of course!" she said. "Bobbie scallopped the oysters."

"Give me some more," said Malcolm.

"Fling over the last biscuit," sang out Oliver. And in a flash Elise picked up the little brown ball and tossed it across the fern-dish straight as an arrow.

"Good shot!" said Oliver, catching it in both hands.

"Oh," piped up Ruthie, "make Malcolm stop. He took a cookie and it isn't time for them."

Father just chuckled, and said, "Pretty good! pretty good!" And I tell you it was simply glorious to be natural again!

"Don't eat too much," said Elise, "for dessert's coming and it's awfully good."

"And chocolate layer-cake with it!" said I.

"Oh, bully!" shouted Malcolm and Oliver together.

"Say," asked Alec, "isn't this a good deal better than last night when Nellie's cap fell into your butter?"

We all burst into sudden laughter and Nellie, who was filling the glasses, had to set down the pitcher. She was shaking with mirth. We laughed until it hurt; we simply roared; and suddenly Elise gasped, when she was able to get her breath:

"Wasn't it funny? I was so frightened by you all then, I didn't know what to say about that old cap. But now—O dear!" and suddenly she turned to Ruth who sat next to her, put her arms around her and kissed her. "Oh, Ruthie," she exclaimed, "isn't it *nice* to know them all!" And I couldn't tell whether the tears in her eyes were from laughing or crying.

We stayed up late that night.

"Run and get my slippers," said Father to Ruth after supper; and all the evening he lay back in his chair and watched us children while we sang college songs to Elise's ripping accompaniment; and poked fun at the twins because they'd just bought their first derbies. It was eleven-thirty when we went up to bed.

"Come here a minute, Bobbie," whispered Elise to me, and I went into the guest-room. "Do unhook the back of this dress." When I had finished she said, "I'll be down at six-thirty" (we were going to get breakfast too), "and don't you dare to be late! I'm going to make the omelet. You can make the johnny-cake. Bobbie, isn't it nice Delia left?" And she kissed *me* as well as Ruth.

That night the boys all gathered in my room again. I wrapped up in the down comforter, and we were just beginning to talk when Tom appeared.

"Hello," he said, smiling all over. He came in and closed the door. "Well," he asked, "what do you think of her?" And I knew he asked us because he so well knew what we did think. But just the same I wanted to tell him.

I shot out my bare skinny arm at him.

"Tom," I said, "I think she's a corker!"

He first took my hand and then suddenly, very unlike the Vars, he put both arms around me tight.

"Bobbie," he said in a kind of choked voice, "you're a little brick!"

And, my goodness, I just had to kiss Tom then!

CHAPTER IV

IT has been nearly a whole year since I have written in this book of mine. I've been too discouraged and heart-sick even to drag myself up here into my cupola. I've aged dreadfully. I've been disillusioned of all the hopes and dreams I ever had in my life. I've skipped that happy period called girlhood, skipped it entirely, and I had hoped *awfully* to go to at least one college football game before I was grey. I am sitting in my study. It is a lovely day in spring. There are white clouds in the sky, young robins in the wild cherry, but *my* youth, *my* schooldays, *my* aspirations are all over and gone.

Miss Wood said to me one day last winter—Miss Wood is my Sunday-school teacher and was trying to be kind—"You know, Lucy, it is a law of the universe for us all to have a certain amount of trouble before we die. Some have it early, some late. Now *you*, dear, are having your misfortunes when you are young. Just think, later they will all be out of your way." Miss Wood hasn't had a bit of her share of trouble yet. Why, she has a mother, a father, a fiancé, and a bunch of violets every Sunday. She has perfectly lovely clothes, a coachman to drive her around, and was president of her class her senior year in college. Such blessings won't be half as nice, and Miss Wood knows it, when I'm old and grey. I just simply hate having all my troubles dealt out to me before my skirts touch the ground.

Our minister said to me that misfortune is the greatest builder of character in the world. Well, it hasn't worked that way with me. I'm hot-tempered and have an unruly tongue; I don't love a soul except my brother Alec; and the only friend I have in the world is Juliet Adams. I'm not even a genius—I've discovered that—and my religious beliefs are dreadfully unsettled. Years ago I used to lie awake at night and imagine myself in deep sorrow. I was always calm and sweet and dignified then, beautiful and stately in my clinging black, and near me always was a young man, a strong, handsome, clean-shaven young man in riding clothes (I adore men in riding clothes) and I used to play that this man was the son of the governor of the state. Strange as it might seem, he was in love with me and when my entire family had suddenly been killed in a railroad accident—I always had them *all* die—this man came to me in my lonely house and told me of his devotion. It really made sorrow beautiful. But let me state right here that that was one of the many empty dreams of my youth. When misfortune *did* swoop down upon me, I was not sweet and lovely, there was no man within a hundred miles to understand and sympathise, there was nothing beautiful about it. It was just plain hard and bitter. It's only in books that trouble is romantic.

Elise visited us in the spring a year ago about this time (it seems like a century to me) and my misfortunes began to pour in the following fall, when I was a senior, and seventeen years old. That last year of high school had started in to be a very happy one for me. Father had finally allowed me to go to dancing-school; mathematics was a bugbear of the past; and our basket-ball team was a perfect winner.

I loved dancing-school. It came every Saturday night from eight to ten, and Juliet Adams used to call for me in her closed carriage and drop me afterwards at my door. I remember that on that last Saturday night I was particularly full of good-feeling, for I kissed Juliet good-bye—a thing I seldom do—and called back to her as I ran up the steps, "Good-night. See you at Church." I was never so unsuspecting in my life as I opened the front door. But the instant I got inside the house and looked into the sitting-room, I knew something was wrong. The entire family was all sitting about the room doing absolutely nothing. Father was not at his roll-top desk; the twins were not drawn up to the centre table studying by the student-lamp; Alec was not out making his Saturday night call; and, strangest of all, Ruthie was not in bed.

"What's the matter?" I asked.

"Take your things off and come in, Lucy," said Father.

I didn't stir. My heart stood dead still for an instant. I grabbed hold of the portière.

"Something has happened to Tom," I gasped, so sure I didn't even have to ask.

I suppose I must have looked horribly frightened, for one of the twins blurted out, in the twins' frank brutal way, "Oh, say, don't get so everlastingly excited. Tom's all right, for all we know. So's every one else. Do cool off."

Ruthie giggled. She always giggles at the twins, and I knew then that my sudden fear had been for nothing. The angry colour rushed into my face.

"Smarties!" I flung back at the twins with all my might.

"Oh, Lucy!" I heard Father murmur, and I saw Alec drop his eyes as if he were ashamed of such an outburst from his seventeen-year-old sister.

"I don't care," I went on. "Why do you want to frighten me to death? What's the matter with you all, anyway? What are you all doing? Why isn't Ruthie in bed? Why are the twins—"

"It's all about *you*!" Malcolm interrupted in a sort of triumphant manner.

"Me!" I gasped. "What in thunder—"

"Oh, Lucy!" Father again murmured.

"Well, what," I continued, "have you all been saying about *me*?" And I sat down on the piano-stool.

Father cleared his throat the way he does before he asks the blessing, and every one else was quiet. I knew something important was coming.

"Lucy," Father said, "we think the time has come for you to go to boarding-school."

It hit me like a hard baseball and I couldn't have spoken if I were to have died.

Father went on in his sure, unfaltering way.

"I have been considering it for some little while, and now as I talk it over with the others—we always do that, you know—I am more convinced of the wisdom of such a step than ever. Alec has been doing some investigating, and Elise suggested in her last letter that Miss Brown's-on-the-Hudson is an excellent school. I have, therefore, communicated with Miss Brown and a telegram announces to me to-day that a vacancy allows her to accept you, late as it is. Before worrying you unnecessarily, I have made all arrangements. I have written to Aunt Sarah, and she is willing to come and take your place here. So, my dear child, I am only waiting now for your careful and womanly consideration." I think he must have seen the horror on my face, for he added gently, "You needn't decide to-night, Lucy. Think it over and in the morning your duty will seem clear to you."

I have heard of people whose hair grows grey in a single night. It's a wonder mine didn't turn snow-white during that single speech. Boarding-school had never been intimated to me before. I had been away from home for over night only twice in my life, and then stayed only a week. Both times I had almost died of homesickness. I would as soon be sentenced to prison or to death. Oh, I didn't want to go away! I didn't want to! The silence after Father finished was awful. One of the twins broke it.

"When Father told us about this to-night," Malcolm began importantly, "we thought he was dead right. You see," he went on, "we want our sister to be as nice as any other fellow's sister."

"Don't you 'sister' *me*," I managed to murmur, for I wasn't going to be patronised by the twins who are a year younger than I am.

"Well, anyhow," said Oliver, the crueller one of the twins, "you haven't got the right hang of fixing yourself up yet. You go round with tomboys like Juliet Adams, and some others I might mention, that fellows haven't any use for. High school is all right for *us*, but, no siree, not for *you*. Some girls get the knack all right at home; but look at yourself now! You wouldn't think a girl of seventeen would twist her feet around a piano-stool like that!" I twisted them tighter. "Even Toots" (that's Ruthie), he went on, "seems to carry herself more like a young lady."

Ruth giggled at Oliver's last remark and I came back to life.

"I may be plain and awkward and gawky," I began, "and as homely as a hedge fence, but let me tell you two children, if I spent my time primping before the glass, and mincing up and down the street Saturday afternoons before Brimmer's drug-store like your precious Elsie Barnard," I fired, looking straight at Malcolm and bringing the colour to his face, for he was awfully gone on Elsie, "or Doris Abbott, Mister Oliver," I added, and Oliver flushed brilliant red, "you two wouldn't have any stockings mended or any buttons on your coats or any lessons either, for you know without me to explain every little thing you are awful dunces!"

Father said, "Oh, come, Lucy, let us not quarrel;" Ruth went over and sat on the arm of Oliver's chair (she always sides with the twins); and my older brother Alec just looked hard at his magazine.

There was a long silence and then I got up and walked over to Alec. I took the magazine out of his hand. I was calm now.

"Alec, what do *you* think about my going away?" I said.

He looked up and smiled his kind, tired smile at me. Then he took my hand but I drew it away quickly, turned and sat down on the arm of the Morris-chair in which he was sitting, with my back square to him. His gentle voice came to me from over my shoulder.

"Well, Lucy," he said, "you see, you've been working so hard for us all here, for so many years, that I think, too, you've earned a little vacation. You've been such a splendid mother to us—such a perfect little housekeeper, that now I'd like to see you less hard-worked. We don't want to cheat you of your girlhood. We want you to have all the good times, and gaieties, and clothes, and things like that, that other girls have."

Ah, yes! I saw finally. They were ashamed of me. Even Alec was ashamed of me. I was not like other girls. I was plain and awkward and wore ugly clothes. I wasn't pretty. They wanted to send me away as if I were an old dented spoon to be straightened and polished at the jeweller's. When Alec paused he put his arm over in front of me so that it lay in my lap. At the touch of it the sobs seemed suddenly to rise up in my throat, pressing after each other as if they were anxious to get out into the air, and I rose quickly, pushed Alec's arm away and left the room. They mustn't see—oh, no, they mustn't see me cry! I meant to go to my bedroom and have it out by myself, but instead I rushed to the kitchen and buried my face for a minute in the roller-towel. Then before I let myself give way, I drew the dipper full of cold water and swallowed those sobs back, forcing them with the strength of Samson. You see I knew my sudden exit would leave an uncomfortable sensation in the room back there, and I wouldn't have had one of them think I was emotional for anything. So after a minute I went back. They could see for themselves that there wasn't a tear in sight. Standing in the doorway, facing them all, this is what I said, my voice as hard as metal.

"Father, I shall be packed, and ready to go on Monday morning."

When I closed the door to my room that night I did not cry, although my throat ached with wanting to. As I drew my curtain and looked out into the dark night I thought of Juliet Adams, sleeping peacefully like a child, and I realised how little she knew of sorrow. When the big clock in the hall struck twelve I was kneeling before my bureau, stacking my underclothes in neat little piles ready for my trunk. How little I knew that what I then thought my pretty ninety-eight-cent nightgowns, long-sleeved and high-necked, would about die of shame for their plainness, before the beautiful lace and French hand-embroidered lingerie represented at midnight spreads at school. I'm glad I didn't know then that I would come to despise my poor faithful clothes.

I was piling my gloves into a box when there came a soft knock at the door. Alec came in, in his red and grey bath-towel bath-robe.

"Not in bed yet?" he said gently, and came over and sat down near me on the floor with his back against the wall, his knees drawn up almost to his chin and his arms clasped about them. We sat there for a moment silently, and I grimly folded gloves. Then, "Good stuff, Bobbie," he said finally—and oh, so kindly—"Good nerve."

I turned and looked straight at him.

"No, Alec," I said, "there isn't anything good about it. It's horrid feelings and hate that make me go."

He looked away from me as he always does when he disapproves, but he put his hand on my shoulder and I was grateful for that touch.

I turned on him frantically and burst out, "Alec Vars, you are the only one in this whole house I love—you and Father," I amended, for we all adore Father. "You're the only one who is kind or thoughtful. I've tried to do my duty in this place by you and the others, but I guess I haven't succeeded. Now I'm going away and we'll see how the twins enjoy a dose of Aunt Sarah." I paused, then added, "Look here, Alec, don't let Ruth go out to the Country

Club. She is pretty and the older men—why, your friends talk to her and make her vain and hold her on the arms of their chairs. Don't let *her* go. And the twins—I haven't told on them yet—but they're smoking! They're dead scared for fear I'll tell Father, and I said that I should if I caught them at it again."

"Good Bobbie, you'd keep us straight if you could, wouldn't you?"

"No, I wouldn't," I flared back. "It's hate I feel and—"

Alec put his hand over my mouth.

"What shall I do to you?" he laughed.

I rose abruptly, crossed the room and closed the window at my back. There was a big lump in my throat and I stopped at the marble wash-stand built into one corner of my room, and took a drink of water. Then I went back to my glove-sorting. Finally I was able to ask, "Alec, were you at the bottom of this?"

"Oh, I don't know," he smiled. "Possibly—I—or Will Maynard."

"Will Maynard!" I exclaimed. Dr. Maynard is a physician in our town, and was a classmate of Alec's years ago in college. He has nothing to do with *me*.

Alec picked up one of my gloves and began turning it right-side-out, as he explained.

"We dropped into Grand Army Hall one afternoon a week or so ago when you were playing a basket-ball game. I'd never seen you play before. We stayed for a half an hour or more. Going home Will said to me, 'Why don't you send that little wild-cat sister of yours away to school?' I began to mull it over. Of course, Bobbie, old girl," Alec went on, "I admire your pluck and spirit in basket-ball. I like to see you win whatever you set out to. You played a fine game—a bully fine game; but there are other things in life to acquire—other kinds of things, Bobbikins." He stopped. "Oh, you'll like boarding-school," he said.

"I'll like Dr. Maynard not to butt into my affairs," I replied under my breath; then I remarked, "I'm ready for that glove, please."

Alec passed it over and got up.

"Good-night," he said. "Oh, by the way," he added, "here is something you may find a use for. Your tuition and board, of course, will be paid for by Father, but I know there are a lot of extras—girl's things—that you'll need. Possibly this will help." He dropped a piece of paper into my lap and was gone before I could look up.

I unfolded the paper and saw a check dancing before my eyes for one hundred dollars! I knew very well that we were as poor as paupers in spite of our big house, and stable, as empty now as a shell. I knew Father's business was about as lifeless as the stable, and that Alec alone stood by him trying to give a little encouragement. Splendid Alec! I fled after him. He was just groping his way up the stairs to his third-floor room. I caught him and very unlike my even temperament put my arms around him tight.

"O Alec," I blubbered, "it isn't because of the money; it's because of *you*." Then I added, like a great idiot, "Oh, I *will* try not to be such a tomboy! I *will* try to be worth something when I'm away, and all the things you want me to be." And then because I hated to pose as any kind of an angel, I turned, fled back to my room and locked the door.

I made a great impression with my announcement the next day in Sunday-school. Juliet could hardly believe me. She stared at me as open-eyed and awestruck as if I had told her I was going to China. She wouldn't sing the hymns, and during the long prayer she whispered to me: "You'll be going to Spreads!" And later: "You'll have a Room-mate!" And again: "Perhaps you'll be invited to House-parties!"

If I were about to be hanged it would be little comfort to me to be told that in a few hours I would be playing on harps, walking streets of gold and wearing wings. I didn't want to go away—that was the plain truth. I preferred Intelligence-Offices to boarding-schools; I preferred our big brown ugly old house, empty stable, out-of-date carriages, cruel twins, and uncuddleble Ruth to spreads, room-mates and house-parties. I wanted to stay at home! But I was bound that no one should know that my heart was breaking; I was determined that no one should guess that I was being sent away, boosted out of my position, like the poor old minister in the South Baptist church. I would go with my head up, and tearless! Only once did I give way, and that was in poor little Dixie's furry neck when I threw my arms about him in his stall. Poor little dumb Dixie! Poor pitiful dumb carriages gazing silently at me. "*You'll* miss me. *You'll* be sorry," I said.

On that last grey Sunday afternoon I took my good-bye walk, through Buxton's woods back of our house. I gazed for the last time on the precious landmarks that I had grown to love—the two freak chestnut trees, soldered into one like the Siamese twins; the hollow oak where we used to dig the rich dark brown peet and find the big, slimy white worms; the huge fallen pine, struck once by lightning, along whose trunk and in among whose dead branches we used to play "ship" and "pirate-boat." I walked alone—all alone. There was no romantic lover in riding clothes, as in my dreams, to share my sad reflections. Only a scurrying chipmunk or red squirrel, now and then, gazed at me with frightened eyes, then scampered away; only the dead leaves under my feet kept rhythm with my dragging steps. I was awfully lonely and unhappy. It seemed to me that even the sombre sky and the dead quietness of Sunday connived to add to my dreariness.

When I reached our iron gate on my return, it was nearly dark. Dr. Maynard was just coming away from one of his frequent Sunday afternoons with Alec and I met him by the fountain.

"Hello, little Wild-cat," he sang out cheerily. He always has called me Wild-cat, though I never knew why. "Back from one of your walks 'all by your lone'?" I think he copied that from Kipling. "Ears been burning? Al and I have just been talking about you."

I had never as much as peeped in Dr. Maynard's presence before—he's fifteen years older than I—but I couldn't bear his interference in my affairs and I retorted, "I should advise you not to meddle with wild-cats, Dr. Maynard!"

"Whew!" he whistled in mock alarm; and though it was not a pretty thing for a girl of seventeen to say to a man whose hair was beginning to turn grey, I finished hotly, "Or you'll get scratched!" and turned and dashed into the house.

CHAPTER V

IN thinking over my career at boarding-school I always recall three remarks which were made to me in the smoky Hilton Station as I waited for my train. Father and Alec and Juliet who, the dear old trump, had actually cut school to see me off, were at the station.

Alec had said, "Go slowly, Bobbie, and know only the best girls," and I had replied, pop-full of confidence, "Of course, Alec."

"And whatever else you do," exclaimed Juliet, "don't you dare to get a swelled head, Lucy Vars." "I won't," I had assured her.

Father, dear kind Father, his hand on my shoulder, had commanded: "Dear child, discover some one less fortunate than yourself and be kind to her." And I had promised, tussling with the painful lump in my throat, "I will, dear Father."

Father had slipped a paper bag into my hand then—a bag of lemon-drops (Father always buys lemon-drops) and two sticks of colt's-foot. The poor dear man had forgotten that I didn't like colt's-foot, but when I opened the bag in the train and saw those two little brown sticks, somehow I loved dear Father harder than ever. I put them into my travelling bag very tenderly, and have kept them ever since.

I don't know how to explain my impressions of boarding-school. I realise now that in spite of the pain at leaving home I did have buried in the bottom of my heart dreams of the vague, unknown joys of room-mates and spreads. Every young girl has such dreams, I guess. Even as I sped along in the train, trying desperately to dissolve that lump in my throat with Father's lemon-drops, I was wondering about the new bosom friends I should make. Edith Campbell, an awfully popular older girl in our town and a friend of Alec's, had been to a fashionable boarding-school in New York ever since she was a child, and she was forever bringing home girls to visit her, or whisking off herself to ball-games and Proms with "a Room-mate's brother" or "a Best-friend's cousin." I could hardly realise that I, Lucy Vars, was about to step within the same fascinating circle. Fifty girls to eat and sleep and walk with; fifty girls to choose my friends from; fifty girls to bring home with me for over a holiday; fifty girls for me to visit; and fifty girls with brothers or cousins at Harvard and Yale and Princeton. Perhaps that very winter some college man would invite me to a Prom; I would dance till morning, and become such a dazzling belle that by Easter-time I would look upon the twins as mere *boys*. Probably by summer I would be dashing about to house-parties, and talking to real grown-up men over a cup of tea like Dolly in the "Dolly Dialogues." Perhaps I would be president of my class at school, like Tom at college. Perhaps—perhaps—oh, I am forced to smile at myself now as I look back and see the funny little short-skirted, pig-tailed creature that I was, sitting there in the train, gazing out of the window, building my absurd little air-castles by the score, on the very way to the destruction of every dream I ever had. I didn't make a single friend at boarding-school. I didn't meet a man. Here it is almost summer, and house-parties seem as remote from me as they did ten years ago. I must try to explain why I made such a flat failure of things. It isn't a pleasant story, but here goes:

The first instant that I stepped into that school I knew that I was a curiosity to everybody there. Never shall I forget that first evening when Miss Brown ushered me into the big school dining-room and seated me beside her. It looked like fairy-land to me—red candles on a dozen little round tables and all the girls in soft, light dresses with Dutch necks. When I finally dared look up from my plate and glance round, I thought I had never seen such beautiful creatures. I couldn't find a homely girl among them; and such lovely hair as they had, done soft and full and fluffy with large ribbon-bows tied at the back of their necks. The girls at our table had the whitest hands and the prettiest soft arms, with bracelets jingling on them.

After supper Miss Brown seated herself in a big armchair by a low lamp in the drawing-room and read aloud from "Pride and Prejudice." The girls all gathered about her and did fancy work on big hoops. I didn't have any work and tried to make myself comfortable on a little high silk-brocaded chair. I felt horribly embarrassed. Every time a girl looked up from her work and scrutinised me from top to toe, I felt like saying, "I know I'm a perfect mess. I see it. I know my hands are like sandpaper, and my shoes thick-soled, and my dress a sight. I know my hair is ridiculous braided and bobbed up with a black ribbon like a horse's tail. I know it." I couldn't listen to a word that Miss Brown was reading. I was awfully disturbed thinking about my trunk on its way to me, filled with its queer collection, and wondering what in the name of heaven I could put on the next night. My blue cashmere haunted me like a bad dream. I think that first evening at boarding-school was the first time I really missed having a mother. *She* would have known the blue cashmere was ugly; *she* would have known that little bronze slippers with stockings to match were the proper thing; *she* would have known that girls at boarding-school wore Dutch necks and wide ribbons tied low, at the back of their necks. I simply dreaded unpacking that pitiful little trunk of mine. I wished it could be lost.

My room-mate's name was Gabriella Atherton, but when I entered the room which I was supposed to share with her I wished she had been plain Mary Jane. The bureau was simply loaded with silver things—silver brushes and mirrors and powder-boxes, and at least three silver frames with the stunningest men's pictures in them you ever saw. The walls were covered with college flags, and the window-seat was banked with college sofa-cushions. Why, I didn't know a single man, except high school boys, great awkward creatures like the twins. I hoped Gabriella wouldn't find out that I had never been to a college football game in my life, nor been invited to one either. My one last hope for consolation lay in the possibility that Gabriella was older than I. I thought she must be at least twenty to know so many men. When we were finally alone, getting ready to go to bed I asked her. My heart sank when she announced that she was only sixteen. I know exactly how a mother feels now when another person's baby born a month before hers talks first and shows signs of greater intelligence. I remember I was standing before my chiffonier braiding my hair for the night, pulling it flat back as I always did and fixing it in one tight short little braid, when Gabriella announced she was sixteen. Why, she looked old enough to be married, and I—I gazed at my reflection—I looked like poor Sarah Carew in the garret. No wonder the family wanted to send the old spoon away to be polished. No wonder!

"One of the girls," Gabriella went on to say, "has had a Box from home. She's asked the whole school to a Kimono Spread in her room. Do you want to go?"

A Spread! My heart leaped! And then I got a glimpse of Gabriella in the glass before me. She was a vision in a flowing pink silk kimono with white birds on it. She had her hair fluffed up on top and tied with a wide pink taffeta ribbon—she actually slept in it—and little pink shoes on her feet.

"I guess I won't to-night, thanks," I said, not turning around, for I didn't want her to see what a peeled onion I looked like; "the train made me car-sick." And I snapped the elastic band around the end of my braid.

After Gabriella had gone I turned out the light and crawled into the little brass bed, which Miss Brown had said was mine; but I didn't go to sleep. I just lay there listening to the muffled laughter and chatter at the end of the hall. It was only nine o'clock and lights were not due to be out until ten. I hated lying there wide awake and I kept wondering how I could get dressed in the morning without letting my room-mate see all my plain ugly things. Then I remembered that I had left my common cheap little wooden brush, the shellac all washed off with weekly scrubbings, on top of my chiffonier. I jumped up quickly and hid it in the top drawer; then suddenly I turned on the light, sat down in my horrid red wool wrapper, and wrote something like this to Alec, blubbering and dabbing tears all through it:

> *"Dear Alec,*
>
> I'm here safely, I've met all the girls and they are perfectly lovely. I'm going to love it. My room-mate's name is

Gabriella Atherton—isn't that a beautiful name?—and she is a perfect dear! I can't write long for I am due at a spread; so, so-long until I have more time. This place is full of corking girls. They would, however, consider the twins mere babes-in-arms. Tell Aunt Sarah that Father will want his flannel night-shirts as soon as there is a frost. They are in the all-over leather trunk in the storeroom. The girls will be wondering where I am, so good-night.

"Your enthusiastic
"BOBBIE."

Then I went back to bed and bawled like a baby, until I heard Gabriella at the door. Another girl was with her and I heard her say, "Good-night, dear," and Gabriella call back exactly as they do in books and as they did once in my dreams. "Good-night, sweetheart." Thereupon I ducked my head down underneath the covers and pretended to be asleep. A half-hour later, when I felt sure that Gabriella was dead to the world, I opened my eyes and lay awake until almost morning.

But no one needs to think that I was homesick. Wild horses couldn't have dragged me home. I was bound to stick it out or die and I tried not to be a little goose and cry my eyes out. That wouldn't help me to make the best girls my friends and I didn't mean to disappoint Alec if I could help it. I was there for business and I meant to accomplish it. Alec had said he admired that quality.

But Miss Brown's-on-the-Hudson was awfully different from the Hilton Classical High School. They played basket-ball as if it were drop-the-handkerchief: there was no regular team. We exercised by walking two by two for an hour every afternoon. There wasn't the slightest chance for me to shine in athletics.

I was robbed also of my hope of being a genius. There was a girl who could write ten times better than I. It was after one of her poems was read out loud in class, that I discovered I wasn't gifted in the least. She was the marvel of the school, and whenever there were guests she was asked to read her poems herself. They were the deepest things I ever listened to—about the soul, and sorrow, and "swift sweet death." She *looked* like a genius too. She had jet black hair and wore it in long curls tied loosely behind, big dreamy eyes, and pale transparent skin. She wasn't very healthy and always wore black. Her mother was an artist in Florence, and Lucia (think of it, *my* name, but pronounced so differently) Lucia had always lived in Italy until she came to school. I tell you, as soon as I saw her and listened to her poetry, I was terribly thankful that I had never let any one know that I had ever thought *I* could write. I got A on my compositions, and A in everything else, but no one imagined that I was a genius. They considered *me* just a plain everyday shark. But I tried not to be offensively smart. I flunked on purpose once in a while; I passed notes in class whenever I could find any one to pass them to; I got so I could turn off a "darn" as neatly as any of them, and pout and say "The devil!" when I pricked my finger pinning down my belt. For I was determined they shouldn't think me a "goody-goody" or a "teacher's pet." I even crocheted a man's tie and pretended it was for a friend of mine at a fashionable preparatory school in Massachusetts. I went so far in my frantic endeavours, as to cut out from old magazines all the pictures I could find of an actor, whom, by the way, I had never even seen, and stuck them in the corners of the glass over my chiffonier.

Oh, I tried to be like the other girls. I knew they hadn't liked their first impressions of me, but I tried to show them that I wasn't as queer as I looked. I tried to be pleasant and accommodating; I tried to be patient and bide my time; I tried—heaven knows I tried, Alec—but it was no use. From the start it was absolutely no go. I couldn't make even the *worst* of those girls my friends. I tell you I did my level best, but I hadn't the clothes, nor the silver bureau-sets, nor the frames, nor the men's pictures to put into them, nor the college banners, nor the mother to send me boxes of food from home. Those girls treated me as if I were the mud under their feet. If I was in the room, I might as well have been the bed-post for all the attention they paid to me. If I was told to walk with one of them during "Exercise," that one was pitied by the rest. They looked upon my clothes as if I were a Syrian or Turk in strange costume. I used to get hot all over whenever I had to appear in a dress they had never seen. And, O Juliet—good old loyal Juliet—you were afraid I would be spoiled by admiration! I simply have to chortle with glee when I think of your warning to your old chum. A swelled head! My *eyes* got swollen instead, old Jule, with tears! And Father—dear Father—there wasn't a single soul for me to be kind to. *I* was the most miserable one in the whole school, the most unpopular, the most forlorn. And there's the truth in black and white.

After about five weeks of an average of ten insults a day, I got tired. Too long a stretch on the diet of humble-pie doesn't agree with me. There's an end to every one's patience. One day in late November little Japan up and fought; and once started, there was no stopping her. You see the girls had gotten into the habit of asking me to help them with their lessons. At first I was pleased, for I naturally thought that if they would let me see their stupid minds, they would admit me into a few of their intimacies and secret affairs— and oh, I did long to be friends with them! But I discovered they had no such intention.

One night I went into Beatrix Fox's room, by appointment, at quarter of ten. She was waiting and ready for me, but I could see the remains of a spread on the table and desk—crumbs, nutshells, olive-stones, and a half-eaten bunch of Tokays.

"Oh, here you are!" said Beatrix, and with no attempt at concealment, she went on. "I've been having half a dozen girls to a spread," she said. "But I told them to leave one piece of cake for *you*, Lucy. Here it is. Now let's get at the Latin."

I was awfully insulted. Beatrix Fox nor any one else had ever seen the least fire or spunk in Lucy Vars before that night, but I couldn't hold in a minute longer. I took the delicious piece of chocolate layer-cake and went over to the waste-basket. I threw it in. "There's your cake!" Beatrix stared as if I had gone crazy. "There's your old cake, Beatrix Fox!" I repeated, and went out of the room.

After that night I was a changed person. I couldn't be touched with a ten-yard pole. I became a regular bunch of fire-crackers—spurting and going off in everybody's face and eyes at the least spark. And oh, to speak out my mind, and to spit out my feelings at last, was simply glorious! It was like getting the rubber-dam off your tooth after a three hours' sitting at the dentist's. After that experience with Beatrix, there was no more Cicero translated nor French sentences corrected by Lucy Vars for a single one of those stupid-minded, rattle-brained young ladies. I made a notice on pasteboard in black ink and hung it on my door. It read: "A PUBLIC TUTOR CAN BE OBTAINED FROM MISS BROWN. DON'T APPLY HERE! LUCY CHENERY VARS." The girls thought the sign was perfectly horrid and I was glad of it. I wanted to be horrid. I revelled in it. I wanted to be horrid to everybody who had been horrid to me.

Once during "Written Exercise," I wrote a whole page of Latin Composition wrong, so that little cheating snobbish Barbara Porter next to me might copy it off on her paper and pass it in. At the bottom of *my* sheet I wrote, "I've made these mistakes on purpose. You may give me zero." Miss Brown, in a long talk in her private office, told me it was not a kind thing for me to do. But I didn't care. I had let Barbara Porter copy my Latin Comp for five weeks without a murmur, and she had never put *herself* out to be kind to *me*. I wasn't going to be anybody's door-mat!

At Thanksgiving all the girls "double up," which means that the ones who live far away spend the holiday with the ones who live near. Of course no one wanted me. Gabriella, who at times tried to be nice to me, felt conscience-stricken, I suppose, for she said to me one day when we were dressing, "It's too bad you're going to be here alone, Lucy. Don't you suppose

Miss Brown would let you to come down to East Orange" (Gabriella lived in East Orange, New Jersey) "and eat Thanksgiving dinner with us?"

I replied maliciously, "Why, I'm sure Miss Brown would let me spend the entire three days with you, Gabriella."

Gabriella hedged then, as I knew she would. "Oh, I'm so sorry. I'm taking Grace and Barbara home with me, and there's a dance I do want to go to—and—if you—"

"O Gabriella," I broke in, "don't be alarmed. I shan't burden you for one little tiny minute. I just wanted to frighten you. I wouldn't give your friends at home such a shock as the sight of me would be, for anything in the world. I shall enjoy, on the other hand, the quiet of this room after my charming room-mate has departed."

That's the way I talked but I wrote home: "Gabriella wants me awfully to spend Thanksgiving with her. There is a dance and all sorts of plans, but in spite of all her urging I've refused. There's quite a bunch of us staying here" (the bunch were teachers), "and jolly spreads and sprees in store."

I didn't want my family to know—kind Alec, the arrogant twins, pretty Ruth, and Father who used to be so proud of me—I didn't want them to know what a poor little Cinderella I was. When I went home I wanted every one to think I had had a glorious time at school, as all girls do. I wanted my family to open their eyes and say, "My, how you're changed!" and every one at church to whisper when I came in a little late, "There's Lucy Vars home! Hasn't she grown up?" I wanted Dr. Maynard to raise his hat to me when he met me on the street, and call me Miss Vars. I wanted Juliet to gaze at me with envy. If there was any real silver underneath the tarnish on me I was bound it should shine when I went home at Christmas. And so it happened that I made up my mind that if I couldn't make friends with my new schoolmates I could at least learn something from them. I used to observe them very carefully and jot down important points in my memory. Even the things that I derided to their faces, I meant to copy when I went home. My brain became a regular copybook of rules.

"My skirts," I recorded, "should be below my shoe-tops, not above.

"The way to keep a waist down, is to fasten it with a safety-pin behind and a long black steel pin in front.

"My nails should be as shining as a dinner-plate.

"A shining face is not supposed to be pretty.

"Powder is used to remove shine, and isn't wicked like rouge.

"Girls of seventeen use hairpins and rats, and keep their hats on with hatpins instead of elastics.

"Mohair and gingham underskirts and Ferris waists are not worn by girls of seventeen.

"Huge taffeta bows underneath the chin, on the hair, or anywhere in fact, is the rubber-stamp for a girl of my age.

"Automobiles, actors, college football, and allowances are popular subjects for conversation.

"Don't break crackers into your soup.

"Don't butter a whole slice of bread.

"Don't cut up all your meat before beginning to eat."

I used to watch Gabriella dress like a hawk. She had lots of clever little tricks, like pinning up her pompadour to the brim of her hat, or rubbing her cheeks with a hair-brush to make them rosy. She used to put a little cologne just back of her ears, which I thought very queer, and she was forever asking me if I could see light through her hair. Every week she gave her face what she called a cold-cream bath. She said her mother always did, after riding in the automobile.

I planned to spend every cent of Alec's one hundred dollars on clothes. I did all my shopping in New York. I adored New York! Saturday afternoons when the other girls went to the matinée, the chaperone allowed me to spend the time in the big department stores. I didn't buy anything—just looked and looked, priced and priced, and when I had a nice clerk, tried things on. Once I had my nails manicured, so I would know how; once I went to a Fifth Avenue hair dresser, who charged me a dollar and a half to make me look like a sight; and one day I bought Father a necktie for fifty cents and Alec a scarf-pin for seventy-five. That is all I spent until just before Christmas when I blew in the whole hundred. For, you understand, it was not to impress the girls at school, but the people at home, that I bought my new outfit. It was not until after I had made a great many estimates and carefully planned it all out on a piece of paper that I asked one of the younger teachers, who I thought had good taste, if she would help me buy a few trifling clothes on the following Saturday.

We started on the early train and reached New York at nine o'clock. I think that Saturday was the happiest day of my life! I bought a suit for thirty-five dollars at Kirby's; a hat marked down to ten dollars at Earl & Kittredge's; a silk dress for twenty-five dollars; a spotted veil for fifty cents; a barette for twenty cents; pumps for four dollars; one pair of silk stockings for one dollar, and so on. I had just seven dollars and sixty-seven cents left after I had bought my last purchase—a lovely red silk waist for travelling. My suit was dark blue, my boots tan with Cuban heels, and my blue velvet hat had two reddish quills in it. I was awfully pleased with my selections, and I confided to Miss Davis, the teacher, that I wasn't going to wear any of the things until the very day I started for home.

"And now," I said, "I'm going to take you to luncheon, Miss Davis, after which I want you to be my guest at a matinée."

It was simply grand to have money! It makes you feel like a queen to fling it around as if it were paper. After I had spent almost a hundred dollars Miss Davis thought I was an heiress in disguise, and to carry out the part I left the whole of fifty cents as a tip for our waiter at luncheon. I told Miss Davis to pick out the most popular play in New York for us to see. We bought the best seats in the house.

Never, never as long as I live shall I forget those two hours and a half of perfect happiness! I'd never seen anything but vaudeville in my life, and I almost cry now when I think of that play. It was perfectly grand. The hero kept looking right straight at me all the time and what do you think? What do you suppose? He was the very actor whose pictures I had cut out and stuck in my mirror! He was Robert K. Dwinnell, and I hadn't known until I was inside the theatre and looked at the program that he was in New York. It seemed to me too strange a coincidence to be true. I don't believe in omens, but Miss Davis told me afterward she hadn't the slightest idea that I had been collecting his pictures. After that play I could hardly speak. The queer grey light of day after the glow of the footlights, didn't seem real. Boarding-school and all the girls seemed trifling. I couldn't think of anything except Robert Dwinnell and that play all the way back in the train. I felt that I was the beautiful heroine instead of Lucy Vars. I felt her joy at meeting her lover instead of my anguish at going back to a lot of unfriendly girls. I lived and breathed in the action of the plot I had just seen. I couldn't get away from it. Before I boarded the train that night I dragged Miss Davis into a small shop which we passed on the way to the station, and with the last fifty cents of Alec's one hundred dollars I bought a real picture of Robert Dwinnell. The picture is here now in this very cupola, in the top drawer of my desk and is the only comfort that I have. Mr. Dwinnell is sitting on the edge of a table swinging one foot, just as he did in the play—I remember the place in the third act—and his eyes are looking right at me.

I wonder, oh, I wonder sometimes, if he and I will ever meet.

CHAPTER VI

IT was about a week before the Christmas vacation that my last outbreak at boarding-school occurred. It was one noon after lunch when I was passing through the hall on my way upstairs. I had to go by Sarah Platt's room, where the little clique of girls I had once longed to be one of, used often to congregate after luncheon before the two o'clock study-hour. They were gathered there to-day, talking and laughing together in their usual mysterious manner, and I wondered vaguely as I went by, what they were discussing now. I never allowed myself to listen intentionally, but the conversation of those girls, who were still strangers to me, always fascinated me, and I confess I used to overhear all that I could without being dishonourable. As I sauntered by the half-closed door of that room I recognised the voice of Sarah Platt herself, who of all the girls I had aspired to make my best friend. Sarah was a dashing kind of girl and would show off to awfully good advantage before my family if I had invited her to visit me.

"Well," I heard her say, "I think Miss Brown is taking her in on charity."

I knew Sarah must be referring to me and I stopped stock-still.

"Why, she hasn't *anything*, and this horrid place is probably a palace to her!"

I flushed with rage. Palace nothing!

"I think," said a little Jewess by the name of Elsie Weil, "it's too bad for Gabriella. I'd hate to have such a room-mate forced on *me*."

"I don't think Miss Brown ought to take such a girl in at all and make us who pay a thousand dollars a year be intimate with a person we never can know socially," drawled Sarah Platt. "It's hard on her too," she finished patronisingly.

"Oh, don't mind about *me*," I breathed, ready to explode.

"I'm just tired," another girl broke in, "of having all the teachers, and Miss Brown too, talking and lecturing to us about being nice to *Lucy, Lucy, Lucy* all the time."

"And the spite and scorn that the child puts on lately," added Sarah, "is perfectly absurd. As if she had anything to back it up!"

"I know," went on the little Jewess, "her family can't be much. You can see that. Did you ever notice the row of old-fashioned family pictures on the back of her chiffonier?"

At that I caught my breath. My dear good family! And without waiting to hear another word I flung open the door. There were six or seven girls before me crowded together in a bunch on a couch in the corner. I felt myself grow suddenly calm as I stood there before them not saying a word, and they staring back at me as if I were an apparition.

"I heard every single word you said," I began slowly, "every single word!" Then my thoughts collected themselves and filed by in the order of soldiers on parade. "I don't care a straw for your opinions. I feel above every one of you. It makes me smile to think I would be the least disturbed by common and uneducated westerners," for Sarah lived in Missouri, "or Jews!" I spat at Elsie Weil. "You needn't any of you trouble about being kind to me. I don't want your kindness. I'm perfectly indifferent to every one of you. I am *not* here on charity; and as for the pictures on my chiffonier, if you don't like them, lump them, or else keep your eyes at home." I knew I was acting unladylike but I was fired up and couldn't help going on. "My family may not have fashionable photographs, my clothes may be as ugly as mud, but if you *knew* who my older brother is, if you *knew* who my father is, if you *knew*! My father is president of the Vars & Company Woollen Mills; my father is a director in the Hilton County Savings Bank; my father is a state senator; my father—oh, I shan't tell you all he is, because you haven't got enough brains to appreciate it. It would be like telling monkies about Abraham Lincoln!" I stopped just a moment, but no one spoke. All those girls huddled together in a bunch just kept on staring as they would at a rearing horse in a parade, meekly from the sidewalk. "You don't know about anything but clothes and theatres. And let me tell you once for all I don't want anything of *any* of you." Sarah Platt opened her mouth to speak. I cut her off short. "Keep still, Sarah Platt," I said. "Don't you dare address one word to me!" Oh, I wanted to do something insulting, like sticking out my tongue, or making an ugly face. But instead I just said, "And don't one of you in this room ever assume to speak one word to me as long as you live!" And I turned, stalked out of the room, and went straight upstairs.

I don't know how I could have said anything so horrid as all that, and I seventeen years old, but somehow it is always easier for me to roll off spiteful things than anything sweet and kind. I am always less embarrassed about it. Poor Alec would have been awfully disappointed to have heard such an outburst from his sister. Father would have said, "Oh, Lucy!" The arrogant twins wouldn't have wanted to own me. Only my dear old chum Juliet Adams would have been proud. She would have exclaimed, "Bully for you, Bobs!"

When I reached my room on the next floor, I calmly opened the door and went in. Gabriella was standing by her desk. I never shall forget how she looked—perfectly white and staring at me horribly. I wondered what ailed her, for she couldn't have heard my tirade on the floor below.

"What's the matter, Gabriella?" I asked.

"Oh, Lucy," she began, then sank down in a chair by her desk, leaned forward with her head buried in her arms, and began to cry dreadfully.

I went over to her.

"Gabriella," I said, sorry for her somehow, for though she was one of Sarah Platt's clique she had not been talking about me; she was, after all, my roommate, and at least she let me see her cry. "Please, Gabriella, tell me what it is."

"Miss Brown," she choked, "wants—" she stopped, then wailed, "*you*!"

"Me?" I groped blindly. Me? Had my awful words been telegraphed to Miss Brown's office? Did she know already? I couldn't follow. Things were happening too rapidly. "Me, Gabriella," I asked. "But what for? Please stop crying and tell me."

I could barely catch a few words amidst her violent sobs.

"*My* father," she said. (I knew Gabriella's father had died the winter before when she was away at school.) "A telegram," she stumbled on, and I waited, "*your* father—"

My father!

I went to Gabriella quickly, put my arm about her and leaned my head down close to hers.

"Listen, Gabriella. Be quiet for just one minute and answer me. Did you say *my* father?" and then in a fresh torrent of sobs I heard her "Yes."

I left her crying there and went down through the long corridors to Miss Brown's office. I passed Sarah Platt's room without knowing it. I even passed some one in the hall but I have no idea who it was. I kept thinking, "This is your first test. Be ready and don't break."

Miss Brown was at her desk. She started a little when she saw me, then smiled—how could she smile—and said, "Oh, Gabriella found you. Come here, dear," and she put out her hand. I closed the door and then backed up against it. I couldn't go near Miss Brown. I didn't want her tissue-paper sympathy.

"What's happened to my father, Miss Brown?" I asked. "You can tell me the very worst right off."

She didn't hedge any more.

"He is very, very ill," she replied, going straight to the point as I liked to have her.

"Does that mean," I said, "that he is—is—" I couldn't say it—"is worse than very ill?" I finished.

"No," she replied. "No, Lucy. Your father is still living. I have just called up your brother by long distance telephone and they want you to come home immediately. It is your father's heart." Then she added, looking at me firmly, as if she were upholding me by the hand: "It is a long trip. You must be prepared for the worst, Lucy." I didn't answer and she turned to her desk, picked up a piece of paper and passed it to me. "Read it," she said. "It is a telegram for you."

I looked down and these words greeted me like dear, comforting friends:

"*Stand up, Bobbie. Be brave. We need you to be strong. Alec.*"

It was just as if my dear brother Alec were suddenly there like a miracle in the room beside me, and *now*, at last, I would not disappoint him.

I looked up at Miss Brown.

"When is there a train?" I asked calmly; but to myself I was saying over and over again, "Stand up. Be brave. They need you to be strong."

Miss Brown came over to me, and I must say I've always liked her from that day to this. She didn't say anything silly or comforting to me. That would all have been so useless. She just took my hand in a man's sort of way and held it firmly a minute in hers, "Your brother will be proud of you," she said. That was all, but do you think then I would have failed?

"We will go upstairs and pack," she added immediately, and I followed her, bound now to control myself or die.

I don't know how I ever got started. I only know there was a confused half-hour of packing, with Miss Brown helping and Gabriella close by me all the time. Gabriella couldn't seem to do enough. I saw her slip her pink kimono into my suit-case; I saw her pin one of her beautiful pearl bars on my red silk waist. She got out my new blue suit and brushed it; my new hat with the red quills; and while I combed my hair, she laced my new tan shoes. I understood that it was her way of telling me how sorry she was, for every once in a while she'd have to stop and cry. Once she said, "Oh, I am so sorry I've been so mean. I hope—oh, I do *hope* you'll come back, Lucy." But I didn't care now. It was too late. All my thoughts were with my family who needed me. I gathered their dear pictures together in a pile and put them in my suit-case— Father's picture too, but I didn't trust myself to look at it. Dear Father—but I didn't dare let myself think, just at first.

I felt in the air that all the girls knew my news about as soon as I did. Of course they didn't come near me. Even if I had been popular I don't believe they would have come. Sorrow somehow builds up such a barrier, and the one or two girls I met in the corridors kept close to the other wall and tried to avoid meeting my eyes. Gabriella and Miss Brown and the English teacher, whom I had always hated, saw me off. I begged to take the trip alone and Miss Brown finally allowed it.

I thought of everything during that journey, and the more I thought the more I trusted myself to think, I don't know what made me so clear-headed and fearless, but I'd run my thoughts right up to any hard truth, and they wouldn't balk; they'd go right over. My mother had died when I was so little that I did not remember it and so this was the first test I had ever had. Perhaps—oh, perhaps,—I faced it clearly and squarely—perhaps when I was met at the station they would tell me that I had come too late. I knew now that I wouldn't give way. Some great wonderful strength was in me and I wasn't afraid of myself. My home-coming was very different from the one I had planned, but when we drew near to the familiar old station I just said, "Be strong," and I knew that I should.

Dr. Maynard was at the station to meet me. The minute he got hold of my hand he said, "It's all right. You're not too late."

"That's good," I replied, but somehow I couldn't feel any more joy than sorrow. I remember, in the carriage, I asked lots of straight-forward, businesslike questions and Dr. Maynard answered me in the same way. There was no hope. The end might come at any moment. When he stopped before our door and helped me out, he said, "Bobbie, you're a brave girl." But I wasn't. I couldn't have cried. I didn't know how.

I went into the house while Dr. Maynard stopped to hitch and blanket his horse. I found the twins and Ruth and Aunt Sarah all in the sitting-room. It didn't come to my mind then, but now, as I remember it, it was all very different from the triumphant entry I had planned. No one jumped up to greet me, and my new suit and tan shoes and hat with the quills were all unnoticed even by myself. The twins came forward and kissed me—not embarrassed as they usually are, but scarcely realising it. They didn't say anything, just kissed me and turned away. Ruth lay prostrate on the couch. She didn't stir at sight of me and I went up to her and kissed her on the temple. At that she buried her face deeper into the cushions and began to sob. Aunt Sarah looked as if she had been crying for weeks. She sat quietly rocking by the west window and her big, dyed-out, blue eyes were swimming in tears, brimming over, and running down her wrinkled face. It's something awful to me, to see a grown person cry. It's like an old wreck at sea, and I just couldn't kiss her. Everybody so horrible and silent and dismal, was worse somehow than death, and just for a moment I stood kind of helpless in the middle of the room. Then the door into the library opened and I saw my dear tired, patient Alec, and suddenly his arms were around me tight, holding me close—close to him and I heard him murmur, "Good Bobbie, good, brave Bobbie," and oh, if I can hate people awfully, I can love them too. When he let me go, he said calmly, "Don't you want to come and see Father?" and I followed him upstairs.

Dr. Maynard led me to the side of Father's bed and I took one of Father's dear, familiar hands in mine. Alec sat down on the other side and for a while we three waited silently until Father should wake up. I wasn't frightened. It all seemed very natural, and none of the heart-breaking thoughts that came to me all during the weeks after he left us came to me then. It really seemed almost beautiful to be waiting there until Father should wake up. When finally he opened his eyes and saw me, he smiled, and pressed my hand a very little. Then he spoke.

"Lucy!" he said; and after a long pause, "Do you like school?" he asked, just as naturally as if we were having a nice little talk downstairs.

"Oh, yes, dear Father, I do!" I answered, and he pressed my hand again. It didn't strike me so very deeply then that my last word to my father was a lie, but afterward I used to cry about it for hours and hours. After a moment my father turned to Alec, "Stand by the business, my son," he murmured.

And without a moment's hesitation my brother promised, "I will, Father."

I didn't think Father would say anything more, for he closed his eyes again, but after a while he opened them and I saw he was actually noticing my hat and red waist, and the pearl pin Gabriella had given me. He smiled and I heard him murmur, "Pretty!" That was all; and oh, since, I have been so glad that my new clothes did so much more than I had ever hoped. For that was the last word my father said. I felt his hand grow limp in mine, and just then Dr. Maynard touched my shoulder and led me quietly away. He told me to lie down on the bed in the guest-room. I obeyed him and when, a little later, he came to me I understood the message in his eyes. I didn't feel the awfulness of it then nor I didn't have the least inclination to cry. I lay there very quietly for half an hour, then of my own accord I got up and went downstairs.

I found Aunt Sarah by the window still crying without the grace of covering her tear-stained face. The twins were not there. Ruth jumped up when I came in and clung to me frantically.

"Aunt Sarah," I asked, annoyed, "*why* do you sit there and cry?"

"Unnatural girl," she answered, "have you no heart, no tears? Don't you know your father has died?"

At those awful words poor little Ruth clung to me still tighter and wailed, "Oh, send her away, make her go off!"

I replied to my aunt, "Aunt Sarah, don't you know you shouldn't speak like that before Ruth? I'm surprised."

A little later Alec came quietly into the room. Poor Ruthie flung herself upon him just as she had upon me, and as he held her and patted her shoulder, he said, looking at me in a way that made me stronger, "Lucy, you will find Oliver in the alcove under the stairs. Go to him and give him something to do."

Poor Oliver was crying as only a boy of sixteen who isn't used to it can, I guess—dreadfully uncontrolled. He was sitting on the leather couch, leaning forward with his face in his hands. I went straight over to him and sinking down beside him, put my arms right around him. Poor Oliver—poor big broken Oliver! All the hate in my heart for that cruel twin rolled right away when I felt his great big body leaning up against me. I loved him just as if he were my son come home. We sat there together a long while—just Oliver and I—and finally when he was a little quieter he managed to say, "Don't—don't tell Alec and Malcolm—that I—I—"

"Of course I won't, Oliver," I assured him, and then I added just as if nothing had happened, "My trunk is still at the station, Oliver. I need it awfully. Here's the check. It's dark out now. Will you go down and see about it?"

He looked away and replied in a voice that tried to sound natural, "Sure, I'll go," and stood up and blew his nose very hard. I saw him glance into the mirror over the fireplace. Then, "Will you get my overcoat and hat?" he asked shamefacedly. When he went out of the house he had the visor of his cap pulled well down over his eyes, and his hands shoved deep into his pockets. We hadn't said a word about Father.

As for myself, I don't know what was the matter. I honestly didn't seem to feel a thing. I was just like a soulless machine. During the three following days I wrote notes, sent telegrams, saw about a black dress for Ruth, Aunt Sarah and myself, planned good nourishing meals for the family, went on errands, and "picked up" every room in the house, for they certainly looked awful. I didn't sleep and I wasn't hungry. I was wound up pretty tight, I guess, for it took me a long while to run down. On the second afternoon Dr. Maynard took me out to drive and then shut me up in my bedroom with the curtains all drawn tight and a little white sleeping-powder to take in fifteen minutes if I didn't go to sleep. I took the powder and stayed awake all night besides. Once during those blind, confused three days Juliet came to see me, to tell me how sorry she was I suppose, but I wasn't glad to have her. I remember I just said, "Hello, Juliet, how's basket-ball and high school?" I wasn't glad to see even Tom and Elise. When Elise held me tight in her arms and whispered, "Poor little Bobbie!" I felt like a hypocrite, and pulled away. Every time the door-bell rang and I knew that it was some one else who had come to try and comfort us, I wanted to lock myself in my room. My head ached and my eyes felt like chunks of lead. But I didn't want sympathy. I didn't need it.

The end came the night after the funeral. It hadn't occurred to me but that I would go back to boarding-school after Christmas. We were all in the sitting-room—all but Aunt Sarah who finally had stopped crying and was recuperating in her bed upstairs. Tom and Alec were discussing all sorts of plans, and I remember that Dr. Maynard, who seemed to be one of the family now, was there too. I wasn't following the conversation very closely, and suddenly I heard Tom say, "Well certainly the sooner Aunt Sarah packs up, the better."

"Why, who then," I asked, "will take her place?"

Alec looked up.

"What do you mean, Bobbie," he asked. "You'll be here, won't you?"

"Why, no. I shall be at boarding-school," I replied.

At that Ruth suddenly flopped over on the couch and began her usual torrent of crying. "I hate Aunt Sarah! I hate Aunt Sarah! I hate Aunt Sarah!" she wailed.

"The whole fall was rotten!" put in Malcolm. "Do you mean to say, Lucy, that you're going back to that school?" he fired.

"I guess your duty is *here*, Bobbie, old girl," said Tom; and Elise got up and came over to my chair.

"I know how hard it is to give up school," she said sweetly, "but they do need you, don't they, dear? Later, perhaps—"

"Well, I must say," interrupted Oliver, who was master of himself without any doubt now, "if this isn't the greatest! Look here, Alec," he asked, "do you intend to allow Bobbie to neglect us in this fashion?"

And Alec, dear Alec, across the room just smiled and said, looking straight at me, "I am going to let her do as she thinks best," and his eyes were full of kindness.

I got up then. My knees were trembling. I thought at last I was going to break down and cry. They wanted—oh, finally my family wanted me! I didn't know whether to trust my voice or not.

"Well," I said a little wobbly, trying to smile back at Alec, "I'll think it over." And as soon as I could, I sneaked out of the room, on the pretense of getting a drink of water. I went into the little back hall off the kitchen, took an old golf cape that was hanging there, threw it over my shoulders, and went outdoors. It didn't seem as if I could get my breath inside the house. It was dark, the stars had come out, and I went out of the back gate, walking as hard and fast as I could. I knew I must do something, for as wicked as it seems I was almost crazy with happiness, and I was afraid that at any moment, now at the very last, I should give up entirely, lie down at the side of the road and cry and cry. I almost ran as I hurried along, and all the time I kept saying, "Hold on. Be strong. Don't let go." Yet I knew the storm was gathering and I was losing my grip. I didn't plan to go to Juliet's house, but suddenly I saw it looming up in front of me, and it occurred to me to stop and tell Juliet my beautiful good news. So I hurried to the back door and burst into the kitchen. The Adams's cook gave an awful start.

"Good Lord!" she exclaimed.

"Hannah," I asked, and my voice was strange and hoarse, "where's Juliet?"

"Why, at dinner," gasped Hannah, staring at me. "What is it, Miss Lucy?"

"Tell her to come up to her room," I managed to say, and in our usual informal way I dashed up the back stairs to Juliet's room, which I knew so well. I waited impatiently in the dark and in a minute I heard Juliet pounding up the stairs. Then I saw her coming through the hall, her white napkin in her hand. I grabbed her.

"Juliet," I cried, "Juliet, I'm not going back to boarding-school! They want me here! I'm so happy I don't know what to do. It's horrible to be happy but I am, I *am*!" And then it struck me so funny to be happy on such a day that I laughed! I laughed simply dreadfully. All my pent-up feelings burst forth then, and I laughed till I cried. I could hear myself laugh and that made me laugh more, and then Juliet looked so queer and thunderstruck that that added to it. Pretty soon Mrs. Adams was there and they were putting cold water on my face, which struck me as the hugest joke I ever heard of, for they must have thought I was hysterical. I laughed so hard that actually I hadn't enough will or strength left to stop if I tried—I, who am usually so controlled. I got down on the floor finally, and then I don't remember anything more.

When I woke up it must have been hours later, for I was all undressed lying quietly in Juliet's bed, and there was Mrs. Adams going out of the door, and there—yes—there was Dr. Maynard behind her. There was a low light on the table by the bed and beside it sat my dear stolid Juliet. I thought at first I would burst out laughing again to see her sitting there with her funny little tight pig-tails braided for the night, with me in her bed getting her sheets all hot. Just then she looked up.

"Hello, Bob," she said in her commonplace, natural way. "Want a drink of water?" and she came over and gave me a little sip out of a glass. I didn't remember anything then, only that it was good to have old Juliet around.

"There was no one as nice as you at school, Juliet," I said.

"I guess that's a merry jest," she replied in her usual way. She took the glass away and I heard her go out of the room. I lay there very quietly and watched the dim light flickering. There was a little clock somewhere that was ticking quietly.

Then—oh, then I came back to life, and suddenly the thought of my dear, dear father returned to me. I began to cry softly for the first time, and finally fell asleep.

As I sit here this soft spring day and listen for the noon-whistle on Father's factory to blow, I shall not wait for the sight of Dixie and the phaeton coming up the hill, for Alec will be alone and I hate to be reminded of too many places left empty by Father. Father had so many favourite chairs. In every room in the house it seems as if he had his special place. And his roll-top desk closed and locked, his various pairs of shoes and slippers which he used to keep underneath all put away, makes the dear spot look as if it were for rent. I hate the neat orderly air of the sitting-room. It seems to be reproaching me. Father used to love to fill the room with all kinds and descriptions of papers. Everything, from a folder left at the front door directed to "The Lady of the House" to year-old newspapers, Father wanted preserved. There were three piles of the *Scientific Machinist*, four feet high, stacked up in one corner. I used to beg Father to let me carry off those *Scientific Machinists* at least— they collected dust fearfully—but he wouldn't allow me even to suggest such an idea. So on my own responsibility one day, I stealthily took away some of the bottom ones and packed them in the storeroom. I knew he'd never miss them and the pile was growing. Every month I'd clear out the paper case, preferring to annoy the kindest father a girl ever had to having an untidy room. I cry when I think of the kind of daughter I was; I cry and cry in the middle of the night. I wasn't good! I wasn't good! I write it down for every one to see. Of course it's too late now, but I've taken down the muslin curtains from Father's room, and the lace ones from the sitting-room. Father never approved of hangings of any kind. I don't allow the cat in the front of the house. I haven't destroyed a single folder, pamphlet or catalogue. The pile of *Scientific Machinists* I wouldn't move from the corner for anything in the world.

Oh, Father, if you were only here to be pleased; if you were only here to scatter papers around; if you were only here to ring the gong for dinner, call Ruthie "baby," me "chicken," say "Hello, boys!" to the twins, and then sit down opposite me, clear your throat and ask the blessing; if you were here again I would be a better oldest daughter. I wouldn't tease for a rubber-tired runabout, for new wallpaper, nor for that brass bed for my room.

I don't know where you are, nor where my mother is, but somehow up here in this cupola on a starry night, when I sit on the window-seat, lie flat back with my head out of the open window, and look up into that great dome of a sky, I feel as if you two may be together somewhere, perhaps seeing me.

But I don't *know*. There are times when I'm dreadfully doubtful; there are times that I don't believe anything. I think I may be an atheist! I have never discussed the subject with anybody, but occasionally it comes to me, just as the fear used to come that I was adopted, that religion is all a lie. I know I'm a member of the church, and it may be horribly wicked of me, but once in a while right in the middle of my prayers at night, I'll stop and think, "Perhaps no one is hearing me at all."

Really, I wonder sometimes if any other girl ever had such awful thoughts.

CHAPTER VII

ONE day last fall I received an important letter from Oliver. The twins are in college now, perfectly great fellows and awfully prominent. I don't know what they don't belong to down there at that university; and good-looking—well, I just wish Gabriella or Sarah Platt or horrid little Elsie Weil could lay their eyes on Oliver's last photograph. He's stunning! The big loose baggy clothes that college men wear, suit those two boys perfectly, and though I refuse to put on the worshipful air that Ruth assumes in the twins' presence, I'm just exactly as proud of my brothers as any girl in this world. Oliver is the better-looking of the two and the more athletic. He's a member of the crew now, and it gave me an awfully funny feeling up and down my spine when I saw my younger brother's picture in one of the Boston papers. Malcolm is the more studious, wears glasses and sings in the Glee Club. He isn't "a greasy grind" at all—not that sort, but he never gets into scrapes or mix-ups, and doesn't seem to need so much money.

Money was what Oliver's important letter to me was about. Usually he wrote to Alec but this time he appealed to me. When I tore open his letter at the breakfast table and started to read it out-loud to Alec and Ruthie as usual, I was confronted with great printed notices at the top and on the margins—PRIVATE! PERSONAL! DO NOT READ OUT LOUD! SECRET! and so forth. I assure you I shuffled that letter back into its envelope as quickly as I could and waited for a quiet hour by myself. This is what the letter said:

> "*Dear Bobbie,*
>
> "This is *very* important. So shut the door and read it carefully. I'm writing to you because you have influence with Alec, and you've *got* to use it. Alec doesn't seem to realise the demands on a man down here. When he and Tom were at college they had all the money they wanted, and they don't in the least understand the mighty embarrassing position it puts a fellow in to have *no cash*. I get pretty sick of sponging. There are certain class and society dues, Athletic Association fees, etc., that any kind of a good fellow must ante up on. Alec doesn't in the least appreciate the situation. He's getting mighty close lately, it seems to me, and every time he sends me my measly monthly allowance, he seems to think it's a good chance to drool out a sermon on economy. Economy! Heavens, I've been known time and time again to walk out from town after the theatre, to save a five-cent car-fare. I've been to some of the swellest dances that are given in a hired dress-

suit. *Of course* I had to have some evening clothes. *You* would know that.

Now look here, Bobbie, it so happens that I've got to have something that resembles a hundred dollars! Don't jump. I'll pay it all back—every cent. But it's serious, and I *must have it*. If you can't get it from Alec, can't you borrow it out of the Household Account which you have charge of? I'll make it right with you in a week or so, and be more than grateful.

"Your affectionate brother,
"OLIVER."

"P. S.

"Don't let Malcolm know I need this money, nor tell Alec what you want it for. And by the way, I must have seventy-five of the hundred by December third at the latest *absolutely*. Understand this is no ordinary matter. If I don't get the money somehow it will mean public disgrace. Comprenez-vous?"

Now Oliver knew as well as I that we were dreadfully poor. Ever since Father died, Alec had made it very plain to us that we were on the ragged edge of financial disaster. We had never been what any one could call prosperous—at least not since I could remember—but when Alec took hold of the reins at Father's woollen mills he found things in a pretty bad condition, I guess. He explained to Malcolm and Oliver just exactly how uncertain our financial future was, before they even started in at college. He told them that they must let it be known, early in their college course, that they couldn't afford the luxuries of well-to-do men's sons. He said that college must mean to them a period of serious preparation. It was only due to Tom's generosity, he explained, that it was possible for the twins to go to college at all. Tom assumed the responsibility of the twins' tuition. "And sometime," announced Alec emphatically, "both you boys are to pay back that loan, every cent." "Sure. Certainly. Count on us!" were the replies they made. They were overwhelming in their assurances. There was no grumbling *then* when Alec preached to them about economy.

It was just before the twins went to college that we were all put on an allowance. Alec called us together one day in the sitting-room and we talked it over. Alec conducts those discussions of ours with a lot of ceremony. He sits in Father's big chair and allows each one of us to state his or her opinion, while the rest sit quietly and listen. Even little Ruth may say what she thinks and no one is allowed to break in or interrupt. Alec is the jury and the judge all in one, and when he has heard both sides and weighed the question carefully he makes the decision. Tom is the higher court, but I've never known Tom once to disagree with Alec's verdict, so it doesn't do much good to appeal your case. At that meeting in the sitting-room it was arranged that Ruth and I should receive each twelve dollars a month, and when it came to the twins we all agreed that they ought to have a great deal more than two girls living at home. Alec said that he would start them on twenty-five apiece, and out of that amount everything, except board and room and doctor's bills, should be paid. At the same time Alec also arranged a household allowance, and I was very proud when he appointed me keeper of the Household Account. I was glad he thought me old and able enough for such a position and was bound to prove myself worthy. Every month he made out a check to me for fifty dollars and put it in the bank under my name. I paid the grocery and provision bill on the tenth of every month, submitted a report of the different items to Alec on a long ruled sheet of paper, which he, when he had time, examined and O.K'd. He impressed upon me again and again the absolute necessity of keeping the Household Account separate from my own. He told me in a long talk how awfully dishonest it would be if I ever used a single cent of that deposit for anything but household expenses. He went so far as to give me examples of cashiers in banks who were put in prison because they borrowed a little money now and then from the bank for their own use, fully intending to pay it back as soon as they could. So you see that when Oliver suggested my borrowing from the Household Account it was entirely out of the range of possibility to consider such a thing.

I felt sorry for Oliver. I knew exactly how much he must have wanted a dress-suit. It seemed to me a perfect shame to have two corking fine fellows like the twins cheated out of friends and good times and popularity—like myself at boarding-school—because they couldn't afford the proper clothes or pay their shares on spreads and theatre parties. A hundred dollars was an awfully lot but I put Oliver's letter into my work-bag the evening of the day it came and went down into the sitting-room after supper to join Alec by the drop-light on Father's desk. Every evening I sewed while Alec worked on the factory books. Alec didn't talk much lately. He didn't seem to want to. He was usually too tired for anything but bed, when he finally closed the big ledgers, but I was always there beside him just the same. The twins sent their laundry home every two weeks in an extension-bag, and it's quite a job keeping two strapping college boys sewed up. To-night as I weaved in and out across a delicate little hole in a mauve-coloured sock of Oliver's it looked to me as if it were an expensive sock: it had silk clocks embroidered up the side. I was so busy, planning just how I would approach Alec for that hundred dollars, that he startled me when he turned around in Father's revolving desk-chair.

"Bobbie, I want to talk with you," he said.

"All right," I replied gladly. "Go on." Perhaps, I thought to myself, there will be a chance to introduce Oliver's letter.

Alec folded his hands on the slide of the desk drawn out between us.

"We're spending too much money," he said simply.

I had heard that same sentiment expressed so often that I wasn't deeply impressed. I had observed in spite of Alec's continued talk about economy that there was always enough to pay the bills. I continued sewing.

"Of course; I know," I said, trying to appear sympathetic.

"No, Bobbie," Alec replied; "I don't think you do. It is different this time. Will you stop sewing?"

"What do you mean?" I asked, dropping my work in my lap.

"Bobbie," Alec said, "perhaps you will understand the seriousness of the situation when I tell you that I do not think that we ought to live in such a big house."

"Not live here?" I exclaimed.

"I'm afraid not, Lucy. It's a big place to keep up for just you and me and Ruth. We can't afford it."

"Has the business failed, Alec?" I interrupted with kind of a sick feeling in my stomach.

"Certainly not," he said in an annoyed sort of manner as if he had not liked me to ask. "We're simply living way beyond what we can afford; that's all. We've got to cut down. I don't know how long it may take to make a favourable sale of this house, but in the meanwhile we can't afford to keep two servants. I'm sorry, Lucy; I'm sorry; but it's a matter of economy *to-day*, not economy *to-morrow*. I've thought it all out," my brother continued, beginning now to pace up and down the room. "I know Nellie has been with us twenty years. We shall miss her; but she's not strong, she can't cook or wash. We must have a good young Irish girl—five dollars a week—not more. It means a big change this time, you see. I had hoped to avoid such a course as this, but if we are to escape a worse catastrophe—"

I don't know what Alec went on talking about as he walked up and down that sitting-room floor; I don't know how long he continued explaining, and trying to make clear to me the seriousness of our situation; I don't know; I really *don't know*. I sat stunned and silent in my chair, not stirring a muscle. *Sell our home!* Why, Father had built it. I had been born in it. *Dismiss Nellie!* Why, Nellie had known my mother. Nellie was part of the foundation of our lives. I couldn't take in the succeeding facts because those two were stuck in my throat. I felt like crying out, "Don't, don't cram any more in. I'm choking!" But Alec kept right on.

"The stable, of course, I shall close immediately. We mustn't keep a horse. I shall have to get rid of Dixie."

It isn't a nice figure, but at that last announcement I gulped up all that I had tried to swallow before.

"O Alec," I interrupted, "poor little Dixie! Please, please, *please* don't sell Dixie!" I pleaded. "Please don't sell our home," I cried. "Why, where shall we live? Don't send Nellie away. Don't! Don't! I'll do anything! I won't buy a stitch for myself. And I'll work—I'll work my hands to the bones! I can earn something. But oh, don't sell dear, poor little Dixie." I leaned forward suddenly and burst into tears. "Oh, everything has always been hard in my life—hard, hard, hard!" I sobbed.

Alec came over and stood in front of me perfectly silent. He hadn't seen me go into a passion like this for years. I could feel his tired kind gaze burrowing through my two hands that covered my face. I wished he wouldn't look so troubled and sad, for though I didn't glance up, I knew exactly how disappointed in me he was—how shocked by my tears. For a full half-minute he said nothing. He waited until I was perfectly quiet, then he spoke very gently.

"Why, Bobbie," he said, "ever since the day that you came from boarding-school when Father was so ill, and I came into the room and found you strong and calm and self-possessed, ever since then I have thought of you as *my partner*." He stopped. "But perhaps this—*this* is too much. Perhaps—"

"No, Alec," I said, ashamed; "no, it isn't too much. Just wait a minute, please."

"I will," said Alec kindly, and walked over to the window.

I guess it might have been two minutes he waited. His back was toward me when I mopped my eyes, when I tucked my handkerchief into the front of my shirt-waist and stood up. I summoned all my strength. Alec is my commander-in-chief, and I tried to rally my forces before him. I must not be a coward before Alec. I took up my sewing.

"I won't be so foolish again," I remarked evenly. "You can tell me *anything* now."

And my general replied, "That's the sort," and smiled. "As to the twins," he went on, taking me at my word, "here's a letter stating the situation to them."

He gave a short laugh with no joy in it. "The twins' allowances are going to be cut down almost half!"

"The twins!" I had completely forgotten Oliver's letter. "The twins! Can't you possibly—O Alec, college boys need so much and—Oliver, you know—"

"I'm tired of Oliver's extravagances," burst forth Alec impatiently. "I don't want to hear another word from Oliver about money. If he can't get along on the amount I am able to send, he can come home and go into the mill."

Just here the cheerful honk-honk of Dr. Maynard's automobile sounded outside the window. Alec went to the door and let him in. As Dr. Maynard entered the room he brought in a big breath of fall evening.

"Hello," he said. "What are you two up to? Come on, Al, put on an overcoat and come out for a run around the reservoir. I've got my engine working like a bird again."

"Thanks, Will, wish I could," said Alec with that tired smile of his, "but I've got a lot of work on hand to-night. I think I'll send Bobbie."

"All right! Fine!" said Dr. Maynard, and though I didn't have much heart for going, I knew that Alec didn't want to talk with even Will Maynard to-night, so without a word I went for my things that were hanging in what we called the "Black Closet."

I was glad to escape for a minute to the protecting dark. I stood pressing up against the old overcoats and ulsters, waiting for my eyes to appear less swollen, and wondering why Oliver needed seventy-five dollars by December third. The vision of Oliver in overalls at work in the mills, disgrace, no home, no Nellie, no Dixie, rags, poverty, wriggled before my eyes like moving pictures. I took hold of the nearest garment at hand and pressed it against my face. It happened to be Father's old overcoat. I recognised it by the feeling, for often I had groped for it when Father had been alive and brought it out to him waiting in the hall. I reached up to-night and touched the dear familiar, worn, velvet collar. "O Father," I whispered, "everything is tumbling down. What shall I do about Oliver?" Probably another girl would have breathed a little prayer to God but I make all *my* requests of Father. It seems to me that Father is more likely to take a personal interest in my affairs than any one else in heaven.

"What are you up to?" Dr. Maynard sang out; and I called back, "Coming," and hustled into my warm overshoes.

It was a beautiful dark starry night, and I wished Alec could have felt a little of the cold air on his hot head. I love an automobile! I'm never happier than when I'm sitting with my two hands on the wheel, one toe on the gas, the other on the brake, a heel on the little pedal that makes the old machine snort up a hill like a horse dug in the side with a spur. But to-night I didn't care to run the car. I suppose I wasn't a very entertaining companion, for on the way home, after we had been out about an hour, Dr. Maynard asked in his friendly manner:

"What is it, Bobbie? You're leaving it to me to have most of the fun to-night."

"Dr. Maynard," I exclaimed, "I'd give anything in the world if I were a man and could earn some money."

"What profession would you follow?" he laughed at me.

"I'm serious. Has Alec ever told you much about the business?"

"Not much, but I know he's been disturbed about something lately."

"Well," I said, "there's one of those pictures in that big Doré book with illustrations of the Old Testament, that reminds me of the Vars' affairs. It's a picture of Samson, and he's standing in a great huge kind of hall, pushing down two perfectly enormous stone pillars. The walls and the ceiling and the roof are all caving in—people headfirst, arms, legs, great blocks of granite, children, men,—oh, everything you can think of—tumbling down in horrible confusion. That picture used to give me the nightmare; and now it seems to me as if some old giant of a Samson had gotten down underneath us. All our underpinnings are giving way and we're all falling down—headfirst a thousand feet, smash, on to rock-bottom."

"Why, what do you mean, Bobbie?" laughed Dr. Maynard, amused.

"I mean," I replied—though perhaps I ought not to have told—"I mean, that Alec is going to sell the house and Dixie and we're going to keep only one girl. I mean that the business is on the ragged edge of nothing, and that we're as poor as paupers."

Dr. Maynard slowed down our speed to ten miles an hour.

"Al's a plucky fellow," he said. "I hadn't an idea!" Then he added, "*You* want to help?"

"Well," I replied, "I've got to have a lot of money right off, and I don't like to ask Alec. It's for an emergency," I added. "Can you think of any possible way for a girl who can't do a thing on earth but scrub and darn stockings, to earn a fortune?"

I think we ran about a mile before Dr. Maynard spoke. Then when he did, he seemed to be almost apologising for his scheme, which seemed to me perfectly lovely.

Dr. Maynard has stacks of money and since his mother died, lives all alone in the big, white-pillared house where he was born. Eliza, their old servant, takes care of him. "But," he explained to me, "cooking and cleaning are Eliza's strong points. Now there are lots of odds and ends she doesn't have time for. She never liked to sew, and I have a pretty hard time keeping socks mended, and linen, and towels, and such things in good condition. I hire a woman now by the day once in a while. But I'm sure I'm way behind now. If the scheme appeals to you at all, I'll have Eliza lay out a pile of stuff that needs a few stitches, and you can sew on it at odd moments. Just keep track of your time and I'll pay you—well, you seem to be a fairly busy person, I'll pay you double what I'm paying now which would be about fifty cents an hour."

"Dr. Maynard," I said, "I think you're the very kindest man I ever knew!"

"Oh, no," he broke in, "this is purely a business transaction."

"But," I went on, "fifty cents is a lot too much. That would be giving me money."

"Well, let it be understood," he said, "I'm not giving you anything. You're earning it in just as businesslike a manner as a stenographer—or Eliza. I'd like you to keep an accurate account of your time, please, and send me an itemised bill. I said fifty cents and I stick to it. Shall I come over to-morrow with your first relay?"

I thanked Dr. Maynard with my whole heart. I was so relieved I didn't know what to do.

"Would you mind," I said as he opened the front door for me, "waiting just a minute? I've a note upstairs that I wish you'd mail on your way home."

I dashed up to my room, directed an envelope in mad haste to Oliver, and on a half-sheet of note-paper I scratched:

> "In spite of Alec's news I may be able to scare up some of the money.
>
> "BOBBIE."

Alec had half a dozen letters for Dr. Maynard to mail also, and I had the satisfaction of laying my note to Oliver on top of the announcement which cut his allowance in half. After the door had closed and Alec and I were alone, I went and kissed my brother good-night.

"Good-girl," he said wearily; "the ride brightened you up."

"Yes," I replied; "and I know we're going to come out all right, Alec." And I felt that we should, now that I was going to put *my* shoulder to the wheel.

CHAPTER VIII

TWO days later I received a frenzied reply to my note to Oliver. The words were underscored, smeared, repeated, blotted and scratched out. I never read such a letter. I think Oliver swore in it. At any rate my heart almost stood still when the words "for God's sake" struck at me like swords from the white paper. I knew at least that Oliver was terribly in earnest. I read and re-read the letter, then locked it away in the cupola in the lowest drawer of my table-desk. No one shall ever see it; no one shall ever know what it contains—no one but Oliver and me. I shall never tell Alec, nor his own twin Malcolm, nor even his wife, if he should ever marry. This is between Oliver and me. He had chosen to tell his older sister about his trouble to the exclusion of every one else, and she would prove to him that he had rightly placed his faith.

I don't want to imply that Oliver had been really dishonest. I am sure he had not been that, but it seems that he was treasurer of something or other down there at college, and had boggled the accounts. He never could keep money straight. Perhaps he had borrowed a little of it—like the bank clerk Alec told me about—and now suddenly he discovered there was more of a shortage than he could make good. He wrote that on December third he must make a report, and if he couldn't account for seventy-five dollars short in the treasury—well—There followed six dashes with three exclamation points at the end.

I wrote back I'd get that seventy-five dollars for him or die.

I scraped money out of every hole and corner I could find. I sold my lavender liberty automobile veil to Juliet Adams for a dollar and a half, and Ruth bought my rhinestone horse-shoe pin, which I paid three-fifty for, for seventy-five cents. I didn't spend a single penny of my own allowance for November and begged Alec for five dollars which I told him, without a quiver, that I'd got to have for the purpose of buying some new stuff for the kitchen. But most of the money had to come from Dr. Maynard. I sewed like mad. Locked in my bedroom with the alarm-clock keeping track of my time I simply devoured holes. I was like a hungry animal. I couldn't get enough of them—and the bigger they were the better they satisfied me. Socks by the dozens; table-clothes gnawed by rats; napkins worn to shreds; blankets to be rebound; sheets to be hemmed; *anything* that required a needle, I welcomed with rejoicing.

But of course a man doesn't need more than three dozen socks on hand, five dozen perfectly whole towels and ten table-clothes. There is an end to a bachelor's equipment, and even after I had finished mending with gummed paper a whole music-rack full of old sheet-music Dr. Maynard used to sing, I had earned only twenty dollars.

I was very unhappy when Dr. Maynard passed me my last receipted bill. He was looking at me out of the corner of his eye.

"Well," he said, "does this close our business transactions? Are you all fixed up now?"

I shook my head and blushed, ashamed somehow to be in need of so much money.

"Oh, I know," I hastened to say, "that there's no more work you can give me, and I do thank you—I do really."

"Let's see," Dr. Maynard said. "Let's see. What kind of a hand do you write? If it's plain and legible, I don't know but what I'll engage you to copy some old letters of my mother's—written to me when I was a small boy at school. The ink is fading and I want them preserved."

"Dr. Maynard," I exclaimed, "I don't know what I'd do if it wasn't for you!" There were almost tears in my eyes I was so grateful.

"Nonsense," he laughed. "But what do you want so much money for?"

"A bill—for some dresses I had made, and I don't want to bother Alec."

Dr. Maynard gave a long low whistle.

"Oh, I see." Then quite seriously he added "Better tell him, Bobbie."

"Dr. Maynard," I said, "if you mention one single word of this to Alec, you don't know the harm you'll do. You don't know!" Why, if Alec had gotten wind of what Oliver had done, there wouldn't be a scrap of lenience shown that poor twin. It would mean clattering looms for Oliver, as surely as the electric chair for a murderer; and I was absolutely fierce in my determination that that brother of mine should graduate from college, as well as all the others. Before Dr. Maynard went home that afternoon he had promised he would not tell Alec a word about our business transactions.

I enjoyed the copying. Dr. Maynard's mother must have been a perfectly lovely woman. She used to write to her son every Sunday, and oh, such sweet companionable little notes—all about what was going on in the town, and always at the end just a sentence or two about honour and ideals, and how she believed in her son and missed him. If Oliver had had a mother to write to him like that—to tell him how she wanted him to grow up in the image of his honoured father who had died, who rejoiced at every success he had, who sympathised at every failure—if Oliver had had a mother to write him letters every Sunday evening by the firelight, I don't believe he would have ever gotten into such a difficulty. I wondered if mothers wrote letters like these to their daughters. Of course they must.

Every once in a while, I would run across a reference to my own mother (for Mrs. Maynard was her neighbour) and, really, it was a little like seeing her for just a minute.

I know I'm neglecting my story, but I must tell about one special letter of Mrs. Maynard's, because it referred to me. It didn't happen to be written to her son but to a woman friend whom I didn't know. It was a chatty letter, that related all the important events and happenings in the town, very long and full of the littlest details you can imagine. It was on the fourth thin sheet that I ran across this: "And our dear neighbour Mrs. Vars has a little daughter three weeks old," I deciphered. "She has named her Lucy for herself. I went in to see her last week and took her a jar of my quince jelly. She is a very happy woman. She has always wanted a little girl. When she took the little baby in her arms she said with tears in her eyes, 'My little daughter and I are going to be "best friends" all our lives.'"

I read that precious sentence over and over again. My mother and I 'best friends all our lives'—and oh, I couldn't remember her smile. 'Best friends all our lives'—and she had gone before we could share a single secret. I leaned right forward over my copying and cried, "If you'd lived I wouldn't care if we were poor. If you and I were 'best friends,' I wouldn't care if I never had a good time. Oh, if you were here! If you were here!"

And yet, although I cried so hard, I was strangely happy that evening. Of course I don't believe in miracles. They don't happen nowadays, and yet it seems almost as if my mother might have sent that message to me, to console me in my struggle, to tell me that I wasn't all alone. I gazed at her picture—the only one she had ever had taken—under its cold glass over my bed, before I went to sleep that night. It is a profile, clear-cut and a little sad. They tell me she was only nineteen in the picture—my age, just my age now.

"My best friend," I whispered, "my best friend all my life!"

As the dreary days wore on, all the sympathy that I possessed yearned over my patient brother Alec. But I couldn't help him any. Time and time again I tried to cheer him up, but my attempts fell flat. There was a time when Alec used to go out among the young people in Hilton quite a good deal, but I observed that lately he had nothing but business engagements to take him away.

Alec had never talked to me about a certain young lady named Edith Campbell—I don't know that he had ever mentioned her name to me—but I knew that he had always entertained a sneaking admiration for her. Since father died he hadn't seen her so much and I had been glad of it. I don't like Edith Campbell. There is so much show about her, and she always contrives to make Alec look so forlorn and pathetic. I remember one morning not long after Alec's serious talk with me, that he went out of the door gloomier than ever with his green felt bag filled with the ledgers that he'd been working over till midnight. Just as he was going down the front steps who should appear but Edith Campbell in a sporty little rig, driving a new cob of hers—round and plump and shiny. She had some little out-of-town whippersnapper of a man beside her, and as she drew her horse to a standstill right by Alec, she looked trig and sporty enough for the front cover of a magazine. She gave Alec a play salute from the brim of her perky little hat, and my poor tired brother took off his limp grey felt. He went over and leaned one hand on the horse's brilliant flank, and gazed up at Edith. His overcoat that used to be black looked greenish in the bright sunlight and the velvet collar was worn about the edges.

"Hello, Al Vars!" exclaimed Miss Campbell. I could hear her through the open door, hidden behind the lace. "I haven't seen you for *one age*. You ought to come out of that shell of yours. Al *used* to be a pal of mine," she laughed to the man beside her and introduced them. The stiffly-starched little out-of-town man gave Alec a hand gloved in yellow dog-skin and Alec turned and said something I couldn't hear to Miss Campbell. She called her reply back over her shoulder as she drove off. "Sorry, Al. Can't. Too bad. I'm going to Florida with Mother and Dad for the winter next week!"

Alec stood forlorn in the middle of the street, watching her descend the hill. The back of the highly-shellacked little waggonette flashed in the sunlight. Miss Campbell sat erect, sleek as her horse. My feelings grew savage against her, and when Alec finally shifted the heavy green bag to the other hand and moved slowly off down the street toward the factory I wanted to run after him and tell him she wasn't worth a single thought of his. I wished that my life-long devotion might make up for this single morning's sting of Edith Campbell's heartless exhibition of prosperity. But it couldn't. It couldn't break through my brother's brooding silence for even an interval.

Ruth took our change of circumstances very philosophically at first. Ruth is sixteen now, and awfully pretty. She has boy-callers about three times a week. She's very popular. She can sing like a little prima-donna, and can dance a cake-walk like a young vaudeville performer. The twins think Ruth is the cleverest little creature alive. She's a very independent sort of girl. No one can give any advice to Ruth on what is the proper thing for her to wear; no one can tell *her* what is the correct way for girls of sixteen to act; at least, *I* can't. Ruth loves fashion and style. She was glad to have Alec dispose of Dixie.

"Why," she said to me in her little sophisticated way, "Dixie is eating his *head* off, and he *limps*! I'd be ashamed to be seen at a funeral driving Dixie! You may have noticed *I* never use him." She was delighted to learn that Alec was going to sell the house. "For he says," she announced to me gleefully, "that perhaps *now* we can live in one of those darling little shingled houses on the south side. Those houses have the loveliest little dens in them with a stained-glass window, where I could have my callers. I just hate the parlour here. There's a big new crack over the marble mantel, and I have a dreadful time making people sit with their backs to it."

"And Nellie?" I questioned.

"Good riddance, I think. She's the bane of my life, and she hasn't a scrap of style. She's been here so long she thinks she can boss me as if she were my mother."

Ruth's chief source of sorrow was the announcement that she couldn't attend dancing-school. That brought the tears and for three days she'd hardly speak a word. When I told her that she ought to be cheerful for Alec's sake, she slammed the door in my face and told me not to preach.

I am afraid Ruth and I aren't very congenial sisters. I try very hard to be helpful and sympathetic, for Ruth, of course, is as motherless as I am. But she's a difficult younger sister. She never wanted me to take her to places when she was a little girl. She hates to be petted. It troubles me a little to think we aren't closer friends, because we each are the only sister in the world that the other has.

It was Ruth who stepped in and upset my whole scheme with Dr. Maynard. She can be dreadfully annoying, and cause as much trouble as any grown-up person I ever knew. It was when I was within ten dollars of the end of my struggle. I had finished the copying, and now I was working Dr. Maynard's initials on about everything that that man owned.

It was on a Saturday afternoon, and Juliet Adams, who had come down from college to spend Sunday with her family (Juliet goes to a girl's big college now), had dropped over to see me. I was sitting by the west window sewing on some things of my own, for of course all Dr. Maynard's work I was careful to do in private. Ruth was upstairs getting dressed to go out to a party with one of her numerous boy-friends. Suddenly, with her hair down her back, and dressed only in her white petticoat and dressing-sack, she appeared in the doorway.

"Got a thimble?" she asked. "I want to baste in a ruching," and without asking leave she grabbed my work-bag that was on the couch. It was open and she caught hold of it in such a way that the contents all went tumbling out on the floor. A dozen new socks done up in balls, on which I had been working initials, rolled out in all directions. The red monogram stared me in the face.

"I'll pick them up," I said hurriedly, but Ruth was too quick for me and she pounced upon them before I could stop her. Very little of importance escapes Ruth.

"W. F. M.!" she exclaimed. "Who's that? W. F. M.! As I live, on *every* one of them! Who's W. F. M.?" She unrolled one pair. "Men's socks too," she said, holding them up to plain view. "W. F. M.!" Then suddenly she broke into hilarious laughter. "I have it!" she burst out, waving the socks over her head and triumphantly dancing around the room. "William Ford Maynard! W. F. M. William Ford Maynard!"

"Stop, Ruth!" I cried, my old anger beginning to surge up in me. "*Stop*, I tell you!"

But Ruth was deaf to me. She simply kept on tearing around the room like a wild Indian. "How do you do, Mrs. Maynard," she shouted at me in silly school-girl fashion, and amidst her mad laughter sang out, full of derision, "Juliet, let me introduce Mrs. William Ford Maynard!"

I was standing up in a minute and was at Ruth with all my might and main. I was firing mad.

"Ruth Chenery Vars," I cried, "stop, *stop*, STOP!" and then suddenly there was Alec standing quietly in the doorway in his overcoat and hat.

Ruth and I went out like flames.

There was a dead silence for an instant, then Alec asked quietly:

"What does this mean?"

Ruth answered him.

"I tipped over Lucy's work-bag and all these men's socks fell out. Every one of them is marked with Dr. Maynard's initials, and Lucy got mad because I made fun of her."

"Will's initials, Lucy?" asked Alec perplexed.

"Yes, W. F. M.," went on Ruth delightedly. "See?" She gave the socks to Alec. "Nobody is W. F. M. in this town, but William Ford Maynard," she finished and sat down on the piano-stool in a satisfied way, as if she had cleared *herself* of any blame, and now was ready for some fun.

I think it was here that Juliet got up and slipped out of the room. Anyhow I know she wasn't there during the whole interview.

"Well, Lucy?" said Alec, looking at me.

"I was paid for it," I exclaimed. "I was paid for every single initial and every single stitch I ever took for him! Oh, there was nothing sentimental about it. Ruth makes me sick! I did it simply to earn money."

Alec looked down at the initials.

"How much were you paid?" he asked.

"I was paid," I went on, still on the defensive, "I was paid fifty cents an hour. It was all business from beginning to end. Oh, there was nothing silly in it!"

"Fifty cents an hour?" Alec repeated.

"Oh, yes," I said. "Ruth is absurd. I made out bills and receipts and everything. It was absolutely businesslike."

"And how much has Will already given you?"

The colour for some reason rose to my cheeks. Alec looked as if he wasn't pleased and I was suddenly ashamed.

"About—sixty dollars," I murmured.

"Sixty dollars!" Alec flashed. "Why did you need so much money?" he asked me sternly.

I saw my danger then. It was as if I had had my hands on the steering-wheel of Dr. Maynard's automobile, and suddenly saw an enormous limousine headed for me around a curve.

"Why," I stammered, trying to keep calm, "I thought the business was doing so—poorly, that I—I—"

"Why did you think it necessary not to tell me about this—enterprise of yours?" asked Alec.

The limousine kept coming straight for me, you see.

I hesitated just a moment. I had no idea of telling about Oliver. After you've worked for a cause, you'll protect it if it kills you. But I was at a loss to know which way to turn, and I had to act quickly. An inspiration came to me. It wasn't a good one, but I was excited.

"I borrowed seventy-five dollars from the Household Account. I had a dressmaker's bill of my own to pay that had stood a long while, and so—now I'm trying to make it up."

Alec dropped the socks as if they had been hot. He didn't say a single word. He just stood there and stared and stared. I glanced up for a fleeting second and Alec's eyes were terrible. The vision of them remained with me for days, just as the image of the sun will dance before your eyes after you have gazed at its piercing light for an instant. I turned and looked quickly out of the window. The clock in the hall struck five. I counted it to myself. The last stroke died away, and still Alec stood and stared. He seemed to be willing me to bow down in remorse and shame. I couldn't help it. I tried and I couldn't. I wasn't guilty—oh, no, Alec, I wasn't guilty—but suddenly a hot wave spread over me up to my temples and I hung my head before my brother's condemning gaze.

He turned away then, and without a word went out into the hall.

I didn't know a silence could be so eloquent; I didn't know a silence could hurt. It sobered even Ruth. She slunk quietly upstairs. And when I discovered I was quite alone, I drew a long breath. Then I got up, gathered the poor socks that had caused so much trouble together in a pile and put them back into my work-bag.

I didn't go down to supper that night. Alec knocked on my bedroom door about nine o'clock, and came in.

"Please put the household check-book on my desk," he said shortly; "I will take charge of it hereafter."

"Very well," I replied, perfectly calm; and a thick heavy curtain fell quietly down between Alec and me like the curtain after the last act at the theatre.

CHAPTER IX

HOW can I tell about the days that followed—black, blinding days with Alec's silent displeasure following me wherever I went, Ruth looking at me askance and avoiding an encounter, and I, firm, uncommunicative, and dismal as the grave?

To save Oliver from disgrace cost me a big price. I paid Alec's confidence and respect to buy Oliver's honour. Sisters ought not to have preferences among their brothers, but, Father, you know, *you*—before whom now there is no deceiving or pretending—you know that there is no one in the world to me like Alec. Why, Oliver and I used to fight like cats and dogs. Ruth is Oliver's favourite. I don't know why I was putting myself to so much trouble for Oliver, breaking my heart to save his reputation. Father would have put Oliver into the mills; Tom would have put him there; Alec also; but at night when I look at the sad profile over my bed, that face which only until lately had been simply an old-fashioned picture of my mother, I wonder what *she* would have done. I know Mrs. Maynard would have sold her soul to protect *her* son's reputation. Perhaps I was saving Oliver from disgrace for the sake of my "best friend." At any rate there was no going back now.

Meal-time of course was dreadful. There was no connected conversation. The clatter of the slumpy general-housework girl, as she piled up our plates and took them away, was more annoying than ever, when we all simply sat and listened. It's a difficult thing, too, to ask for the bread, and avoid glancing at the person who passes it. I didn't join Alec in the sitting-room any more by the drop-light; I didn't hurry downstairs to meet him at noon; I didn't ask him if he were tired.

"Please, Alec, say *something*!" I said, almost desperate, at the end of the third day.

I didn't know Alec could be so hard and unforgiving. His reply made me feel awfully sympathetic and kind toward Oliver, or any one else who might have made a mistake. It seems that, besides shattering my brother's entire confidence in my honesty, I had shocked his sense of propriety in accepting money from Dr. Maynard. To call it a business transaction appealed to Alec as absolutely absurd. He assured me that he was going to pay every cent of Will's money back to him. I started to reply, but Alec shrugged his shoulders and turned away.

"I don't want to talk about it, Lucy. Let us not argue about a matter in which your honesty and reliability is so involved. I had such faith in you! I could have forgiven you your lack of pride—your utter ignorance of the proprieties in spite of your nineteen years, in accepting sixty dollars from a friend! But you have been dishonest. You knew as well as I the seriousness of your offence when you borrowed from the Household Account placed in your name at the bank. No, please, do not answer me. For what is there for you to say?"

I didn't know. I went upstairs—not to cry, not to grieve, but to sit down in my black walnut rocker by the window and think bitter thoughts. I didn't care if I had been improper; I didn't care if Alec was unjust and willing to believe the worst of me; *I didn't care!* I had sixty good, crisp dollars tucked safely away in a little chamois bag in the bandbox where I keep my best Sunday-go-to-meeting hat, and when my allowance came due on December first I should have seventy-five. I didn't care if all the world turned against me. I had accomplished what I had set out to do, and no one could rob me of my victory anyhow.

I had it all planned that on December first I would deposit the seventy-five dollars in the bank and make out a check for Oliver immediately. But something happened which made quicker action necessary.

When December third, Oliver's fateful day, was about a week off I received another letter from him. In his haste, in directing it, he had omitted the state, and the letter had travelled to a Hilton, New York, which I never knew was on the map, before it found its way to me three days later.

> "The business meeting has been set forward to November twenty-sixth, so you better send the check on the twenty-fourth, at the latest. You've been a trump to get it for me, and if you're good, I'll have both you and Ruth down for a game sometime, with a spread in my room."

I didn't read any farther. I reached for my calendar. I found the twenty-sixth. I followed the column up to the days of the week. Yes—as sure as I was alive—Saturday! To-day was Saturday. To-day was November twenty-sixth! Oliver must have seventy-five dollars to-day!

It was nine o'clock. Alec was at the factory. Ruth was not in the house. I went down to the roll-top desk and found a timetable. There was a train at nine-fifty. It didn't take me an instant to decide that I would deliver that money to Oliver myself. I would go down to that college town, hunt that boy up, and place my little packet of seventy-five hard-earned dollars in his hands.

I put on my hat and coat—the same old black coat, by the way, that I had had dyed when Father left us—instructed the general-housework girl to tell Alec that I wouldn't be home for lunch, and hurried over to Dr. Maynard's. I buried all the pride I ever had (which Alec had said was a small amount) and pulled the big front bell. I was glad when Eliza said the doctor was in. I had never called there before, and I refused to enter even the hall. I had come to beg for money and it seemed more correct to stand on the doorstep. I had made up my mind after Alec's cutting speech that I would never take another cent from Dr. Maynard as long as I lived. But I had to, you see. My allowance wasn't due for five days. I simply had to have nineteen dollars immediately—four for my railroad fare and fifteen for Oliver. I wasn't going to have that twin even fifteen dollars dishonest. I wasn't going to fail now, at the eleventh hour, even if it cost my reputation.

"Hello," said Dr. Maynard in the doorway. "Good morning! It isn't often I have calls from young ladies so early. Come in!"

"No," I replied. "No, thanks." I stopped a minute then I said, "I know you'll be very much surprised. I know I'm going to do a very improper thing. I must seem to have no pride at all, but—but—can you lend me nineteen dollars?" My cheeks were burning red. Dr. Maynard folded his arms and leaned up against the casement of the door. I could see him smiling. "I'll pay you back," I went on bravely, "in four days—at least fifteen dollars of it. The rest I can give you on January first."

Dr. Maynard sat down on the doorstep and made a place for me.

"Sit down, Bobbie," he said.

"I can't," I replied; "I'm in a hurry."

Dr. Maynard stood up again—he's always very polite with me—and refolded his arms.

"Alec came over last night," he went on, "and it seems, Lucy, that Al didn't approve of our little game. He took it a little more seriously than we did, and perhaps it's better, after all, if you're in any sort of difficulty to go straight to your brother, if you've got as good a one as Alec."

"Aren't you going to lend it to me?" I asked point-blank.

"Well, now, you see," Dr. Maynard smiled, "Al didn't tell me the story, but he implied that you had explained the whole thing to *him*; and of course, Bobbie, if he, your brother, doesn't approve of your cause—"

"I told him a lie," I interrupted; "I told him I'd just the same as stolen seventy-five dollars from the Household Account, which he put me in charge of; and I haven't at all. I simply haven't! I shan't ever need any more money after to-day. I'll never ask another favour after this, but I've got to have it. *I've got to!* If it would do any good to get down on my knees and beg, I'd do it. But it seems to me when I debase myself by asking you for money right out of a clear sky, you must know it's awfully important. Alec tells me I've been improper even to earn money from a friend. It must be worse to beg it. But

I don't care—I *don't care*—just so you give it to me, and quick, because I've got to take a train."

Dr. Maynard looked very sober and serious for him.

"Can't you tell me what you need it for?" he asked.

For a moment I was tempted, but men are so queer and severe with boys who make mistakes, so terribly correct about honesty, how did I know but perhaps Dr. Maynard, too, would think Oliver ought to go into the mills.

I shook my head.

"I can't," I said; "I wish I could,—but, I'm sorry, I can't."

"How much do you need for your railroad fare?" he inquired, irrelevantly, and when I had told him he asked, "And what time does your train leave?"

"At nine-fifty," I burst out impatiently; "and I shall lose it if you don't hurry. We are wasting time. Oh, please decide quickly."

He didn't answer for a minute. He was biting his under lip, beneath his moustache, and gazing far away beyond my head. His arms were still folded.

"Four dollars; the nine-fifty," he contemplated out loud, unmindful of my precious minutes.

The frown between his eyes looked dreadfully unfavourable to me. I stepped toward him, and looking up to him on the step above I said, "Dr. Maynard, I copied all those letters of your mother's, and it seems as if I almost knew her now. I just know *she* would think my cause was worthy."

Dr. Maynard simply adored his mother, and I suppose it was the sudden thought of her that brought a kind of mist into his eyes. He stepped down beside me, took out his leather bill-book, and passed me two ten-dollar bills. "Then, Bobbie, here it is!" he said gravely.

I thanked him quietly, opened my bag, and put them away.

I have always thought Dr. Maynard was a mind-reader. His next speech simply staggered me.

"I should go to the train immediately," he said; "the nine-fifty will be crowded this morning, with people going to the game. And by the way, if by any chance, you have a notion of passing through any college town on the day of a big football game, you'll find it very confusing. Why not let me go with you? I'll ask no questions. Or will the twins meet you?"

"How did you know? How did you guess?" was on the tip of my tongue; but I replied instead, "Oh, thank you. I *must* go alone. I shall be back by dark—and—and some one will meet me," I stammered.

All the way to the station I kept thinking, "Why couldn't Alec have believed me worthy of good motives too? Why couldn't Alec have surmised and understood? Why couldn't it have been my brother who trusted and had faith?"

Before I bought my ticket I sent a telegram to Oliver, so he wouldn't be passing away with anxiety. "*Coming to-day. Bobbie*" I said, and five minutes later sank into a seat in the train with a sigh of relief.

It was nearly twelve o'clock when the last friendly, blue-coated policeman left me with a pleasant nod near the end of my destination. I didn't have a bit of difficulty changing trains, crossing Boston and weaving my way in and out and up and down a labyrinth of subway passages and various street-car lines. Everybody was awfully helpful and as long as I have a tongue I could travel around the world, I believe, without the least bit of trouble. It wasn't until I neared the end of my journey that I felt any nervousness at all. Oliver roomed at number 204 Grey Street and as I reached the nineties my uneasiness became quite apparent. I could feel it in my chest, as if I were hungry. I did hope Oliver would be in. I did hope I was doing the right thing. Probably my growing excitement was a little due to the gala spirit of the football day. It pervaded everything. It thrilled me. Crowds of people with steamer-rugs and overcoats over their arms had thronged the trains and street-cars all along my route—a good-natured crowd, prosperous-looking young men and stunning girls wearing great bunches of flowers and carrying flags. Everybody was excited, even down to the small boys selling programmes and banners in the square I had just left; everybody glowed with enthusiasm and with the foretaste of a triumph. I had never been to a football game in my life, and I had always wanted to. Perhaps Oliver would take me; perhaps we would have lunch together somewhere! I should adore to see the college buildings! Possibly—oh, possibly, he would introduce me to some of his friends!! The thought of the thrilling things that might be in store for me made me swallow to keep myself calm. As I hurried along Grey Street I was so excited that I somehow wished that the wonderful time was all over, and that I was speeding safely and victoriously home again, wearing a faded bunch of chrysanthemums that Oliver would buy for me, and hoarding in my memory the brand-new acquisition of a real College Football Game.

I was rather disappointed in the appearance of number 204. It was a big brick building and not at all my idea of a College Dormitory. It was just as plain and ordinary as it could be, with the door opening right square on to the brick sidewalk, and a horrid little tailor-shop and drug-store opposite. I didn't know what I ought to do. The big front door was wide open, and I could see into the hall. It looked like a prison—all brick and masonry, and bare granolithic stairs with an iron railing. I didn't know whether to go in or not. If there had been a policeman in sight I would have asked his advice, or an old lady, or a girl, but there was only a very good-looking young man on the other side of the street, so I rang the bell and waited. No one came. I rang again; I rang that old bell—at least I pushed the button—six times! No one answered, so I finally started up the stairs. Perhaps I was waiting at the basement door (the interior certainly looked like a cellar) and the parlours or reception-rooms were possibly on the floor above. It was while I was standing, hesitating on the second landing, gazing up interminable flights of cement stairs and brick walls, wondering how in the world I could dig Oliver out of such a tomb, that a door opened somewhere up above and down those stairs—bump-bump, clappity-clap, pell-mell, like ten barrels falling down one over another, shouting, laughing, guffawing—I heard what I thought must be a regiment charging down upon me. I drew back a little into the corner and suddenly four men—four stunning young college men appeared before me.

They all stopped shouting as if I had been a vision, and though they didn't say a word I could feel they observed me with a start of surprise as if young ladies in their corridors were a great curiosity. I blushed for no particular reason; they passed on quietly down the stairs; and would have left me there without a word if I hadn't spoken.

"Excuse me," I said to the back of the last young man. "Could you tell me—I'm sorry to stop you—but does Oliver Vars room here?"

They all halted and looked up at me. I blushed worse than ever. I suddenly felt as if I ought not to have been there, and though the young men were just as courteous and polite as they could be I was awfully embarrassed.

"Why, yes, he does room here," said the young man nearest me, taking off his hat. "Did you want to see him?"

"Yes," I stammered. "It's—it's very important. I'm sorry but I—"

"That's all right," he assured me quickly, for I guess he heard my voice tremble; "I'll find him for you." And oh, he had the nicest, straightest, cleanest look. "You go on," he said to his friends; "I'll be with you in a minute." Then to me, "Vars rooms here, but I am about sure he's out now. If you'll come with me perhaps—Must you see him right off?" he inquired.

"Oh, yes, thank you. I must. I *must*! I've come on the train to see him. I've got to see him if I sit here and wait for him."

"Oh, I'll get him all right," the young man said. "We haven't much of a place here to wait, but if you'll come with me, we'll find him," he assured me.

He stepped back to let me pass out in front of him to the street, and once on the sidewalk, he fell behind me a moment so that he might walk next to the curbing. Oh, that young man had beautiful manners! I'll always remember them. It was just the noon hour and he met lots of men that he knew. To each one he raised his hat as if he'd had a princess with him. They returned his bow in the same manner, with a curious look at me.

"They think," he laughed pleasantly, "I'm taking you to the game this afternoon!"

I flushed. I wanted to say, "I wish you were." If I had been the pretty girl whom we had just passed, in the black lynx, with a little round fur hat with a red flower on it, it would have been easy to smile, glance sidewise, and say pretty things. But from under my black felt sailor, side glances wouldn't be attractive. I kept my eyes straight ahead. "You can explain to them afterward," I said.

He left me in a drug-store. "I'll get him!" were his last words as he raised his hat.

I waited three quarters of an hour. It was after one o'clock when I saw Oliver push open the big plate-glass door. He had been hurrying. His face was red, his eyes startled and frightened, his hair tossed a little under the cap he wore. At sight of me he stopped, then strode up to me, where I was sitting on a stool by the soda-fountain.

"You!" he gasped. "You! For heaven's sake, Bobbie, what are you here for?"

"I telegraphed," I explained. "Didn't you—"

"No," he broke in, "I've had no telegram. What's the trouble anyhow? Who's dead? Who—"

"Why, Oliver," I replied calmly, "nobody's dead." Then in a lower tone, "I've come with the money," I said.

"The money! Why didn't you mail it?" he fired.

"Your letter didn't come till this morning, and—isn't the meeting to-day?"

"Oh, yes," he said still annoyed; "but there was no such rush. I've managed to borrow enough to fix *that* up. Oh, I knew I better not rely on your getting it here, and so a friend of mine lent me enough to tide me over." We had moved away from the soda-fountain and were talking in low tones beside a display of fancy soap.

"Then why—?" I began.

"Oh, because," he took me up, "I've got to pay Holmes back. No man of any respect owes money to a friend for a longer time than he can help. But Holmes didn't expect it till next week. It was absolutely crazy, your coming way down here. You went to my room, didn't you? What do you suppose the men will think? Do you know who it was told me you were here? Blanchard! Blanchard! A Senior! One of the biggest men here! Heavens, when he told me a girl wanted to see me—You don't have any idea of propriety, Lucy!"

"Oliver Vars," I returned, "I've brought seventy-five dollars down here in this bag for you, and you had better stop talking like that to me. If it wasn't for me and my impropriety, you'd be working in the mills, let me tell you. And I don't know but what it would be better. If Alec knew what you'd done—if Tom knew—"

Oliver's attitude changed immediately.

"Oh, I know," he interrupted. "It's been bully of you, Bobbie. I tell you I appreciate it. I suppose you had a hard time squeezing even such an amount out of old Al, and just now too, when business is so rotten. But I'll pay you back some day, you'll see. You've helped me out of a devil of a scrape. I'm going to have you down to a game or a tea soon."

"There's a game this afternoon!" I exclaimed. "Oh, Oliver—I've never seen a football game."

My brother frowned. "I'm more than sorry, but I'm taking some one this afternoon. Malcolm and I, two other fellows and four girls, a party of eight of us, are all going together."

"Couldn't I sit alone somewhere, off in a corner? I wouldn't mind a bit. I want to see the crowds and be able to say that I have been. Oh, I'd love to hear the cheering. You could call for me afterward, and—"

"Oh, no, Lucy; oh, no. That's out of the question. Why even if I could get a ticket, which I can't, it wouldn't do. You don't understand in the least."

There was something about the way Oliver glanced at my old rusty laced boots that made me say fiercely, "I don't suppose I'm dressed well enough!"

"Oh, it isn't that—not at all," he assured me, and suddenly I felt that it was. "Of course it isn't, though the girls do put on the best things they have. It's simply that no girl ever goes alone to a game."

"Well, then, here's the money," I said in a hard voice.

"Say, Bobbie, I'm awfully sorry. If you only had let me know. If you only—"

"Oh, never mind," I interrupted.

A young man in a grey sweater entered the store. Oliver glanced around at him, then flushed and finally raised his cap. The young man returned the bow generously. If I had been less sensitive I wouldn't have noticed how Oliver stood so as to shield me from the young man's gaze. If I hadn't walked that three blocks and a half with that young god Blanchard, whoever he was, I wouldn't have minded Oliver's half-apologetic bow. Mr. Blanchard hadn't been ashamed of me; *he* hadn't hidden me; *he* hadn't flushed when he met his friends. I wanted to get away from Oliver as soon as I could. I wanted to go home.

"Well, I might as well be starting along," I said. "I found my way down here without any trouble, and I guess I'll get home all right."

"Say, Bobbie, I'm more than sorry. I wish I could put you safely on the Hilton train, but I've got to rush like mad as it is—change my clothes, get some food, and call for Miss Beresford, all before two o'clock. So if you're sure—"

"I am," I tucked in.

"I'll put you on the electric car. Say—" his face brightened, "don't you want some hot chocolate?"

"Oh, I couldn't, Oliver. No thanks. Please."

I was glad to be alone again. I was glad of the protection of the crowds and the stream of strange faces. I sat in the corner of the car, where Oliver had left me, with a hard look about my mouth—at least I felt as if it were hard. There is no such thing as reward. Everything in life is unfair. Who was Miss Beresford? Would she wear coon-skin and velvet? Would Oliver buy her a stunning bunch of flowers to wear at her waist? Perhaps one of the actual dollars that I had earned would purchase a little flag for her to wave. Why should I pay for Miss Beresford's good time? Why should I have to work so hard, and wear ugly black? Why should I be going home—hungry and faint, and ashamed—while every one else was thronging in the other direction?

It was while I was changing cars, standing alone on the edge of the sidewalk, taking in all I could see of the excitement, that my eyes fell on a stunning creature in a long luxurious fur coat. She wore a huge bunch of violets, as big as a cauliflower. A great big sweeping plume streamed out behind. She was bubbling with laughter, and the young man striding along beside her was laughing too. They were a lovely pair, both of them full of the joy of living. The girl (I looked twice to make sure) was some one I knew. The girl, as sure as I was alive, was no other than Sarah Platt—Sarah Platt, whom I had longed to know at boarding-school; Sarah Platt who had always scorned the very sight of Lucy Vars; Sarah Platt whom finally I had almost spat upon as contemptible and mean. A half an hour ago, Oliver had tried to hide me, and now I tried to hide myself. I slunk behind a telegraph-pole. Sarah swept by like a gilded chariot; I heard her voice; I smelled the odor of her violets. "She'll always be glorious and happy," I thought savagely. "She'll always have a good time. She'll marry that young man. I know she will. And I—I'll always be poor and miserable and forgotten."

It was half-past two when I re-entered the big station, inquired of a news-stand girl the way to the restaurant, and found my way to the lunch counter. Instead of luncheon with Oliver, at a small table in some darling little college-town restaurant, I hoisted myself up on a stool and ordered a ham sandwich and a cup of coffee. The girl who drew the steaming black liquid out of the shining metal tank looked sour and dissatisfied. She slopped some of it on the saucer as she shoved the thick crockery toward me. She slammed down my check and slung a towel up over her shoulder with a sort of vehemence that expressed my feelings exactly. I don't know why she was so miserable; I never knew; but I sympathised just the same. When she dropped a glass and it shattered and broke at her feet, she merely shrugged her shoulders, and kicked the pieces as if she didn't care a rap if the whole station fell down and broke. Oh, I just loved that girl, somehow. I knew she thought life was cruel, hard as iron, and terribly unjust. I wasn't the only one who at that moment was not cheering with the crowds at the football game. I wasn't the only wretched person in the world.

CHAPTER X

ABOUT a week after I had been down to see Oliver, I observed that something strange had come over Dr. Maynard. The first time I noticed it was the day I hailed him when he was passing the house one noon, and gave him an envelope with my December allowance sealed up inside. I explained it was in part payment of the loan he had made me the week before. He didn't laugh; he didn't even smile; he was as solemn as a judge, as he took that envelope and put it in his breast-pocket. Usually there is a joke on the tip of Dr. Maynard's tongue. He is always saving situations from becoming serious by a bit of fun. I never knew what it was to feel uncomfortable with Dr. Maynard. The next day when he passed me alone in his automobile, when I was coming home from downtown, it flashed upon me as very odd that he didn't stop and take me in as usual. Then it occurred to me that he hadn't taken me out for a ride, for days. I got to thinking! The next Sunday at church he and Alec seemed friendly enough, but I observed that Dr. Maynard didn't drop in on us in the afternoon. The grave look that had come into his eyes when he passed those two bills to me that morning on his front porch, the solemn tone in his voice when he said, "Then, here it is, Bobbie," seemed to be there every time he spoke to me. I was sorry. It made me uneasy. It didn't seem as if I could bear it if Dr. Maynard should go back on me—along with the business, and Alec, and everything and everybody I ever cared a cent about.

I wondered what was the cause of Dr. Maynard's coolness. Perhaps he felt that Alec was blaming him for allowing me to take so much of his money; perhaps he was nursing the idea that he was responsible for the strangeness between my older brother and myself; or else, possibly Dr. Maynard thought that since I had committed such an unheard-of act as to ask him for money I would naturally feel embarrassed and ill-at-ease in his presence. But that was all nonsense. I didn't regret a thing that I had done. In spite of what Alec might consider my shocking impropriety, I didn't feel ashamed. I adored Dr. Maynard's cheerfulness! It seemed as if I must go and tell him that the only fun I had left now was the fun I had with him. I used to love his jokes and merry-making. I believe Dr. Maynard could make the worst catastrophe in the world a lark, if he wanted to. Why, whenever we had a puncture in the automobile, Dr. Maynard was so good-natured about it that any one would have thought he enjoyed punctures. "You've got a flat tire, George," he'd sing out to me (he calls me George when I am running the car), or, "Sorry, Miss; sounds mighty like a blow-out," he'd say, if he happened to be at the wheel; and while he was jacking-up, I'd flax around and unlock the tools. Before he had the shoe off, I was ready with the new inner tube, and thirty minutes from the time we had stopped we were zinging along again as good as new. Most of the sunshine in my life—literal sunshine and the other kind too—came through Dr. Maynard.

As I became more and more convinced that he was acting queerly, I began to realise how kind he had been to me. I suppose Dr. Maynard is really a better friend of mine than Juliet Adams, to whom I write twice every week, and for whom I make a stunning Christmas present every year. He has surely done more to fill my heart with gratitude and everlasting appreciation. It flashed upon me, one day, that I had never done a thing in my life, without pay, for Dr. Maynard. I began thinking and thinking what a girl of nineteen could do anyhow, for a man of thirty-five, who lives all alone and has all the money he wants.

It was when I was working on Juliet's Christmas present that it occurred to me that possibly it might please an older man, who didn't have any family, if some one gave *him* a Christmas present. The more I thought about it the better I liked the idea. It seemed to me a delicate way of expressing my thanks to Dr. Maynard for all that he had done.

I had an awful time deciding on the present. First I wanted to buy a wind-shield for his automobile but the price of wind-shields is something terrific. Fur robes, automobile clocks, a Gabriel horn all were delightful possibilities, but beyond the limits of my purse. My oldest brother Tom likes books, I always give Alec socks or handkerchiefs. The twins adore sofa-pillows for their rooms. Sofa pillows! Would Dr. Maynard like a sofa-pillow for his room? For a week I hesitated between a sofa-pillow and a hand-embroidered picture frame, but finally decided on the pillow.

I knew exactly how I was going to make it. I had seen one of my friends, who attends a big boarding-school near Philadelphia, embroidering a perfectly stunning one at Thanksgiving for a college man she knew. I copied hers. Of course I realised that Dr. Maynard had been out of college for years, but he is very loyal to his Alma Mater. He told me all about the fifteenth reunion he attended last June as soon as he got home, and seemed awfully enthusiastic. So I bought and had charged to myself, two yards of the most expensive and shiniest satin in the Hilton stores, had it stamped on one side with the seal of Dr. Maynard's college, and on the other with his initials and the numerals of his class beneath. It wasn't very complimentary to Dr. Maynard I suppose, but as I worked, I wondered if I would ever embroider a sofa-pillow for a real college man. I wished this one was destined for some one who was in college now. I should have enjoyed the thought that a pillow made by my hands would be piled high on a couch in the corner of a college boy's room, beneath posters and signs and flags, and that college men would lean up against it and play banjos and guitars. I wished I had half an excuse for making a sofa-pillow for Mr. Blanchard. Dr. Maynard graduated perfect ages ago, in the class of '90—three years before the World's Fair in Chicago, which is one of my earliest recollections. The pillow that I copied mine from has on it a big '09, and Mr. Blanchard is a member of the class of '06. I had only to turn my pillow upside down and it would have been perfect for Mr. Blanchard.

After I had finished the embroidery, I bought the best down-pillow for the thing that I could find—for I wasn't going to skimp on Dr. Maynard's Christmas present, after all his generosity—and also a heavy black silk cord to go around the edge. I must confess when it was all done—the black letters standing up so that they cast a shadow on the red satin, and the surface as round and full as a raised biscuit—I must confess it was perfectly lovely. I think Mr. Blanchard would have liked it very much. I wrapped it up very carefully in tissue paper, over that a layer of brown paper held together by pins, and put it well out of sight on my closet shelf. I was determined that Ruth shouldn't see it.

Christmas used to be a great day with us. Tom always came home from the West; and we had fricasseed chicken for breakfast; turkey and pies for dinner; figs, nuts and Malaga grapes for supper. We never celebrated with a Christmas tree (we considered them childish) and the younger ones of us—Ruth and I and the twins—never hung our stockings. Since Mother died there was no one to keep up the fiction of Santa Claus, and I remember we used to feel awfully set-up and superior at the church supper on Christmas Eve when we, with grown-ups, knew that the person in the old red coat and white beard was just the Sunday-school superintendent dressed up. We always opened our presents in the sitting-room directly after breakfast. Each member of the family had a chair of his own, with his presents piled in it. When we all finally got started on the opening, I don't know whether we were more interested in seeing the presents we had given, opened, or opening the ones we had received. It was a wonderful hour anyhow, and I can't even remember it without getting a thrill.

It's different now; everything is different—Memorial Day, Fourth of July and Thanksgiving—with Father gone. We can't seem to fill up the rooms without Father. When we try to celebrate a holiday I think it must be something like acting or preaching to an empty house. Father was a beautiful audience, and his applause made the day worth while. Since Tom has been married he hasn't been here for Christmas either. Elise's family wants her with them. Besides, she has two little daughters now and can't possibly come East anyhow. You can imagine with only Ruth, the twins, heart-sick Alec, and me—no Dixie, no Nellie, no money for presents, and the "For Sale" sign still outside the parlour window—it wasn't a very merry Christmas for the Vars family. It just dragged, I can tell you. I had to cook the dinner myself because Bridget, the general-housework girl, had too soft a heart to disappoint her second cousin, who had invited her to spend the day with her. Ruth and the twins started off on a skating-party about three in the afternoon, after we'd done up the dishes together. As soon as I was sure they were all safely out of the way—Alec was sound asleep on the third floor—I stuck on my red tam and sweater, and took my present over to Dr. Maynard.

I was dreadfully afraid I'd meet some one I knew on the way, and they'd inquire what I had in the bundle. It was the awkwardest thing I ever attempted to carry in my life. Try it sometime. When I struggled up to Dr. Maynard's front door, I wondered if he had been watching me from the windows, and asking himself what in the name of heaven was coming now. But he wasn't at home. Eliza who came to the door explained that Dr. Maynard had gone out horseback riding, but wouldn't I come in and wait?

I thanked Eliza—I'd never been inside Dr. Maynard's house before—and entered the hall. She showed me into a big square room at the left, and told me to sit down.

"I won't stop, I think," I said. "I'll just leave this. It's a Christmas present for Dr. Maynard. Don't tell him who left it. There's a card inside."

"I'll lay it right here on his desk," said Eliza, grinning with pleasure.

She'd no sooner put my bundle down than I heard the clatter of horse's hoofs on the hard driveway outside.

"I believe he's coming," I exclaimed. "How lucky! I'll wait."

After Eliza had gone back to the kitchen and I was alone, I gazed about the room. It was a dark, dull room with bronze-coloured walls. Low, black walnut bookcases were built in around two sides, and over them hung two solitary pictures—steel engravings of battle scenes. There were several huge leather armchairs, and a bare leather couch in one corner. There wasn't a single sofa-pillow on it. I didn't believe Dr. Maynard liked sofa-pillows after all. Everything was so big and dark and stiff in that room, I was afraid a pillow would look out of place. I walked over to Dr. Maynard's desk. It was just like the room—nothing pretty on it—a book or two, a big bronze horse, a piece of black onyx for a paperweight. There was also a small, dark leather frame, and in it a kodak picture of Alec on horseback. The horse was poor dear little Dixie, who had gone away. I remembered when Dr. Maynard had taken that picture. It was in our back yard last summer. The smoke-bush had been in full plumage. Just before he snapped the picture, he had called to me, "You get into it, too, Bobbie. Stand up here, in front, by Dixie's head." And there I was, as sure as life, pinching the dear little horse's soft under lip, and smiling at Dr. Maynard.

As I stood looking at the picture, wondering where Dixie had gone—for Alec hadn't told me and I dreaded to ask—Dr. Maynard passed by the window by my side. He was coming in from the stable by way of the front door, and Eliza would have no opportunity for telling him that he had a caller. As I heard him fitting his key into the lock of the outside door, it occurred to me that it would be fun to hide. I glanced around the room. There wasn't a drapery in sight. There wasn't a hanging of any description that I could crawl behind. So finally I dashed into what proved to be a closet—dark as pitch.

Dr. Maynard didn't stop in the hall. He didn't call Eliza. He came directly toward the library door and entered the room. The sun was just setting, and a few last rays came slanting through the windows. They burnished the room like magic brass-polish. The bronze-coloured walls shone like dull copper; the brown leather armchairs, the black walnut woodwork, the old camel-shaded rugs were absolutely golden. As Dr. Maynard stood in the late sunshine in his khaki coloured riding things, his face all aglow and ruddy with the cold, he too glowed like everything else. He looked very handsome in his riding boots (I could see him through the crack in the door) and much sportier than in automobile goggles and a visored cap.

He tossed down his riding whip and soft felt hat in a chair, rubbed his bare hands together as if they were cold, blew through his fingers, then abruptly flung himself full length on the leather couch. He clasped his two hands underneath his head, and lay there with his eyes wide open, staring up at the ceiling. I hoped he wouldn't keep me waiting long. A small travelling clock on the desk struck four-thirty, and he turned toward it. It was then that he saw the big white bundle resting on his blotter. He frowned a moment, as his gaze fell upon it (I was shaking with laughter) then got up and walked over to it. He picked it up, turned it over, and laid it down again. He examined the outside closely—for an address, I suppose—gave it up, then shoving his hands into his pockets, stood looking down at the bundle, as if some stranger had left a baby at his door and he didn't know what to do with it. Finally, he decided to open the thing at least, and began taking out the pins. Beneath the brown paper was the layer of white tissue paper, tied with red Christmas ribbon. I didn't think Dr. Maynard would ever get beneath that tissue paper. You would have thought that there was something explosive inside. He lifted up the rustling package gingerly by the red ribbon and looked it all over. My card was hanging from the under side. Dr. Maynard took it off at last and read it.

It was a plain white card with simply the words: "Merry Christmas to W. F. M. from his discharged chauffeur, George." Dr. Maynard gazed at that card as if there had been volumes written on it. He turned it over, searched on the back, and examined again its face. Then he went to the window, put the shade up to the top, and came back to the desk. His back was toward me; I couldn't see the expression on his face as he folded back the tissue paper, and my pillow finally shone up at him. He didn't speak nor make a single sound as he stood looking down at the initials and his class numeral. He didn't stir—just looked until the silence grew uncomfortable. Suddenly he sat down in his desk-chair, leaned forward, picked up Alec's picture and began looking at that in the same awfully still, quiet way. I couldn't bear it a minute longer. The tensity was something like a shrill, long-drawn-out note on a violin. I can't explain it, but it made me want to scream.

Suddenly I burst out upon him.

"Well," I exclaimed, "do you like it?"

He wheeled about, as if he'd heard a shot.

"Lucy!" he said, "Where did you—?"

"In the closet," I interrupted, "watching."

He still had the picture in his hands. He glanced at it, then laid it down, and for the first time in my life I saw the dark colour come into Dr. Maynard's face. He came over to me.

"Did you make it?" he asked me quietly.

"Every stitch for you!" I said, laughing.

He didn't answer at first. He just kept looking at me, with that queer, new look of his. He didn't joke. His eyes didn't twinkle with fun. When he spoke his voice trembled. He took one of my hands very kindly and gently in both of his cold ones.

"You have made my Christmas the very happiest one in my life, Lucy," he said solemnly.

I glanced up surprised. I wish I could write down how his eyes looked. I can't. I only know I was suddenly afraid. I drew my hand away and laughed, for no reason. I was actually embarrassed before Dr. Maynard!

"I guess I must go," I said nervously. The sun had set and the glow had all gone out of the room.

Dr. Maynard didn't answer me. He just stood there like a stone man. Oh, I think that silences are the most awfully eloquent things in the world!

"It's getting dark," I added desperately.

Without a word Dr. Maynard went to the library door and opened it. I followed. Then to the front door and opened that. He stood holding it back, still not speaking (but I could feel his gaze burning into me) and I sped past him out into the dusk, like a wild bird out of a cage.

I don't know how I got home. I half ran, half stumbled along the frozen road. My heart was thumping, and though I wasn't a bit cold (my cheeks fairly burned) my teeth chattered as if I were chilled through. When I reached the house there was a funny, choking feeling in my throat, and I dashed up to my room and locked myself in.

All this last took place not eight hours ago and it is very late Christmas night.

When I write down what has happened it seems absurd to be excited. But when I think of it—when I close my eyes, see his gaze, hear his voice, I can't sleep. So I have climbed up into my cupola. I have been sitting looking up at the stars. They are very bright to-night. There are millions shining.

I can see most all the houses in Hilton from my eyrie. They are dark now. It is after twelve. But there are two windows aglow. I can see them shining, side by side like eyes, through the bare limbs of our apple orchard. They are western windows, in a white house, and eight hours ago the setting sun shone into them, upon Dr. Maynard in his riding clothes. I wonder what he is doing so late.

It's a lovely night—cold, clear and so still. I'd like to walk twenty miles before morning. I'd like to fly a thousand.

O Father, I don't know why it is—it doesn't seem right, for the awful shadow is still over our house and Alec hasn't smiled all day—but this—oh, this is *my* happiest Christmas too!

CHAPTER XI

ON a certain night in April I was in the sitting-room trying to keep awake until Alec came home. His train was not due until midnight. I was awfully anxious to wait up for him, but at ten o'clock I was so sleepy that I couldn't keep my eyes open another minute. So I went to Father's roll-top desk and scribbled this on a piece of paper: "*Dear Alec—Be sure and stop at my room when you come in. Bobbie,*" and fastened it with a wire hairpin on the light that I left burning.

Alec and I were on friendly terms again, and the whole world was smiling for me. I didn't care if the "For Sale" was still hitting me in the face every time I entered the yard, since Alec had put me back in charge of the Household Account. I might have known my cheque-book wouldn't have lied for me. Alec didn't get around to look into my bookkeeping until about the first of January, and then he was so delighted to discover that I hadn't failed in my trust, after all, that he couldn't reinstate me quickly enough. It was so good to be friends again, such a relief to have his faith in me restored and made whole, that I guess he didn't want to risk urging me to explain what I really wanted the seventy-five dollars for. "I know you'll explain all about it, sometime," he said. And I replied, "Sometime, Alec." That was the way our quarrel ended. The next morning I walked to the factory with my brother; the next evening I sat with him by the drop-light and when he went to bed I carried to his room some hot milk and crackers so that he would sleep. Since then we have been nearer to each other than ever before.

There is something beautiful about our relations. I'd die for Alec. I don't believe there ever has been a brother and sister more congenial than Alec and I. I know just how to please him, and he knows better than any one in this world how to manage me. There isn't a prouder girl alive than I, when Alec confides his business affairs to me. I do not understand them very well. Companies and Coöperations, Preferred and Common Stock, Bonds and Bank-notes are all a perfect jumble in my mind. But I've learned long ago, that nothing will shut a man up more quickly than a comment on a girl's part that shows him how ignorant she is. So now I keep still; listen as hard and closely as I can; sympathise with my whole heart when Alec is worried, and rejoice with him when he announces that some Boston bank or other has lent him twenty-five thousand dollars, although I *am* frightened to death of borrowing. I never give my brother a chance to scoff at a girl's comprehension of business transactions. The result is, he talks to me by the hour, and thinks I understand a great deal more than I do.

Ever since last Christmas Alec has been running down to New York about every two weeks. There was a big order that he was trying to secure, besides some sort of an arrangement he wanted to work up with some rich men down there to increase the capital stock of the business, I think he said. I have an idea, though I never asked, that if he could have worked that arrangement it would have saved the business from peril of failing. Alec used to stay in New York about three days usually, and always came home a little more worried, anxious, and discouraged than when he started.

This time he had been away almost two weeks. I had had only one short note from him written the day after he left home. Since then I had not heard from him until his telegram had arrived announcing he would reach Hilton on the midnight from New York.

It was a cold blustering night for April, and before I went to bed myself, I went up into Alec's third-floor room, turned on the heat, filled a hot-water bag and stuck it down between the cold sheets of his bed.

I must have been sleeping very soundly when Alec stole into my room at twelve-thirty. I didn't know he was in the house, until I felt his hand on my shoulder and his gentle, "Hello, Bobbie!" I woke up with a glad start and found him sitting on the side of my bed. "My, what a sleeper!" he said and leaned down and kissed my forehead.

I knew from the first whiff that Alec must have been sitting in the smoking-car (he doesn't smoke himself) and I drew in a fine, long breath before I spoke.

"Oh, Alec," I exclaimed, "how beautifully New Yorky you smell!"

"Do I, funny Bobbikins?" he laughed at me, and at the sound of that name which Alec had not called me by for six months, a thrill of new courage ran through me.

I sat up.

"Alec," I said, "you've brought good news. I *know* it! I *know* it! I knew we couldn't fail. I've felt it all along. I knew Father's dear old business wouldn't go back on us. I had a feeling that *this* trip to New York would be a lucky one."

"I've been farther than New York, Bobbie. I've been to Pinehurst, North Carolina," Alec announced.

"To Pinehurst! Mercy! Whatever in the world—do tell me *every* word. I'm simply crazy to hear all about it."

"Well—" he began. "Say, Bobbikins," he broke off, "would you be very much surprised to know that it is—all right between Edith and me?"

Alec might as well have struck off on a tangent about George Washington or Joan of Arc.

"Edith?" I gasped.

"Yes," went on Alec gently; "Edith Campbell. Of course you've known I've cared for no one else for the last ten years. The business and our large family have always made it seem rather hopeless. But when I was in New York I had a common little picture post-card from Edith, who was at Pinehurst, and your disgraceful old brother here dropped everything and went down there. I was there for six whole days, and she and her family and I all came home together to-night after two rather nice days in New York. She's actually got a ring in a little blue velvet box which she's going to wear for me a little later, Bobbie." He tried to say it lightly but his whole voice was exulting. "You see, I had to come in and tell my partner, didn't I? She would have to know first of all about such a great piece of news."

He stopped and I sat perfectly silent, stunned for an instant, not knowing quite what had struck me and knocked me down with my breath all gone. Alec waited and I tried to jump up, as it were, and speak, so he would know I wasn't dead.

"Why, Alec Vars!" I managed to gasp, and then the horror of his news flashed over me. The man I loved best in the whole world had just told me that he was engaged to be married to a girl whom I abhorred! I wanted to scream; I wanted to bury my face in my pillow and cry; I wanted to say, "Oh, go away, go away, Alexander Vars. Leave me alone. I want to die." But instead I remarked quite calmly, "You engaged? To Edith Campbell? My goodness, but I'm surprised." And then warned by the choke in my voice, I switched off into something commonplace. "Say, would you mind," I said jovially enough, "just removing your hundred and seventy-five pounds off my left foot there? You're crushing the bones in it."

Alec leaned forward and kissed me hard.

"You little brick of a Bobbie! I knew you'd take it like a soldier."

I gulped down a disgusting sob.

"But wasn't I the goose," I hurried like mad to say, for I was afraid I'd break down and bawl like a baby before his very eyes, "wasn't I the little goose to think it was the business that made you so happy?"

"Oh, the business," Alec announced, "is bound to succeed *now*."

"Sure," I broke in hastily, "just bound to. It's awfully nice, all around, isn't it? And I—" I floundered on, "I am just—just *pleased*!"

The hall clock struck one. I grasped the blessed sound like a sinking man.

"Is that twelve-thirty, one, or one-thirty? I haven't the ghost of an idea," I said lightly. Then desperately, at the breaking point, I gasped, "Is it cold out?"

Alec patted my hand.

"Brave girl! I understand. But don't you worry. Everything will work out all right. Now I'll say good-night."

I think Alec must have seen I couldn't hold in much longer. I was, in fact, using every atom of strength that I possessed to fight that pushing, shoving, tumbling crowd of lumps and sobs in my throat. Just as Alec was closing my door I managed to call after him, so that he might know that I wasn't crying, "Be sure and turn out the lights."

"All right, General-manager."

"And say," I added, "you know I think it's perfectly fine."

"Surely! Good-night."

Then my door closed, and I sank down on my pillow, opened the gates wide, and let the torrent of sobs rush through.

Can any one realise the torture of my mind during the long dark hours of that night? I hardly can realise it now, myself. The fact, "ALEC IS ENGAGED TO EDITH CAMPBELL!" glared at me horribly as if it were printed in enormous white letters on a black ground, like a big sign on a factory, and I stared and stared, hypnotised, beyond power of thought. I was so stunned and overcome by the fact itself that at first I was unable to comprehend what it would mean to me. I hated Edith Campbell. All my life I had hated her. She had always treated Alec like the dirt under her feet—forever flaunting Palm Beach and Poland Springs in his face and eyes, parading to church every other Sunday with smart stylish-looking men and planting them down in the pew two rows in front of ours to show them off.

Of course I had guessed that Alec had liked Edith Campbell. As long ago as I can remember he used to call on her when she came home from her fashionable New York boarding-school. Alec invited her to be his special guest, at his Class-Day, when he graduated from college. But she elected to go with somebody else, and pranced down there with a millionaire's son. Poor Alec didn't invite any other girl. I was in knee skirts then, but I was old enough to hate her for it. Not that I wanted such a creature to be nice to Alec. I didn't. I knew my brother was miles too good for her, but I couldn't bear to have such a flashy, worldly, inferior girl show scorn toward a prince. I never understood why Alec had admired her. She's absolutely opposite from my brother in every possible way. She has the most confident, cock-surest manner I ever witnessed. Her clothes are dreadfully flashy and her father is a mere upstart who squeezes money out of everybody he knows.

Hilton used to criticise Edith Campbell before it commenced bowing and scraping to her. When she came home from boarding-school, she let it be known that her intimate friends lived outside of Hilton. She advertised that she visited at some of the big places in the Berkshires. She merely tolerated Hilton and its people.

Oh, I hate her! I never saw why men ran after her so frantically. It used to make me absolutely sick when the younger girls in Hilton got the Edith Campbell craze. They used to try to copy everything she wore. But *I* didn't. I wouldn't as much as turn my head to look at her. I was delighted when Alec stopped going to see her. I had thought, when Alec announced his engagement to me, that that little romance of his had been dead and buried for five years. It hadn't even worried me.

When I awoke the morning after Alec told me his astonishing news, and saw the sun shining in a square on the wall opposite me, I lay very still for a moment. "You've had a horrible dream," I said. "Alec didn't come home last night. Just a minute, and things will get themselves fixed." I sat up, but the dream didn't fade. There was the tell-tale towel with which I had bathed my eyes; there the glass of water; there the dissipated-looking candle burned down to its very last; here the confused tossed bed-clothes, and when I staggered to the mirror, there were my swollen red eyes and awful tangled hair. I dressed slowly, with a very heavy heart, and unable to cry any more, smiled at myself once or twice in the glass out of grim spite.

I had not gone to sleep until it had begun to grow light. I remembered now. And it was nine o'clock when I went downstairs for an attempt at breakfast. Ruth was devouring eggs when I went into the dining-room. I had thought she would be at school, but I had forgotten that it was Saturday. Alec had already gone to the factory. His eggy plate and half-filled coffee-cup stood at his deserted place.

"My, but you're late," said Ruth, emptying the cream-pitcher into her coffee. "Say, isn't it corking about Alec? We've been sitting here hours talking about it. I think it's simply dandy. Just imagine—Edith Campbell!"

I became very busy fixing my cuff-link, for I was ashamed of my swollen eyes; but Ruth was sure to see them. She glanced up.

"I might have known you'd take it like that," she broke out, though I hadn't said a word; "always acting like a thunder-cloud, and throwing wet blankets on everything. Now why in the world shouldn't Alec get married?"

"I didn't say he shouldn't," I murmured.

"Well," went on Ruth, "Edith Campbell is *great*. I can't get over the fact, that with all the men she's known, she likes Alec better than any of them. She's dreadfully popular. I'll bet she's had a dozen proposals. Oh, I think Al's done awfully well. The Campbells have piles of money. I know her younger sister Millicent, and their house beats anything I ever saw. You ought to see it. And besides, Edith Campbell is the best-looking thing! She's stunning on a horse."

Ruth always antagonises me when she talks about people she admires.

"*I* think," I said in a low voice, "that Edith Campbell is common and loud and vulgar."

"Oh, nonsense!" retorted Ruth. "I'm simply wild about the whole thing. The Campbells are going to do this tumbledown old ark all over, for a wedding present, and Al says her father is going to insist on Edith's bringing her horses with her. I don't call that common or vulgar. I call it generous!"

"Is she going to live here?" I gasped.

"Of course she is. Where else? And Alec says that you and I will each have a perfectly lovely room, and divide our time between here and Tom's. I tell you what, I'm glad for one, that we won't have to live like pigs any more. Edith Campbell is used to piles of servants!"

I don't know why Ruth's words made me so terribly angry.

"Ruth Chenery Vars," I said, "I hate Edith Campbell, and I'll never live under the same roof with her. I never will. Do you hear me? I never will!"

Ruth glanced up and met my fiery eyes.

"Mercy," she said, simply disgusted, "why get so everlasting mad?"

I shoved back my chair and left the table quietly, hurried up the stairs straight to my disheveled room, and locked the door tight. My mind was clear now all right; I could comprehend the meaning of the awful black and white sign *now*, without any difficulty. I was no goose not to know perfectly well that Alec's engagement meant that Miss Lucy Vars would be requested to hand in her resignation as General-manager, Keeper-of-the-Household-Account, Bosser-of-the-meals, Mother-of-the-family, and oh, too, Partner-of-Alec. Why, I had poured the coffee at our table ever since the day Father had put me there in Mother's empty chair. I had always sat there, pushed the bell, and told the maid to take off the plates for dessert. My place had always been opposite Father, and after he had gone, Alec had sat there. Ever since, he and I had held the reins together. There wasn't a chair nor a rug, nor a table in the house that I hadn't put in position. There wasn't a pound of sugar, nor a half-dozen oranges in the pantry that I had not ordered. For five years there hadn't been a servant engaged by any one but me. Now, suddenly, all such an arrangement was to be at an end. Ruth was delighted; Alec was supremely happy; the twins, who worship anything that means more cash, would be transported with joy. Everybody, in fact, would delight in a change in administration—everybody but the poor old dethroned ruler, who was locked in her desolate room trying to find consolation in vigorously making her bed.

When Alec came home at noon I saw him scanning my impassive face, for I had not been crying since the night before, and the trace of tears was gone. After our regular Saturday boiled dinner he asked me to come into the sitting-room. He closed the doors carefully and sat down beside me on the couch. I wished he wouldn't take my hand for it was chapped and red, and of course he had held hers, for which he had bought the beautiful ring in the little blue velvet box, and hers would be soft and white. I drew mine away. Alec talked to me gently and told me about the arrangements. I heard him say with a dull shock, that they would be married in the early fall. I remember wondering how they had decided such details in the course of ten days. I soon discovered that they had managed to go over the whole ground. There seemed to be no question undecided, no points untouched. Ruth, he said, would start in at boarding-school in the fall; the twins of course would continue at college and their vacations would, as usual, be spent at home. He repeated what I already very well knew that after the twins graduated they would probably go out West and start into one of Tom's lumber camps.

"So there'll just be me left," I hurried to say, kind of to help him out.

"And, of course, *you'll* live right along here with us," he said, "except, once in a while, when Tom and Elise want you there with them."

"I'm worse to dispose of than a mother-in-law," I half laughed, sorry in a moment that I had spoken so, for Alec looked hurt, and exclaimed, "Oh, Bobbie dear!"

"Oh, I'll try, Alec, I really will," I reassured him, for Alec always brings out the best in me.

"And go and see Edith very soon?" he said, following me up cruelly. "She'll be expecting you."

"Oh, yes, I'll try," I murmured, biting my trembling under lip.

"Good girl! I knew I could count on you. You'll like Edith," he said. "And she wants to be awfully kind to you and Ruth. I know you'll try and make it easy for her, Bobbie," he added, and left me as cheerfully as a summer's breeze.

Late that afternoon, about five I think, I started out for a walk in Buxton's woods, a quarter of a mile back of our house. I hadn't been gone very long when I heard a step behind me, and turning around I saw, mounted on her stunning black Kentucky thoroughbred, Edith Campbell, coming toward me. I wanted to run away, to hide perhaps behind a tree and let her pass, but I couldn't for she had caught sight of me.

"Hold on," she called. "Wait a minute," and she drew up beside me. "Hello, Lucy," she said in her familiar, breezy way. "Now isn't this luck?" Her dark, crisp hair was neat and firm beneath the little black derby—an affectation in dress that no one wears riding in Hilton except Edith Campbell. She didn't have them on to-day, but usually she wears long green drop-earrings, screwed on, I think—too New Yorky for anything. "Wait a jiffy," she laughed, "and I'll walk along with you. Pierre here, can mosey along behind." She sprang down from her saddle like a sporty horse-woman, came up and thrust out a gauntlet-gloved hand to me. She gave me a Hercules grip. "Has Al told you?" she asked, plunging straight ahead, with no delicacy.

"Yes, he has," I stammered, "and—I congratulate you both," I finished desperately.

It did sound stiff and formal and schoolgirlish, but I was angry with Edith Campbell when she laughed at me and exclaimed, "You funny old-fashioned child!"

She arranged one pair of reins over her horse's neck and used the other pair for a lead, slipping her arm through the loop.

"Come on now, let's walk," she said and put her free arm through mine, a familiarity from the wonderful Edith Campbell for which even sensible Juliet would envy me. *I* wanted to edge away from her. "Alec," she went on, "thinks the world and all of you, Bobbie," (as if she had to inform me!) "and I want you to know right off, you won't be losing a brother, simply gaining a sister." (Usual, meaningless words! As if Ruth wasn't more than enough anyhow.) "And another thing," she ploughed ahead, "there will always be a room in our house for Bobbie. One of the things I told Alec was that he must look out for his sisters."

"Alec would do that anyway," I said.

"Of course. Nice old Al! He's as good as gold."

I couldn't bear her patronising manner. She has always treated Alec like that, just because she had money and he had nothing but goodness. I turned to her seriously.

"Miss Campbell," I asked, "how did you come to want to marry Alec?"

"You amusing chicken!" she laughed, then pinching me disgustingly on the arm, she added in a sly way, "You wait, you'll know when the right one comes."

I flushed but held my peace.

"I was only wondering," I said. "Alec has so little money, and you—I mean our business—our success is so uncertain."

"Alec is bound to succeed *now*," she replied in her cock-sure way. "I told Al there was no such word in my vocabulary as failure. Besides *Father* is going to look into the business, and Father never touched a thing that wasn't successful."

"Your father!" I gasped with the colour again in my face. Her father used to collect junk-iron. "Our business!"

"Oh, come, come. Just like Al at first. This Vars pride! Don't you see, my dear, that, independent of weddings, a man can put a little life into a dead business if he wants to?"

"My father's business isn't dead," I exclaimed, now filled with indignation.

"Oh, come, Bobbikins!"

"Don't call me that, please," I said and drew away my arm.

"Tut, tut! Come now! You and I are going to be friends." She treated me as if I were aged five. "You know," she went on, "when I come, I think there'll be an extra saddle horse, in one of the stalls in your stable." She used that mysterious tone you do to children when talking about Santa Claus. "I think if you will look very hard you will find your initials on him somewhere, Bobbie."

"I wouldn't touch it, Miss Campbell. I wouldn't touch one hair of the horse; and please call me Lucy."

We were breaking out of the narrow wood-path, and coming to a travelled road. We walked in silence till we reached the highway. It was almost dark. Suddenly Edith Campbell spoke.

"I must be hustling homeward," she said glibly, and as if nothing unpleasant had occurred between us she asked, "Lend me your hand, will you, Bobbie, please?"

I helped her mount, in silence.

"That's the way," she said. "Thanks. Now look here, poor little childie," she broke off, looking down at me like a queen from her saddle, "whenever you're ready to be friends, remember, so am I. All right, Pierre!" and she cantered off in the dusk.

I stood quite still for a moment, and then right to that lonely, empty road, I said out loud, "I can't live with her. I can't—I can't! Dear Alec, I tried. Dear Father and Tom and Elise, I tried, but I can't, I can't!" And all the dark way home, all the long night through, I ran over and over the words like a squirrel in a revolving cage.

CHAPTER XII

FOR three days and nights I wandered over the ruins of my life, back and forth, helpless, almost driven mad by the horror of it; and then at last Dr. Maynard came. I had not realised that he had been out of town. I had been so stunned by Alec's announcement that I had not missed him. He had been down to Baltimore for three days attending some sort of a medical conference and I had not known that he had been outside of Hilton.

Dr. Maynard and I were as good friends as ever now. Three whole months had passed since that Christmas Day when he discovered my sofa-pillow on his desk, and I had come to the conclusion that he had been merely surprised into his queer behaviour that day. He had never shown a scrap of the same emotion since. I remember the very next time I saw him he had dropped that newly acquired gravity of his. Somehow I had been disappointed. When he referred to my pillow in his old natural, jovial way, I had been hurt. "I tell you what," he had said, "I feel like an undergraduate again. Nice girl like Lucy Vars making me a pillow for my room! Won't you come to my Class-Day?" he had laughed. It was I who had flushed then. I managed to throw back some sort of a careless rejoinder, but I tell you, I didn't waste any more madly happy moments on Dr. Maynard. Grey-haired old bachelor! He was old enough to be my uncle anyhow! We had resumed our automobile rides just as naturally as if he'd never acted queerly at all. We took up our jolly repartee, returned to our old plane of good-comradeship, exactly as if I had never seen him gaze at my picture, and heard his voice tremble when he told me I had made his Christmas the very happiest in his life. *I* didn't care. I was glad of it. I had never wanted Dr. Maynard for a lover! But I wanted him for a friend.

I don't believe I quite appreciated how much I wanted him, until he came back from Baltimore and discovered me wandering about my ruins like a maniac. When I found myself bundled up in Father's old ulster, again beside him in his automobile, flashing through the cool night air, a great wave of relief ran over me. Dr. Maynard has seen me through so much trouble, brought me safely over so many difficulties, that it was a comfort just to sit beside him in silence. When we had reached a good clear stretch of road, he settled down comfortably behind the wheel.

"Now go ahead," he said heartily; "the whole story, please," and I knew that Alec had broken his news to him.

"Well," I started in, "since you've been gone, there's been a dreadful earthquake around here." (Dr. Maynard and I adore to talk in similes.) "My house has been smashed up, and I'm a pitiful refugee. I am cold and hungry and without a home."

"I've come with supplies," laughed Dr. Maynard, taking it up delightfully. "I'm a little late, but I've brought bread and meat and a tent, and want you to crawl in and warm up."

"I can't live with her, Dr. Maynard. I can't!" I broke out, too heart-sick to play with similes any more. "I hate her and I can't help it. She's taken Alec away, she's pushed herself into my dear father's business, and there's no place for me, as I can see, anywhere."

"Tell me all about it," said Dr. Maynard, and I related every single word of my whole pitiful story, growing sorrier and sorrier for myself as I went along, and finally at the end breaking down completely, repeating my old time-worn phrase, "I can't live with her. I can't, can't!" I covered my face with both hands. There were tears trickling down my cheeks.

Without a word of advice or comfort, Dr. Maynard shut off the power and brought the car to a standstill by the side of the bleak country road. He took hold of my hands and gently drew them away from my face down into my lap. Then in a low voice with the play and banter all gone out of it he said, "Could you live with *me*, Lucy?"

"Oh, yes," I replied quickly enough, "fifty times easier!"

Perhaps he smiled, for he added half laughing and yet gravely, too, "I would like to have you, if you want to."

"I only wish I could," I said desperately.

And then very seriously and very solemnly he told me his story. I can't say that I was exactly surprised. I had half guessed it for the last two years; but then I had half guessed a lot of preposterous things that never came true. "I talked with Alec last night," I heard Dr. Maynard telling me gently, "and if you would like—that is if you want to come with me, Lucy, your brother would be glad to have you, I am certain. This isn't the only talk Alec and I have had about you. I wanted to speak to you about this last fall, but Al thought it better to wait. And I wanted to speak again after—the sofa-pillow, and again Al couldn't quite make up his mind that you had grown up, and wanted me to wait again. So I did. You see," he smiled, "it isn't a *new* idea with me."

I listened calmly as Dr. Maynard went on talking in his quiet, unexcited manner. I didn't interrupt his long, well-planned speech. I simply sat dumb with my hands clasped tightly in my lap. I don't remember that I felt a single sensation during the entire explanation except at the end a kind of shock as I thought to myself: "So after all it's going to be just Dr. Maynard!" For when he had finally finished, I said evenly, with the moon standing there like a clergyman before us, and all the watching stars like witnesses behind, "I will come, Dr. Maynard," and I added, "and I think you are the very kindest man I know." For you see he had offered me his home, his protection, and his love, he said, for all my life.

There was something awfully silent and ominous about the gentle still way he turned the machine around and started for home. It was entirely different from what I had guessed might take place. In the dreams that I had woven I had never accepted Dr. Maynard. I had been grateful for his devotion, honoured by his proposal, deeply sorry for his disappointment, but like the girl in an old play called "Rosemary," my heart belonged to one who possessed youth and passion. In those absurd imaginings of mine I used to frame letters which I should write to Juliet Adams about poor Will Maynard. I used to plan just how I should break the news to my brother Alec. But now—Oh, now, I couldn't write Juliet at all; I couldn't tell Alec; I couldn't tell any one about my first proposal. I had accepted it in the first half-hour. There was nothing thrilling about it. I sat like a stone image beside Dr. Maynard. I couldn't speak.

"It took you an awfully long while to grow up," he said at last, half laughing. "I've actually grown grey waiting for you. Alec said to me the first time, 'Wait till she's nineteen,' and then, 'Good heavens, Will, she's nothing but a child yet. Wait till she's twenty,' and so on, and so on. Awful hindrance, because for the last two years I've been wanting to do some important research work in Germany. But I couldn't leave you to the wolves. How did I know but that some good-looking young chap would come along and snatch you up? But now, we'll go to Germany together, and, Lucy," he said, "Lucy—" but I didn't want Dr. Maynard to grow serious. I think he must have seen me kind of cringe away for he broke off lightly enough, "and perhaps some fine day the refugee and I will be seeing Paris together."

I stole into the house that night very quietly, crept up to my room and closed the door without a sound. I wanted to be alone. I was suddenly filled with a kind of panic-stricken wonder, for there had been actual tears in Dr. Maynard's eyes when he took my hand at the door (I hadn't known how to say good-night to him), a tremble in his voice that awed and frightened me. He acted very much as he had about my Christmas present. It had made me happy then, but, you see *then* I hadn't just promised to marry him. Oh, I hated having him look so serious and solemn about it, and now as I stood a moment with my back against my closed door, my hat and coat still on, I pressed my two cool hands against my burning cheeks and tried to comprehend a little of what it all meant. Suddenly I crossed the room, pulled on the gas by my bureau, leaned forward and gazed grimly at my familiar old face in the glass before me. So this was what was to become of Lucy Chenery Vars, I thought calmly; this was her story; this was her end; and oh, to think that all the beautiful unknown future of the person in the glass before me was wiped out and decided in one fell swoop, made me want to throw my arms about her image and kiss her for pity. I turned away.

Of course I liked Dr. Maynard—I had always liked him. And his big, empty, white-pillared house was in the very town, on the very street of my dear beloved home. There was a place for me there. Alec had given Dr. Maynard to understand that there would be no objection from him. Probably it seemed to Alec a good way to dispose of me. Oh, there was everything in favour of the arrangement. I had always longed to go to Europe. Germany and Paris were sparkling ahead, and here—*here* nothing but the nightmare of Edith Campbell everywhere I turned. I drew a long breath—there was no other course for me to follow—looked once more sadly into the glass, pulled down my curtain and began to get ready for bed.

I never shall forget that night. I don't believe I slept at all. I don't know what time it was when I got up and, lighting my candle, sat down at my desk, shivering in my long white nightgown. I just sat and sat; and gazed and gazed; and thought and thought; and dropped, I remember, little drops of melted wax along my bare arm, as I turned over my problem in my mind. "If only I didn't actually have to marry him!" I said out loud and turned and sank again into troubled silence. I got up once and carried the candle close to the cold, glass-covered picture of my mother that hung over my bed. Why did she have to die so long ago? What would she say—she who was to have been my best friend—what would she say if she could turn that clear-cut profile around and let me look into her eyes? I didn't know. I hadn't been old enough to remember even her smile. Shouldn't a girl be glad on the night of her betrothal? Shouldn't there be ardent looks, passionate words, tender caresses for her to live through again in thought? Shouldn't she long for the sight of the man whom she had promised to marry? "What shall I do, Father?" I said out loud. "What shall I do?" But only my clock answered me with its steady, unintelligible tick. No one could help me—no one in the wide world. I asked them, and they couldn't. Even Edith Campbell had said, "you'll know"; but oh, I didn't, I didn't.

So that is why, near morning, I got up again, went to my desk, opened a little secret drawer, and took out a picture. The picture was the one I had bought in New York after I had seen Robert Dwinnell at the theatre in the afternoon. Of course it is silly and very absurd for a girl of my years to treasure a picture of an actor in a secret drawer in her desk. I can't help it. That picture had been my ideal for almost five years now. It wasn't the actor that I liked so much (for of course I have been told that actors aren't nice); it wasn't Robert Dwinnell himself I admired. It was simply the jolly look in his eyes and the way he had—I remembered it so well—of striding across the stage, sitting carelessly on the edge of a table and swinging one foot. It had just about torn the heart out of me to watch that man make love. He had a kind of lingering way with his hands, and with his eyes too, every time the heroine was in his presence. Even before he had proposed to her, I knew he adored her and afterward—oh, really I think Robert Dwinnell must have loved that actress off the stage as well as on. Dr. Maynard's hands had never lingered about my shoulders when he helped me on with a coat; he had never gazed at me eloquently across a crowded room; and even after I had promised to marry him he hadn't crushed me to him in any mad wave of joy. I gazed for a whole half-minute at Robert Dwinnell's picture. I forgot all my problems for a little while—I forgot everything in the memory of that man's image. Call it absurd if you want to, ridiculous and impossible, but when I raised my eyes at last and rose, clear as the day that was just breaking, bright as a new-born vision, I knew—I *knew* I couldn't marry just everyday, kind Dr. Maynard. It was just as if Robert Dwinnell had gotten up from out of that picture, walked over to me, taken my hand and said, "You must wait for some one like me." And I looked up and knew that I must. It was like a miracle, and I shall never forget the sudden trembling assurance in my heart, as I found my way to my desk and in the light of that lovely new morning, drew out a sheet of paper and wrote to Edith Campbell and told her I was ready to be friends. For suddenly, brought face to face with the thrilling image of the man of my dreams, I was ready to live with twenty Edith Campbells. Of course, *of course*, I couldn't marry Dr. Maynard, and with a little pang of regret or something like it in my heart, I finally wrote him this note:

"*Dear Dr. Maynard,*

The refugee has thought it all over very carefully and has decided to gather the pieces of her house together and rebuild on the same spot, like San Francisco."

Then I added, dropping all play and with something I knew to be pain:

"I can't do it, Dr. Maynard, I've tried and I can't. But you'll always be the very kindest man I know.

"LUCY CHENERY VARS."

"*Now* if you don't come!" I said to the picture, and leaned forward and buried my head in my arms.

So that is how it happened that Dr. Maynard went away to Germany alone and I remained at home to fight my battle. It was a dull, grey morning that he sailed, some three weeks after that wakeful night of mine, and I was sitting alone in my room at precisely eleven o'clock—the sailing hour—trying to imagine Dr. Maynard down there in New York on the big, white-decked liner, waving good-bye in his Oxford grey overcoat.

I was wondering if the nicest, cheerfullest steamer letter I could write had reached him when suddenly Mary, the general-housework girl, pushed open my door and shoved in a long white box that had come by express. I opened it wonderingly and gasped at the big mass of fresh red roses that met my gaze. I lifted them into my arms. It was exactly as if the kindest man I know had thrown them to poor me upon the shore, just at the moment that the big boat was pulling out, and I had caught them safely in my arms. There was a little limp card that came with them. The stick had all come off the envelope and it fell out on the bed like a loose rose petal. I leaned and picked it up. The ink had begun to run a little as if the message had been written on blotting-paper, but I could make it out all right. The three little words brought burning tears to my eyes.

The card said: "For plucky San Francisco."

CHAPTER XIII

MANY months have passed since Dr. Maynard went to Europe. There have been two crops of chestnuts for me to gather alone in October since he sailed away—two dull, grey, unimportant Christmas nights since my ridiculous happiest one. Edith has been in command of my father's house for so long now that all the difficult adjustments have been made, the machinery is running without an audible squeak, and the house itself has developed into a plant as imposing and prosperous as a modern factory. As I write to-day I am sitting in my elaborate new bedroom, built on over the new porte-cochère—my old room was cut up into two baths and a shower—and am surrounded with rose cretonne hangings, lacy curtains, and delicately shaded electric lights.

Even the people in my life have changed so radically that I hardly recognise them as the ones that I once worked and cared for. Ruth has grown into a charming young lady; the twins have graduated from college and are earning their own way—Malcolm in New York and Oliver in a lumber camp out West; Tom is middle-aged; Elise, whom I visited last winter, is becoming a little stout and her hair is sprinkled through with grey; Alec has buried his personality in Edith; nothing is as it was. Even Hilton is different. The old Brooks Hotel on Main Street, where George Washington once stopped for over night, has been torn down; there's a new postoffice, a new City Hall; there's a double-tracked electric-car line to Boston. There are two taxicabs in the town now and a new theatre. Dr. Maynard's house looks like a tomb. The wisteria vine is the only live thing about it. Like hair it keeps on growing after death—winding, coiling, across the doors and window-panes with no hand to push it back. A young man just graduated from medical school has taken Dr. Maynard's practice; and as for kind, gentle Dr. Maynard himself I begin to doubt if such a person ever existed. When he went away he sold his automobile to Jake Pickens, a plumber down on Blondell Street, and to-day as I glided grandly by in Edith's limousine I observed Mr. Pickens wheezing up Main Street, chugging along with awful difficulty. The poor old machine looked about ready for the junk heap. A great wave of pity for it swept over me that brought tears to my eyes. Oh, I wish I could have kept right straight on with my old story. But I suppose everything has got to change, houses and towns and automobiles, as well as people and their histories.

I can hardly believe it was only two years ago that I used to climb into the cupola and lock myself away from everything below. There *is* no cupola now. It was cut off, like an offending wart. I was surprised to discover what a perfectly enormous thing it was as it stood upon the lawn waiting to be carried off. It reminded me of a horse that has fallen down on the pavement—symmetrical enough in its proper position, but dreadfully awkward and absolutely colossal sprawling about on the ground. Why, it took four horses to drag it up to old Silas Morton's. Silas Morton is a farmer up near Sag Hill and he bought my sacred temple for fifteen dollars. He uses it for a hen-house! It seemed to me like sacrilege, but the hens laid eggs in it, Mr. Morton said, as if they were possessed. The upper part of the window-panes in the cupola are made of yellow stained-glass, and he thinks—Silas Morton is kind of an inventor—that the hens have an idea it's sunshine and that spring is coming. I tell him the cupola is inspired. I saw a picture once of a common little farmhouse where Mrs. Eddy wrote her book, "Science and Health." If my book were to be published, and some photographer took a picture of the house in which I wrote it, I guess that old hen-coop would win the prize for an odd spot in which to have an inspiration.

With the cupola gone and the French roof entirely obliterated, the iron fence and the iron fountain sold to a junk man, a spreading porte-cochère at one side of the house, a billiard-room at the other, low verandas like a wide brim to a hat surrounding the entire structure, and everything painted a bright yellow trimmed with green, you never in this world would recognise 240 Main Street, once brown and square and ugly. There's a new stable a quarter of a mile back of the house; there are lawns where the vegetable garden used to be; the old apple orchard is now a sunken garden with a pool in the centre. As I write I can hear the trickle of a stream of water that spouts out of the little artificial pond, and catch the prosperous sound of the hum of a lawn-mower run by a motor. The name that Edith has chosen to give to all this grandeur is "The Homestead." It is engraved at the head of every sheet of note-paper in the establishment. The Homestead! You might as well call Windsor Castle the "Bide a Wee" or the "Dewdrop Inn" as this glaring, officious, stone-gated palace anything that suggests plainness and sweet homely comfort. The last time I wrote to Juliet I drew a big black ink line through the words "The Homestead" and wrote above "The Waldorf-Ritz-Plaza."

I've tried not to interfere with the changes Edith has made. I will confess I appealed to Alec about the apple orchard. But it was of no use. It seemed a shame to me, to go among that little company of old friends—twenty or thirty bent and bowing apple-trees grown up now side by side, touching branches and blooming together beautifully every spring just as if they were not far too old to bear anything to be called a harvest. I told Alec that I thought an apple orchard and a stone wall with poison ivy climbing over it was the loveliest garden for a New England homestead that any one could lay out. Alec must have told Edith, for the next day she asked me, in her laughing way, if I wouldn't like chickens scratching in the front yard, and yellow pumpkins piled on the back porch. New England homesteads even managed, she added, to keep pigs near enough the house so that the family could breathe the healthy odour in the parlour. "Dear child," she said, "of course we can't let the place be run over with poison ivy! How funny you are!" And the apple-trees came down. There are formal paths in the apple orchard now, the imported shrubs are tagged with labels, the pond is lined with cement. I simply have to escape to the woods, every once in a while, to make sure that nature is still having her way somewhere in the world.

You must think from this description that Edith Campbell is something of an heiress. Now that word to me has a kind of aristocratic sound, and so I prefer to say in regard to the Campbells, that they have simply oodles and oodles of money. I hate the word "oodles," but it just fits Edith Campbell. It describes her worldly possessions to a T. Her father, old Dave Campbell, is rolling up a fortune that is attracting attention. Why, the cost of all the improvements on old "two-forty" here didn't make a dent in his bank account they say. Alec tells me that if it wasn't for Mr. Campbell, Father's woollen business would not have endured another twelve months. Mr. Campbell has gone into the business heart and soul, and I don't know whether to be glad or sorry. Father never had any use at all for Mr. Campbell. He used to call him "scurvy." I remember the word because as a child I thought it a funny adjective to apply to a man who had a perfectly flawless complexion. I had to muster up all the control I had when I first saw David Campbell's big, fat, voluminous body occupying Father's revolving desk-chair in the private office down at the factory. I didn't think Father would like it. But Alec says that Father would much prefer to have Mr. Campbell elected as a president of the Vars & Company Woollen Mills than that any concern bearing his, Father's, name should fail to pay its creditors a hundred cents on the dollar. Perhaps he would; I don't know much about business. Anyhow I try to be nice to Mr. Campbell.

I try to be nice to Edith, too. It isn't easy. I don't like her, and I don't like her methods, but I don't tell her so. We don't quarrel, although we mix about like oil and water. Of course Edith has her good points. For instance she is the most generous person I ever knew, and she's good-nature itself. She'll take an insult from you, pay you back in your own coin and then exclaim: "Oh, come on, let's not fight. There's a dear! Let's go to the matinée this afternoon." She has a lot of practical ability too. She's a born manager, and as systematic as a machine. The trouble with Edith is her ambition. She wants to stand at the head of all society in the world, and to get there she is ready to work till she drops. Just as soon as she struggles up on top of one heap of people she begins on another, and so on. I don't know where she'll stop. Juliet Adams' mother told me that she could remember when people in Hilton didn't like to invite Mrs. Campbell to their houses. That was years ago, of course, for now they thank their lucky stars if they are invited to hers. There used to be, and are still, lots of beautiful country places sprinkled around Hilton. These summer people never mingled very much with Hiltonites, but as soon as Edith was able to walk she was bound to mingle with them. Well, she has realised that ambition. The summer colony, which is the set that gives social distinction to Hilton, includes Edith in all of its big functions now, in spite of the damning fact that she is a "native" and an "all-the-year-round."

Edith's social activities are simply marvellous to me. She has her plan of campaign—the various combinations of people to be invited to dinner-parties, bridges, or small teas, all mapped out and written down in a book at the beginning of each season. Then she manages to inveigle, by means of big fat cheques, I imagine, lions—pianists, and authors, and lecturers, whom everybody wants to see and hear—to act as her guest of honour. So her parties are always rather popular, you see. Oh, Edith is clever. She may not understand my nature very well, but to the likes and dislikes, pet ambitions and pleasures of human-nature generally she can cater to the queen's taste.

She has fairly hypnotised Ruth. My little sister thinks there is no one like her. As soon as Edith married Alec, she took complete possession of Ruth, provided her with a lot of lovely clothes and sent her off, for the first winter, to a fashionable boarding-school in New York. After eight dazzling months of that sort of life she ordained that Ruth should return to Hilton and "come out." Last fall she gave her a reception that fairly thrilled the town. Edith's word is sacred law to Ruth; Edith's opinion the ultimatum to any doubt on any question whatsoever. *I* am a mere speck on Ruth's outlook on life; *my* ideas don't count; I am so old-fashioned and so easily shocked; I don't know what style is; I don't possess a scrap of what Edith calls social-sense. Perhaps as much as anything else it is Edith's complete possession of Ruth that hurts me. It seems a shame that she couldn't have been satisfied with Alec. I don't see why she had to rob me of my only sister too. I don't cry about it (I won't let myself) but I think I've missed my own mother more since I was twenty than before I was ten. It may be a comfort to mothers whose little children have grown out of the helpless age to know this from a grown-up daughter.

I don't know what to say to you about my brother Alec. I wonder sometimes what has become of him. I see him, I hear him speak, I reply, but I might as well be gazing at his picture and talking with him over the long distance 'phone. I have no idea what he thinks about this new life of ours. He doesn't confide in me any more; we are almost strangers now. Of course I should expect him to be loyal to his wife—he's such a thoughtful man that he wouldn't hurt Edith's feelings for anything—but I wonder and wonder where all his old qualities have gone. Alec used to be so firm and determined, so frugal and economical. Are those qualities still smouldering away down deep in him somewhere, or when Edith took possession of his house, did she take possession of his soul too, and sweep out everything she didn't like, just as she cut off the cupola and sold the iron fence? Some men let women do that with them, especially if it's a woman they've wanted terribly for a dozen years, and never thought themselves good enough for her to accept. Why, Alec simply wants to please Edith and her family in every human way that he can. I have an idea that he feels so grateful to Edith for accepting him, and to Mr. Campbell for saving the business, that he doesn't dare disagree with a single solitary thing the Campbells ever do or think or suggest. I believe my brother is so overcome by living in such continual grandeur, sleeping in a bed with gold trimmings—Napoleonic, Edith says—bathing in a bathroom with Florentine tiles, entertaining all the big bugs within a hundred miles, and travelling to the office every morning in a limousine, that he feels that he must have been a mere worm when Edith picked him up. *I* think he's more of a worm *now*! Anyhow he doesn't show any backbone.

Sometimes at the table I glance at him across the flowers, and once in a long, long while there's a look in his eyes when they meet mine that I recognise as my dear brother's. Usually it's when Ruth and Edith are discussing society; and after one of these clandestine meetings of Alec's and mine across the flowers, I always come up here to my room wonderfully comforted, with a feeling that I am not absolutely deserted, after all.

Perhaps that sounds as if I were unhappy. Please do not think so, because I'm not. I'm *bound* not to be. I should be ashamed of myself, if just because I happened to be ousted from my job and didn't fancy my successor, I simply "went out into the back yard and ate worms." That isn't what I'm doing at all. Once Alec was married and I had made up my mind that I couldn't run away to New York and earn my way, or hire a house of my own and live by myself, I buckled down and did my level best to adjust my likes and habits to the conditions of Edith's reign. One can get used to anything, I believe. I accepted Edith as a person ought to accept any circumstance that can't be avoided. What if her ambitions do seem to me unworthy? What if she has crowded me out of my little niche? What if the customs and the things I liked are desecrated before my very eyes? All this will not cripple me, as a chance railroad accident might. I'm not enduring physical torture. I can still see, and hear, and use my two unhampered feet for long sweet walks in the country. What if, indeed, Edith has robbed me of Alec, and Ruth too? She cannot rob me of the joys of out-of-doors, the messages to me in books, the thrill I feel at the sound of distant music.

I can generally find several hours every day when I am able to steal away somewhere by myself with a book. I never had much time to read when I was younger and no one to suggest and guide as I grew up. I had never read *Vanity Fair* even, nor *Silas Marner*, nor *David Copperfield*. So after Alec was married, I made it my task to catch up with other girls of my age. I have my nose buried inside a novel most all of the time now. At first I used to drive myself to it, allot myself a certain number of chapters to read each day and accomplish it as if it were a stint. Now I simply devour a book in great hungry bites and wish there were more when I am finished. I don't know what I should do if I hadn't learned to love to read. I wonder if it would open up other sources of joy if I should learn to appreciate symphony or Italian Art. Perhaps Beethoven and Leonardo da Vinci, mere names to me now, would become as individual and inspire me with their messages as deeply as dear old Stevenson, whom I couldn't live without.

I think you must have surmised by this time that I haven't proved a great belle in society. You're exactly right. In the first place I hate bridge! Whenever I attempt to play, I get hot all over, and I wish I could unhook my tight collar and roll up my prickly sleeves. When it comes my turn to play, and I find myself desperately at a loss to know whether to trump or not—my partner looking daggers at me across the table and everybody waiting in dead silence—I simply give up all responsibility in the matter, repeat to myself: "Eenie, meenie, mynie moe, Catch a nigger by the toe," etc., and fling down the card that's "it," in utter abandon. Of course, that isn't good bridge, and Edith says I'll never make a player. She says I don't possess any more card-sense than social-sense. I wonder what kind of sense I do possess anyhow! It was a big consolation when I learned that the emptiest-headed women often make the best card players, simply because no superfluous ideas are at work in their brains to interrupt the train of concentrated card thought.

I'm not much more successful in conversation than I am in bridge. I seem to be always on the outside of women's intimacies somehow. Edith's set know one another so confidentially—keep tabs on the gowns, the hats, the jewellery, the number of servants each one has, and guess at one another's incomes. And then they use such a lot of mysterious signs! Sometimes raised eyebrows, a little nod toward a person's back, very tightly pursed lips, somebody abruptly twirling her two thumbs, will set off a whole roomful into peals of laughter, while I simply sit dazed and blank. It's just so with Ruth's younger crowd too. They're always giggling or making unintelligible remarks. You see I'm a kind of an in-between age, not old enough for Edith's set, nor young enough for Ruth's. The girls I used to know in the high school have not proved to be of the fashionable society here in Hilton, and Edith won't let me have them at the house. I've drifted away from most of them, except Juliet Adams, who is doing settlement work in New York, and I can't find any one to take their place.

I've come to the sad conclusion that I'm not popular with men either. At the little dances given here in Hilton occasionally, I'm not a wall-flower, possibly because I'm Edith Vars' sister-in-law, but I'm never "rushed." I can't be very brilliant in conversation at a dance when I'm anxiously watching for some kind, charitable soul to deliver my partner from the fear of two numbers in succession with me. And I have a sneaking conviction that I don't dance very well. You see all Ruth's set "Boston" to a waltz and two-step, and I don't know how. When a man is good enough to ask me to dance it seems too bad to make him exercise until he perspires. No one knows that I don't enjoy dances very much. It looks as if I were having a good time, I suppose, but down in my heart I'm worried and afraid.

At first I used to be eagerly on the lookout for my ideal—for a fleeting glimpse of a face that resembled the picture locked away in my secret desk-drawer. But such a quest is mere nonsense. I go to Boston to shop with Edith quite often; but never, in all the trains, railroad stations, restaurants, or elevators in law-office buildings (where one runs across so many good-looking men) have I seen even once the face of my desire. Why, I searched for that face throughout Oliver's and Malcolm's entire class when they graduated from college; I look for it among the new young men that come to call on Ruth, but I can't find it. Yet if I ever do marry, the man must be born by this time, I suppose. Sometimes, especially when I listen to music, I wonder where he is, in just what city, what house, what room he is sitting at that particular moment. I smile to think how unconscious he is of me, who some day will fill his life completely, and how surprised he'd be if he knew that I was loving him even now.

I wonder what he's doing this very minute—three o'clock on a Saturday afternoon. Perhaps he's playing golf in a Norfolk Scotch tweed; perhaps he's oiling an engine in blue overalls; perhaps he's at the point of death with typhoid fever and is lying in bed with a thermometer in his mouth, and I am going to lose him! Oh, I hope he will be spared! I'll love him, overalls and all, and be proud too, to stand at the back-door and wave my apron when his train goes by, just as they do in magazine stories. I don't believe, after all, I'm a bit ambitious when it comes to marrying.

I suppose every reader of this résumé chapter of mine is simply skipping paragraphs by the dozen in the fond hope that he'll run across some exciting reference to Dr. Maynard. People are always so suspicious of an old love-affair. Let me relieve your mind. As much as you may be disappointed, I must announce that I am not reserving any sweet sentimental morsel, for a climactic finale. Far from it. I haven't got it to reserve. I only wish I had. A sweet memory is such a comforting possession, a thrilling romance of the past such a reassurance. But it is very evident that Dr. Maynard has no intention of providing me with sweet memories or thrilling romances. All the balm and comfort that his proposal may have given me in the beginning he has destroyed by being hopelessly commonplace ever since. I wish you could read his letters! Impersonal? Why, they might easily be addressed to a maiden aunt. Never once has he referred to that starry night, when he asked me to go to Germany with him; never intimated that he wished that I were there to see the castles on the Rhine, or hear the music in the gardens above Heidelberg; never asked, as any normal man would do, if I had changed my mind. Not that I have in the least. I haven't! Only it seems to me almost impolite not as much as to inquire.

Dr. William Ford Maynard is becoming quite well known here in America. There have been several articles already in the magazines about him and the remarkable results of his scientific research. I ought to be flattered to receive envelopes addressed to *me* from *him* at all, I suppose. We write about once a month. His letters are full of descriptions of pensions, and cafés, and queer people at his boarding-place. I know some of his guinea-pigs by name—the ones who have the typhoid, the scarlet-fever, and the spinal meningitis; the convalescents, the fatalities, and the triumphant recoveries are reported to me monthly. But as honoured as I ought to feel, I suppose, to share the results of this man's famous work, the truth is I don't enjoy his letters one bit! I am glad I was foresighted enough not to marry such a passionless man. I never would have been satisfied. I see it clearly now.

My letters to him are regular works of art. I'm bound not to let him pity me, at any rate, and if he can write cheerful and enthusiastic descriptions so can I. To Dr. Maynard I am simply delighted over our burst into prosperity and social splendour. Edith's improvements on the house I rave over. I describe bridge parties, teas and dances as if I gloried in them. I refer to various men— mostly Ruth's suitors, I must confess—frequently and with familiarity. I am simply "Living," with a big capital L, in my letters to Dr. Maynard, and my stub pen crosses its T's and ends its sentences with great broad, militant dashes that are bold with triumph.

Once only did Dr. Maynard condescend to refer to the past, and that was in a little insignificant postscript at the end of a long humorous description of a German family that he saw in a café. This is what he wrote, all cramped up in a little bit of space, after he had signed his name:

> "How is San Francisco progressing in her reconstruction? Does she need any outside help in building up her beautiful city? Please let me know when she does!"

I tell you I wrote him the gayest, most flippant little note I could compose— all about how busy I was with engagements, etc., etc.; and then after I had signed my name, along the margin of the paper I said:

> "About San Francisco—she is progressing wonderfully, she doesn't need any help from any one, unless possibly lead

weights to keep her from soaring. The earthquake did her good. She's becoming very modernised and when you see her next I doubt if you recognise her on account of all the changes. Is Lizzie better? Or was it Nibbles who had the typhoid?"

If Dr. Maynard couldn't afford a fresh sheet of paper, go upstairs and shut himself in his room, and ask me seriously and quietly if I were unhappy or lonely, I would starve first before I'd ask bread of him.

I have it all planned just how I shall treat Dr. Maynard when he comes home—very distantly and as if so much society had made me a little blasé. When his name is sent up I shall keep him waiting in the little gold reception-room for about five minutes, and then glide into his presence, in a long clinging crêpe-de-chine dress. After I have shaken hands and said, "How pleasant it is to have you with us again," I'll ring for tea, then go back and sit down in the carved Italian armchair with the high back, dangle the ivory paper-cutter in one hand the way Ruth does, and inquire what sort of a passage he has had.

If he should come this year I've just the gown to wear. It's black, with a gold cord around the waist. I look about twenty-nine in it, and awfully sophisticated.

CHAPTER XIV

RUTH'S coming-out party cost over two thousand dollars, they say. Her dress alone was made by a dressmaker in Boston who won't "touch a thing" under a hundred and fifty; and Edith's—shimmering blue, draped with chiffon covered with green spangles, and here and there a crimson one (it looked just like the shining sides of a little wet brook trout)—simply spelled money.

I tell you the whole party lived up to the gorgeousness of Edith's gown too. There were orchids frozen in ice, for a punch bowl, in the dining-room; Killarney roses by the dozens in the reception-room; chrysanthemums in big round red bunches in the living-room; and the stairway was wound with smilax and asparagus fern, with real birch trees—silvery bark and all—at intervals of four or five feet. There were extra electric lights, extra maids, extra everything; and on the morning of Wednesday, the twenty-fifth of October, there arrived a whole squad of caterers from Boston with cases large as trunks filled with pattie shells, a thousand tiny brown pyramids of potato croquettes, tanksful of mushrooms, crab meat, and sweet-breads, cratesful of Malaga grapes and actual strawberries imported from somewhere which they dipped in white fondant and then set away to cool in little frilled paper holders, all over the butler's pantry.

It took Edith and Ruth two solid weeks of discussion and consultation to complete the invitation list. You see Edith was careful to give the party early in the fall before the summer colony had gone back home to its winter quarters. After the reception itself there was to be a small dance, and the elect were invited to remain. It was a source of satisfaction to Edith that only a dozen native Hilton men were invited to the dance, and but eight girls. Of course such partiality and ruthless slight and scorn of the people of her own native city caused a good deal of feeling in Hilton, but I observed that most every one who was invited to the reception came, in spite of the fact that they had been omitted from the dance to follow. Every living woman in Hilton was anxious, I suppose, to prove by her presence that she had the distinction of a portion of the engraved invitation at least.

I remember one name was under discussion for a week—a Mrs. Hugh Fullerton who was simply crazy "to get into things," Edith said—an officious, showy little bride from the West, she explained, who had married that young Yale graduate, Hugh Fullerton. Hugh Fullerton had been invited everywhere before he was married. He had been in Hilton only three years, but he had taken well. New young men usually do take well in Hilton. It's the women and the girls who have to climb and scramble. Mr. Fullerton was from Milwaukee, Wisconsin, and was learning the boiler business in the Hilton Boiler Works. He was a fine, tall, athletic, bronzed sort of fellow;

Edith used to invite him to The Homestead very often; he'd ridden every one of her hunters; he was supposed to be one of her favourites. Then he married, and Edith's invitations came to an abrupt end. I had never seen Mrs. Fullerton, but I felt sorry for her.

"She has been married only since June," I said to Edith; "why not invite the poor thing to the dance? What harm would it do? She may be a little homesick way on here in the East, and it might cheer her up a lot to have a little distinction if she's so awfully anxious for it."

"Bobbie, dear child, I'm not running an institution for homesick girls," replied Edith. "I know what I'm about. I rather liked the girl at first, I confess. She's got a lot of style, but she simply isn't being taken up—that's all. The Ogdens live in St. Louis in the winter and this Mrs. Fullerton lived there before she was married. The Ogdens know everybody in St. Louis of any importance, but they never even heard of Mrs. Fullerton. I'm not going to try to float a girl in society, whom I know nothing about. You may be sure of *that*."

"I should think your position would be secure enough after a while, for you to show a little independence," I murmured.

"Independence! Why, child, I'm inviting her to the reception, as it is. Anyhow what can *you* know about it? I'll settle the invitations, dearie." That was an example of the manner with which my ideas were usually treated.

There was a house-party planned at The Homestead in addition to the tea and dance. Edith always does a thing up good and brown. She wrote to about a dozen out-of-town people and invited them to become the guests of the house for over the twenty-fifth. These consisted of boarding-school friends of Ruth's, several of Edith's; and Oliver and Malcolm, who of course came home for the event, provided a generous supply of men from their crowd at college.

The three automobiles were kept busy meeting trains all the day before the tea, and the expressmen were tramping up and down the stairs with dozens of various trunks of all styles and sizes. The guest-rooms in The Homestead looked very festive, all decked out in real lace and silver, with Edith's best embroidered trousseau-spreads stretched out gorgeously upon the beds. It really grew quite exciting as the time for the tea drew near—even I felt a little of the pervading delight. Of course I hated meeting so many new people, but everybody's attention was centered upon Ruth, and I was perfectly free to withdraw to my room at any time I desired. I, thank goodness, was only Ruth's sister.

The tea was on a Wednesday, October twenty-fifth, from five until seven o'clock. Edith had bought a lovely dress for me—pink and soft and shining—and about three o'clock she sent the professional hair dresser, who had been spending the day at the house, to puff and marcel Bobbie, she said.

I hardly knew myself when I gazed into my mirror after I was all dressed. My hair was done up high like a queen's, and there were two little sparkling pink wings in it. My dress was cut into a V in front, and my neck looked so long and slender with my hair drawn away from its usual place in the back, and piled up in a soft puffy pyramid on top, that I seemed almost stately. I just wished Dr. Maynard could see San Francisco then!

As I walked out into the hall, my train made a lovely sound on the soft oriental rugs. I stood at the top of the stairs and gazed about me. Everything was in readiness—maids in black and white stationed at the bedroom doors, the musicians below already beginning to tune their instruments, the dark draperies drawn, a soft illumination of electricity everywhere, and the faint delicious odour of coffee mixed with the perfume of roses. I was overwhelmed with the spirit of prosperity that filled every corner and cranny of my father's house. I wondered what Father would think of it all—big, calm, quiet Father whose tastes were so plain, habits so simple, and whose words of advice to us his children always so eloquent with the wickedness of extravagance. I put him out of my mind just as quickly as I could. I didn't want to think of him just now. I wanted to have a good time for once in my life; I wanted everybody to see that I wasn't shy and quiet and plain; I wanted to be clever and admired; and I would be too! I caught a glimpse of myself, whole length, in the long hall-mirror. My cheeks were flushed and rosy, my eyes were dark and bright. I really believed I was pretty! I could have shouted, I felt so happy. I ran down the side stairway, that leads to the hall off the porte-cochère, through the chrysanthemum-laden living-room and hall, into the rose-perfumed reception-room, where I found Edith and Ruth ready for the first arrival. I felt suddenly generous-hearted toward all the prosperity and luxury that made such a palace of our old house and such a new creature of me. I wanted to tell Edith how lovely I thought it all was.

I had more reason than ever to feel grateful to Edith about an hour later. It was at the very height of the afternoon rush, about quarter past five. I happened to be standing just back of Edith, waiting for a chance to offer her some lemonade which one of the ladies assisting had been thoughtful enough to send to her by me. There was a long line of women that stretched way out into the hall, just like a line in front of a ticket window at the theatre, each waiting her turn for a chance to shake hands with Edith, though most of them she sees every time she goes out anyhow. Edith was very gracious and cordial this afternoon. I've heard very often that she makes a lovely hostess. I watched her closely, trying to see just where the charm lay.

"Ah, good afternoon! Mrs. Fullerton, I believe?" suddenly broke in on my reflections, and I glanced up quickly, curious to see the poor little neglected bride whom I championed. There really was nothing very poor nor very neglected about her appearance. I couldn't see her face beneath her plumed picture-hat, but her costume was very costly and elegant—a lot of Irish lace over something dark.

"Yes, Mrs. Hugh Fullerton," she replied effusively. "Hugh has told me so much about his good times here at The Homestead, Mrs. Vars, and how kind and cordial you've been to him, and I *do* want to thank you. Haven't you a gorgeous afternoon? I'm so glad to meet you, after all Hugh has said. Why, I know some of your horses by name even—Regal, for instance—the one that threw Hugh—do you remember?"

Edith's manner cooled, hostess though she was.

"Regal has thrown so many!" she remarked. "Ruth, Mrs. Fullerton," she finished.

"Oh," went on Mrs. Fullerton to Ruth, not at all abashed, "I've met Miss Vars already. A bride remembers everybody new she meets, you know, and then of course I couldn't help but remember *you*." There was something hauntingly familiar about Mrs. Fullerton's manner and voice. I put the lemonade on a table near by and drew nearer. "It was at Mrs. Jaynes' bridge-party last week," she went on; "don't you remember? We played at the same table, Miss Vars."

"Did we?" inquired Ruth in her sweet, icy, little way; "I don't remember."

"Of course," flushed Mrs. Fullerton. "Débutantes meet so many new people. I know just how it is—I was there once myself. I don't wonder one bit. I remember *I* couldn't keep even the men straight, to say nothing of the women."

"O Lucy," suddenly exclaimed Edith, catching sight of me, "this is Mrs. Fullerton. My other sister, Miss Vars, Mrs. Fullerton. She'll take you to the dining-room and serve you some tea or an ice."

I raised my eyes to Mrs. Fullerton's. No, I hadn't been mistaken. I should have recognised that voice in China. Mrs. Fullerton's mouth opened in amazement as she gazed at me.

"Lucy Vars," she finally ejaculated. "Lucy Vars! Why, Lucy, don't you remember Sarah Platt?"

"Yes, I remember," I nodded.

"How lovely! How perfectly lovely!" exploded Sarah. "Why, Mrs. Vars," she sparkled, "Lucy and I are old pals! Isn't it too nice for anything? We were at Miss Brown's-on-the-Hudson the same year, and I guess if you've ever been to boarding-school yourself, you know what that means. Why, Lucy, you old trump, how are you anyway? I'm simply pleased to pieces!" And the once much-envied Sarah Platt of years ago, the successful, the glorious Sarah Platt, enveloped me at last in a huge schoolgirl embrace!

"Hypocrite!" I thought.

"I'd lost track of Lucy completely," she went on to Edith and Ruth, linking her arm familiarly through mine. "I'd forgotten your home was in Hilton, though I certainly knew it was in Massachusetts somewhere. Wasn't it stupid? Here I've been living for three months in the same place with you, Lucy Vars, and never knew it! Here you were all the time a sister to Mrs. Alexander Vars, whom Hugh wrote me so much about that I almost grew jealous," she laughed. "Isn't this world just the smallest place you ever heard of, Mrs. Vars? You must come right over and see me, Lucy, and make up for lost time, and I hope you'll both come with her," smiled Sarah upon my sisters; "I'd simply love to have you."

We moved away toward the dining-room.

"Oh, Lucy," went on Sarah, "I am so glad to see you again! It's just like discovering somebody from home. I haven't any friend here my own age at all. You've grown so pretty! You're looking splendid; and aren't your sister and sister-in-law just stunning!"

I drew my arm away from Sarah's. I remembered what she had thought about my family once.

"Don't leave me," she exclaimed, "please, or I'll perish. Stay while I have my ice. I don't know one soul in that dining-room."

Life works out its patterns very cunningly, I think. Once I had hidden in shame behind a telegraph-pole from this majestic creature; once she had looked upon me as mean and insignificant, unworthy of even her pity; now she actually plead for my favour, toadied to my family, palavered me with flatteries. I drew in deep breaths of satisfaction.

"Dear, dear life, how kind and just you are after all!" I said half an hour later, gazing into my mirror, in my own closed room. "*My* day is dawning now—mine, mine, at last! And I'm so happy! I'm going to have a wonderful time at the dance to-night. I feel it. Oh, it's good after all to have money and prosperity; it's good to wear soft, pink shimmering dresses that are becoming and make people gaze and whisper; it's good to hold such a position in a community that even Sarah Platts bow and scrape and try to please; it's more than good—it's exhilarating!"

I went out into the hall and started to go down the main stairway. It was deserted now. The hour was seven-thirty, just before the men were due to arrive for the supper and the evening celebrations to follow.

Half-way down this stairway, on the landing, there is a large portrait of my father. Amid all the preparations going on in the house I had not known that Edith had had the electricians adjust a row of shielded electric lights at the top of the heavy frame of Father's picture. The portrait had always hung on the landing where the light is very dim. We had had it for years. It was painted when we were prosperous, but I had never examined it very closely. It was an awfully black sort of picture, and before Ruth's tea I could not have definitely said whether Father was standing or sitting in it. I didn't know that a row of lights could make such a difference. As I turned on the landing that night and came suddenly upon the painting I stopped stock-still. Why, it wasn't a picture! I didn't see the frame, nor the canvas, nor the paint. It was Father, dear Father himself, sitting at his roll-top desk down in the sitting-room. I could see every little wrinkle in his face, the crows-feet at the corners of his eyes, the fine, tired-looking lines along his forehead. He was sitting in his big leather armchair, and I remembered exactly how the leather had worn brown and velvety like that, along the edges. As usual he wore across his breast his heavy gold watch-chain, with the black onyx fob—the one he used to let me play with in church, when I was very little—and in one hand, which was resting easily along the arm of the chair, Father held his glasses just as he used to hold them when he took them off to glance up at me before I dashed off to dancing-school on Saturday nights. "Can't you keep that hair a little smoother?" he'd say to me, and "Isn't there a good deal of trimming on that dress? Your mother always wore plain things with a little white at her neck. Keep your tastes simple, my girl, and your clothes neat and nicely sewed." They were plain, homely words. Any man could say them, but as I remembered them that night, they seemed terribly sweet—almost sacred—and I backed up against the wall, and stared at Father there before me, with tears in my eyes. He would not have liked the sparkling wings I was wearing in my hair. The dress that Edith had given me—all shining satin, wasn't like my mother's with a little white at the neck. The silent, sad expression in my father's eyes smote me. He was gazing straight at me, down into my heart. I almost saw his lips move. The words of the verse that he used to repeat so often at our morning prayers after breakfast, I seemed to hear again: "Children, how hard it is for them that trust in riches to enter into the Kingdom of God." Father was always quoting things from the Bible about vanity and riches. His heroes were always big, simple, honest men like Abraham Lincoln and Benjamin Franklin. As I stood and stared at Father's picture the musicians began to play some soft, dreamy melody, and just then Alec from above caught sight of me leaning up against the wall.

"Hello," he called cheerfully; "how do you like the new lights on the picture?" And he came tripping down all dressed up in his evening clothes to join me. I don't believe Alec had seen the portrait lighted before either, for he stopped short beside me when he came in full view of it. He was speechless for a moment. Really those lights made Father look as if he could answer if we spoke to him. He seemed to be actually sitting there amid all the luxury and splendour he had so despised. Alec came over beside me. He took my hand in his and for a long sweet half-minute, my old partner and I stood there together on the landing and gazed up into Father's noble eyes.

"It's miraculous," breathed Alec, softly, at last.

I couldn't answer. It *was* miraculous. I wished I was in my ugly old blue cashmere and could crawl up into Father's lap.

I didn't know anybody was coming up the stairs till suddenly Alec dropped my hand and left me.

"Hello—hello there," he called out jovially. "Come right up, Mr. Campbell. Just gotten here, haven't you? Everything's gone in tip-top shape so far. We're looking pretty fine around here, aren't we? Bobbie and I were passing judgment on Edith's new lights. Here, let me take that coat. Edith discovered that this old portrait of Father was by an artist who has a reputation now, so she had it properly lighted. It is marvellous what a really excellent likeness it is. Come and tell us your opinion."

I slunk away to my room quietly.

All that evening amid the babble of voices and din of violins, pianos and cornets, while girls in gorgeous raiment sat beneath Father's picture between dances with their partners on the top stair of the landing, and just below men gathered around the punch-bowl; while Edith and Ruth shone in jewels, and old Dave Campbell blatantly exhibited the latest improvements in the house to all his friends, Father looked down upon it all from his lofty position silently, disapprovingly, a look of censure in his eyes that I couldn't seem to escape. My little hour of triumph was snuffed out by Father's gaze like a candle in a tempest; my sudden self-satisfaction, my burst of eager joy in prosperity and position, born to feel the throb of life but for an hour.

I didn't enjoy the dance. I couldn't. I tried once or twice to "enter in," but it was masquerade. There had been champagne served at the supper. Girls as well as men were full of the spirit of mad merry-making. Everybody was having a glorious time—everybody but me. I hated the hilarious laughter. I don't mean to imply that any one became intoxicated, I don't think they did exactly, but just the same the whole affair seemed to me like a debauch going on in my father's house beneath his very eyes. I stole up to the landing about eleven o'clock when the music was still shrieking, Ruth's cheeks burning with excitement, Oliver laughing so loudly that I could hear him above the music, and switched off the lights above Father's picture. He shouldn't look on at such festivities—mute, unable to speak his mind, tied there in his chair, helpless and forgotten—he shouldn't if I could help it!

Late that same night—or it must have been the next morning—anyway after every one was quiet, and the house was finally dark I stole out of my room and crept quietly down on the landing. The house was dead still. I heard the big clock with the chimes strike a half-hour, and a second after all the other clocks reply. I was in my nightgown wrapped around with an eiderdown bath-robe. I found my way stealthily to the little button behind the portrait. I pushed it. There was a little click and suddenly Father was before me! I went back and sat down on the lowest stair, close up to the railing, and looked up into his comforting eyes. No one had known that I had spent the last six dances shut up in my room. No one had missed me. I had had a horrid time, but no one cared.

There were the remains of the orgy of the night before scattered all about Father's feet—a discarded bunch of violets, a torn piece of chiffon, a half a macaroon, a girl's handkerchief. As I sat there and wondered how Ruth and the twins and Alec could all go peacefully to sleep, unmindful of their strict and rigid bringing-up, forgetful of Father left here in the midst of the confusion of the things he preached against, I heard from somewhere, way off, a queer long laugh. I listened intently, and in a moment I could catch the rumble of voices from behind closed doors. I wondered who could be awake at such an hour, when a door opened downstairs, and as plain and distinct as day, a man's voice exclaimed, "Come on, boys, we'll have to carry old Ol up. Lend a hand, one of you chaps who can walk straight, and don't make any noise. Wake up, Oliver, old pal. We're going to bed." I heard a horrid guttural sort of rejoinder from Oliver, and I shuddered. Some of the men must have been sitting up in the dining-room and drinking! I knew, oh, I knew now, that Oliver must be intoxicated! I was in my nightgown. There was no time to turn out the lights over Father's picture, to shield Father from the awful sight of his son, drunk—horridly, helplessly drunk, being carried upstairs to bed. I glanced up at Father shining there in his frame. He was looking straight down the long broad stairway. In another minute Oliver and Father would meet face to face. I turned and fled back to my room.

CHAPTER XV

FOUR months later. Twelve o'clock at night. Wrapped up in my eiderdown bath-robe. Sitting at my desk.

It is midnight. I cannot sleep. I have been lying wide awake, listening to a strong April wind, howling around the corner of the house, for two hours! I've repeated the twenty-third Psalm over and over again. I've imagined a flock of sheep going over a stile (though I never saw it done) for ten minutes solid. I've swallowed two Veronal tablets. It's useless. I surrender. I don't want to get up. I shall have an awful headache to-morrow, besides heavy lead weights behind my eyes; and to-morrow—to-morrow of all days—I want to be fresh and bright and as beautiful as nature can make me. Moreover, I'd rather not write. But I can't read. There has never been a book printed that could hold my thoughts to-night. My mind goes back to the events of the day like steel to a magnet. I've tried solitaire, and ended by pushing the silly cards on the floor. You see something has happened—something big and actual and real!

I have seen Dr. Maynard!

I have met him face to face, talked with him, laughed with him, walked with him from Charles Street to the sunken garden, sat with him by the fountain. I am beside myself with excitement. I had better tell how it all happened. If I get it out of my system I may be able to snatch a little sleep, and I *must* sleep. I have an important engagement to-morrow at three.

It occurred at four o'clock this afternoon. I had bought a bunch of primroses from a man on the street five minutes before. I was on my way home from a shopping tour, and with my pretty early-spring flowers tucked in at my waist, and my hands full of packages, I turned up Charles Street as unconcerned as you please. At the corner I bowed to our minister's wife, and the remains of the smile were still on my face, I suppose, when I saw Dr. Maynard. I didn't know that he was on this side of the ocean, and when I observed him coming down the steps of the postoffice—vigorous and strong and buoyant—I stood still in my tracks, and the remains of the smile turned into something startled and afraid. Dr. Maynard approached me all aglow, stretched out his hand and took mine in a warm, firm grasp. A thrill went through me like a knife. He was as natural as day, beautifully tanned, smiling, big, broad-shouldered as ever, and yet different—oh, awfully different.

"Hello, Bobbie," he said in his hearty old voice, and I looked back at him, perfectly white—I could feel that I was—and speechless. "Don't be a goose. It's just Dr. Maynard," I tried to reason with myself.

"Am I speaking to Miss Lucy Vars?" I heard asked of me. "Miss Lucy Chenery Vars, of 240 Main Street, Hilton, Mass.?"

I nodded, and somewhere down there in the chaos in my chest, I found my poor little voice. "Is it *you*?" I asked shakily.

"Well, I'm not quite sure. Nothing looks very natural around here. I'm beginning to think I'm somebody else."

"Well, I *am* surprised!" I exploded. "I certainly *am* surprised! Why, I never *was* so surprised!" I stopped a minute. Dr. Maynard was smiling right down into my eyes. "I never was so surprised in all my life!" I repeated, as if I hadn't another idea in my head.

He leaned down just here and picked up a half-dozen bundles, more or less, that I had dropped when we shook hands.

"I better help you carry some of these home, hadn't I?" he suggested.

"Oh, yes, *do*," I replied eagerly, and somehow we managed to walk back to the house together.

I don't know through what streets we went, past what houses. I can scarcely recall of what we talked. "He's come home! He's come home! He's come home!" kept ringing in my ears over and over again, like jubilant chimes. "Dr. Maynard has come home!" And whenever I looked up and saw him smiling down at me—so naturally, so beautifully—it seemed as if I should have to make a pirouette or two, right there on the sidewalk. Every time he laughed I wanted to shout; every time he remarked upon a new building or a new house, and especially when he exclaimed, "Good heavens! What have we here?" at the sight of one of the taxicabs, I wanted to turn a handspring. When he first came in view of 240 Main Street and stood stock-still in his tracks, and gasped, "Where's the cupola, and the French roof, and the iron fountain, and the barn, and the apple orchard?" I wanted to throw my arms around him for joy. I must have felt like a dog at the sight of his beloved master whom he hasn't seen for months. It was so intoxicating to have Dr. Maynard beside me again that it seemed as if I must express my joy by jumping up on him, and half knocking him down. Which, of course, I didn't do. My voice broke a dozen times, my underlip trembled, my cheeks burned with excitement, but otherwise I walked along as sedately as if it were an everyday occurrence to run across a man I believed was hopelessly buried in a laboratory in Europe.

It was in the sunken garden that the most important part of our conversation took place. You remember, don't you, that in my letters to Dr. Maynard I had always been enthusiastic over the improvements Edith has made on old

240. So now it was with apparent pride that I led my old friend down the granolithic steps into the one-time apple orchard. I showed him the cement-lined pool in the centre, the Italian garden-seat, the rare shrubbery now bound up in yellow straw, with something like delight. I was so full of exultation at the mere sight of dear, kind, understanding Dr. Maynard that I could have rejoiced about anything. When I exclaimed, "And there's a squash-court connected with the garage, and a tennis-court as *smooth* as *glass* beside the stable; and where the old potato-patch used to be, there's a pergola!" my eyes fairly sparkled. "That sun-dial over there," I boasted, "was designed especially for Edith; and oh, there's the dearest, slimmest little stream of water that spouts out of the centre of the pool, in the summer. You ought to see it!" I was all enthusiasm. Edith wouldn't have recognised me. Ruth would have thought I had lost my reason. Even Dr. Maynard looked at me curiously.

"It certainly is all very fine, I've no doubt," he remarked.

"Yes, isn't it?" I exclaimed.

"But I must confess," he went on. "*I* never objected to the old apple orchard. Just about where the pool is now, there used to grow the best old Baldwins I ever tasted."

"Oh, my," I scoffed, "you ought to see the bouncing big Oregon apples Edith buys by the crate."

Dr. Maynard shook his head and smiled. Then he came over and sat down beside me on the Italian seat.

"Well, well," he sighed, "I suppose old Rip must get used to the changes that have taken place since he's been asleep—squash-courts and pergolas, great sweeping estates with granolithic drives and sunken gardens; new hotels; new postoffices; instead of the roomy, old-fashioned livery-stable hacks, taxicabs; instead of good old snappy New England Baldwins, apples imported from Oregon; and instead of a girl in a red Tam-o-Shanter and her father's old weather-beaten ulster, sitting behind the wheel of a little one-lunger automobile, running it, in all sorts of weather, like a young breeze—instead of that girl," said Dr. Maynard, looking me up and down closely, "a very correct and up-to-date young lady in kid gloves and a veil, a smart black and white checked suit, a very fashionable hat (*I* should call it), with a bunch of primroses, to cap it all, pinned jauntily at her waist."

I blushed with triumph.

"I've just about come to the conclusion," added Dr. Maynard in a kind of wistful voice, "that I don't know San Francisco at all now."

"Well," I laughed waveringly, "I do hope you'll find it a little more civilised than it was before."

"*I* never thought it was uncivilised," said Dr. Maynard quietly; "*I* rather enjoyed it just as it was, to tell the truth. I shall be sorry to find many changes in it because I shall have to become acquainted with it all over again and my time is so short."

"Short?" I exclaimed. I don't know why I had drawn the sudden conclusion that Dr. Maynard had come back to stay. His very next words put an end to my little half-hour of jubilance like the announcement of a death.

"Yes," he said; "I'm sailing back to Germany in two weeks. I was appointed an executor of a distant relative's will, and it seemed necessary to come to New York and attend to it. Of course I couldn't be so near—San Francisco, without coming to see how it prospered after the earthquake. I'm glad to find you so happy, Bobbie. You've richly earned all this," he glanced around the display that surrounded us, "both you and Al, and it's really fine that the change in your circumstances came about, when *you*, Lucy, were still a young girl, and just ready to appreciate and enjoy good times, and pretty surroundings, and new young people. Sometimes the apparent catastrophes work out for our best happiness. You *are* happy, aren't you, Bobbie?"

"Oh, yes—perfectly happy," I flashed indignantly.

"I thought so. Your enthusiasm brims over in your letters. Well, well," twitted Dr. Maynard, "who ever would have thought Al's little sister, whom I used to call 'wild-cat,' would turn into a society girl—a mighty popular one too, if *I'm* any judge. Parties and engagements all the time, I suppose. Now I'm just curious enough to wonder," went on Dr. Maynard teasingly, while my feelings, hurt and enraged, were working up to one of their habitual explosions, "which one of all those admirers I hear mentioned in your letters sent you your pretty primroses *this* morning."

"No one sent them," I blurted out. "If you *must* know, I bought them myself five minutes before I saw you. Those men in my letters were Ruth's friends, not mine."

Dr. Maynard glanced at me sharply.

"Oh," I went on fiercely, "I'm glad to know if you think that I'm happy. It shows how well you understand me. Happy! I'm perfectly miserable, if you want to know the truth. I hate and loathe and despise all this display you say I've so richly earned. I hate parties, and splurge, and sunken gardens, and pergolas, and I haven't a single solitary admirer in the world. I thought you knew me, but I see you don't. I thought if you ever came back *you'd* understand, but you don't—not one little single bit. I thought *you—you—*"

I stopped abruptly. There's no use trying to hide tears that run shamelessly down your cheeks. It was absolutely necessary for me to ask for my bag which Dr. Maynard held, and produce a handkerchief. He didn't say anything as I mopped my eyes. I thought perhaps he was too shocked to speak. He didn't offer me a single word of comfort—just sat and waited. I didn't look at him; and still with my face turned away I said, subdued, apologetically, "I don't see what is the matter with me lately. You mustn't mind my being so silly. I'm always getting 'weepy' for no reason at all." I opened my bag, tucked away my handkerchief, as a sign that the storm was over, and stood up. "I hope you won't think that I usually act this way with—with all those admirers of mine," I added, smiling.

Dr. Maynard ignored my attempt at humour.

"Lucy," he said quietly, but in a voice and manner that made me start and catch my breath, "my real reason for coming to America wasn't the will. It was you." He stopped and I looked hard into the centre of the dry pool. "I mistrusted some of your letters lately, though I confess not at first—not until last fall. You've been overdoing your enthusiasm this winter, Bobbie. So I decided to come over and find out for myself if you had been trying to deceive me. The will offered a good excuse, so here I am. And you *have* been deceiving me—for two whole years. Why, Bobbie," he said very softly, "what shall I do to you?"

I glanced up and saw the old piercing tenderness in his eyes.

"Don't be kind to me," I warned hastily; "not *now*—not for anything. *Please*, or I shall cry again."

I heard Dr. Maynard laugh the tenderest, gentlest kind of laugh, and in a second both his arms were around me. Yes, both Dr. Maynard's arms were close around me! I didn't cry. I just stayed there quiet and still and safe; and I've been there in imagination about every moment since.

When he finally let me go he said simply, but in a queer trembling voice, "Will you go to drive with me to-morrow afternoon at three, way off into the country, away from pergolas and cement pools, and people?"

I nodded, unable to speak.

"All right. I'll be here. Good night," he said gently, and turned abruptly and left me there alone in the garden.

I watched him hurry up the garden-steps and out of the gateway. He turned once and waved his hand to the pitiful little wind-blown creature he left behind in the bleak unbeautiful garden. I felt as if he had torn me from my moorings and that I must toss and drift in strange unknown seas until to-morrow at three.

I managed to gather my bundles together somehow, and come up here to the house. My cheeks were flaming when I opened the door. I left my packages in a chair in the hall and hurried up here to my room as quickly as I could. Once here I locked my door tight and threw off my things. "Oh, don't be silly; don't be absurd," I said, and buried my face in the dark of my arms on my desk. "It's just Dr. Maynard," I went on later, "and you know how you felt two years ago. Oh, be reasonable. Be calm." But all the time that I was talking sense to myself, I was feeling strong arms about my shoulders, and a kind of sinking, fainting, going-out feeling that people must experience when they lose consciousness, would steal over me so that I couldn't think.

Finally to put an end to my nonsense I opened a secret compartment and took out Robert Dwinnell's picture. *He* would cure me of my delusion; *he* would keep me true to my ideals. I gazed at Robert Dwinnell for a solid sixty seconds, then deliberately, straight across the forehead, down the nose, through the very smile that once had thrilled me, I tore that poor picture into a thousand bits, and dumped the remains into the waste-basket. It was a dreadful act. I felt like a murderess. I don't know what made me do it, but Robert Dwinnell had lost his charm. Dr. Maynard, glowing with health, his eyes fierce with a tenderness that actually hurt, made my poor old idol look flat and insipid.

Some time later—ten minutes perhaps—an hour—I don't know—a maid knocked and asked if I were coming down to dinner. I got up and followed her mechanically, and for the life of me I don't know whether there was roast-beef or lamb.

Now I am again locked in my room, and my soul is actually on fire. It is as dark as death outdoors. Every one in the house is asleep. But I am sitting here gazing at a little faded picture of an automobile which I finally discovered in an old souvenir-book of mine. That little speck there is Dr. Maynard and I am going to see him to-day at three!

CHAPTER XVI

EVER since I can remember having any ideas on the subject at all, I have always longed to be married in one of those dark, little tucked-away chapels in some cathedral or other, in France or England, like a girl I read about in a book. Perhaps a late afternoon service would be going on up near the big altar; candles would be burning; the priest would be chanting queer minor things; poor women would be stepping in, crossing themselves, to say a prayer; and, all unconscious of me, nearly hidden by the big stone pillars, tourists would be tip-toeing about, gazing at the rose-window and the towering arches. There would be footfalls and whispers in the nave. Echoes everywhere. I should have loved the echoes! "But then," Edith said, "you wouldn't have had a sign of a wedding present, and you can't furnish your house with echoes, crazy Bobbs."

If ever there was a wedding opposite to my ideal of one, it was mine. For of course I am married to Dr. Maynard.

You aren't surprised, I know. It was all decided that afternoon at three, and two weeks later when Will sailed back to Germany it wasn't in imagination that I stood on the dock and waved him good-bye. I was there soul and body this time, and I followed with my fluttering handkerchief every motion that he made with his hat and great spoke of an arm. I watched him till he faded out of sight, and then with Ruth and Edith, who went to New York with me, I returned to the shops to buy my trousseau.

Will had to be back in Germany on May first to deliver a lecture before a very learned assembly of scientists and doctors. They wanted him to tell them about a few of his experiments with his guinea-pigs. It was a great compliment for so young a man, and an American besides, to receive an invitation to address a body of old-world sages. Of course he couldn't disappoint them, but he told me that by the middle of August he would be sailing back again and after a simple little wedding in the dead quiet of midsummer, he would at last carry his refugee back with him to Europe. He was not going to begin work until October. We planned to travel till then.

"So, after all," said Will to me that afternoon at three o'clock, "after all, some day—oh, Lucy—perhaps some day—" and *this* time it was I who finished the sentence.

"Yes, perhaps some day," I said sparkling, "the refugee and you will be seeing Paris together."

Our plans would have been lovely if they had worked out; but they didn't. I haven't seen Paris yet, and there's no prospect that I shall until Will's Sabbatical year comes around. We're going across then, he says, if we have to work our way on a cattle ship. You see Will no sooner got back there to Germany and delivered his lectures to those old sages, than the medical department of one of the biggest universities here in America sent him an invitation to become a member of their faculty. The position was quite to his taste, he wrote me. He could keep right on with his experimenting and guinea-pigs to his heart's content—the university had wonderfully equipped laboratories, the best in America—and what did I say? What *should* I say to a person whose very picture that had been taken for just me to put on my bureau, had appeared in two magazines that month? Such an insignificant tail to the big lion as I, ought cheerfully to go wagging to the North Pole or the Sahara Desert. Of course I didn't say a word.

I never saw anything like the way the magazines burst forth in sudden praise of Will. His appointment to the faculty of the university was reported in every paper published. I didn't know whether my emotions were of pride or fear. After reading an account of what Dr. William Ford Maynard had accomplished and how high his position was in the scientific world, and then, immediately following, seeing the announcement of his engagement to Miss Lucy Chenery Vars, of Hilton, Mass., I was filled with a good deal of apprehension.

Edith was delighted with my engagement. To boast of William Ford Maynard as a future brother-in-law was a great feather in her cap. The plans for an elaborate wedding were formed and crystallised before I had gotten used to wearing my engagement ring. I didn't want a big wedding, but it seemed useless to remonstrate. You see I was under obligations to Edith. All my linen, stiff gorgeous stuff with heavy elaborate monograms, she had given me; bath towels two yards long which I despise, sets of underwear all ruffles, fol-de-rols and satin rosettes, she had bestowed upon me; also my solid silver service, Sheffield tray and flat silver were gifts from Edith. I didn't like my flat silver. The design is awfully elaborate, representing a horn of plenty overflowing with pears and grapes and apples. Edith, however, thought it was stunning. I didn't like my wedding invitations, thick as leather, engraved in enormous block letters, my name staring at me like a sign over a store and a whole pack of cards besides. But Edith did. I didn't want the ceremony to take place in the Episcopal church which Edith has been attending lately, with a boys' choir preceding me up the aisle, when I've always been a plain straight old-fashioned Congregationalist. I didn't want eight bridesmaids of Edith's choosing, selected from the most prominent families that she could find. I didn't want all society invited. But I soon discovered that my wedding was to be Edith's party, not mine.

On the morning of the fifth day before the great occasion I was in the Circassian walnut guest-chamber looking at the overwhelming display of wedding presents. The original furniture had been moved into the stable and a low wide shelf covered with heavy white damask ran around the entire room. Edith had put all the cut-glass together in the bay-window, and under the glare of a dozen extra electric lights it sparkled bright and hard. There were two enormous punch-bowls, a lamp, a vase big enough for an umbrella-stand, thirteen berry dishes, baskets and candlesticks, two ice-cream sets, two dozen finger-bowls and six dozen glasses. I hate cut-glass!

"Lucy, Lucy, you up there?" somebody called as I gazed.

"I suppose so," I sang back, and I heard Edith coming up the stairs. I hadn't a doubt but that she would be staggering under a fresh load of presents and I wasn't mistaken. She appeared with a regular Pisa Tower of them, extending up to her eyes.

"How's this for a haul?" she gasped. "Come on, my dear, hustle up and see what you draw." Then she added, "Gracious, Lucy, where in the world did you resurrect that old dress? Don't you know every one will be dropping in at all hours during these last days?" Edith herself was fairly dazzling in stiff crackling white linen.

"It was so comfortable," I murmured, "and it has no bones in the collar."

"I should say it hadn't! Your bridesmaids will be here any minute. Hurry up and look at these things, and then go and get yourself fixed up. *Do.*"

I began silently on the bottom box, cut the string, removed the cover, and from beneath the tissue-paper drew out a red flannelette bag.

"It's another plateau," I said wearily before I unpulled the draw-string. I had seven already.

"A plateau! From the Elmer Scotts!" She tossed the cards over to me contemptuously. "That girl visited me for two weeks before I was married. They have loads. A plateau! Only the six-fifty size at that, and—how disgusting—*marked!*"

I didn't know the Scotts from Adam. Half my presents were from Edith's friends. I didn't see why the Scotts should give me anything.

"Why, they were invited to the reception, my dear!" said Edith, scandalised. "Come, pass it over! Here goes for three hundred and seventy-two," and she tore off a little number from a sheet of others, touched it with the tip of her tongue and slapped it on to the face of the plateau. She listed it under S in a small book and placed it with my seven other plateaus on the silver table. I hadn't liked putting them all together. "But, nonsense," Edith had said. "Don't you see, little simpleton, if they are together, people can tell how many plateaus you have at a glance? My goodness, three hundred and seventy-two presents so far and three more days yet! I'll bet you get five hundred. Dear me, Lucy," she broke off, "there come your bridesmaids. Do go and change your dress. Put on the embroidered mulle; and hurry, child."

I suppose my blue checked gingham did look faded and plain, but I went to my room with a great swelling loyalty in my heart for every plain thing in the world. I hung my blue gingham in the closet almost tenderly. Already my wedding costume was there, staring at me from the corner—shining satin and expensive lace, little sachet bags sewed into the lining, and, on the belt inside, the name in gold letters of one of the most fashionable dressmakers in New York. I was gazing at it, wishing with all my heart that I hadn't got to take the place of the tissue-paper now stuffed into the waist and sleeves, when my sister-in-law suddenly appeared at the door.

"Hurry, Bobbie," she said. "Hurry, do. Your bridesmaids are all here and the Leonard Jacksons have brought over the John Percivals in their car. Don't forget the Jacksons gave you the dozen silver coquilholders, and the Percivals the Dresden service plates. Be nice to Mrs. Percival. She's going to be one of your neighbours next year. I must run along. They'll be wondering." She started to go, but turned back and added, "Why in the world aren't you more enthusiastic, Lucy? You ought to be the happiest girl in the world, *I* think. I never saw a more elaborate trousseau or a costlier layout of presents in my life. I can't imagine what else you want!"

A maid knocked outside the door and spoke to Edith. I didn't hear the message, but Edith gave a little exclamation and hurried away.

"The King Georges or the Kaiser Wilhelms in their aeroplane, no doubt," I muttered, and made a face at my wedding-gown as I yanked down my embroidered mulle.

I am going to skip the details of my wedding—the broiling condition of the thermometer, the sweltering bridesmaids, the crowds, the push, the funny grown-up feeling in my heart when Alec and Tom kissed me good-bye so gently, the joy when the train finally gave a snort and a jerk, and I knew that Edith in her pearls and satin couldn't possibly follow. I am so anxious to describe the funny old brown house that Will and I leased in the shadow of chemistry buildings, law-schools, and dormitories down here in this university town, and the life—the curious, happy, contented life that I drifted into—that I do not want to waste any time.

The week after my wedding Edith sailed with Ruth for four months in Europe. That is how it happened that she wasn't on the ground to superintend the choice of a residence for Will and me. I knew very well that Edith would never have countenanced for a minute the house that we finally decided to rent for the winter. It was a brown, square affair, a door in the middle with a window on each side, not colonial in the least, nondescript as it could be, with a slate French roof. Will and I thought it would answer the purpose, however—even though the bathtub was tin—and moved into it when the brick sidewalk was sprinkled with yellow maple-leaves, and the gutter was collecting dry ones.

I didn't know a soul in the town. I didn't know the name of a single street except our own. I didn't know where to go to buy even a spool of thread. But I wasn't homesick—oh, no, I wasn't homesick. You see I had forgotten the joy of my own kitchen and pantry; I had forgotten what a collander looked like; I had forgotten how sweet a row of cups are hanging by their handles, underneath a shelf edged with scalloped paper!

I enjoyed acting as my own mistress too; though I am sure if Edith had known what I was up to, she would have left all the pleasures of Paris to set me in the right path. For I didn't even unpack some of my wedding presents. They didn't fit in very well with Will's furniture which he had freighted down from the old white-pillared house in Hilton, and every sliver of which I simply adored. It wasn't colonial furniture, understand, which is so fashionable nowadays, but black walnut of the seventies—high-backed armchairs and sofas and marble-topped bedroom tables. There were funny old steel engravings of the United States Senate, battle scenes, and Abraham Lincoln, besides some big heavy bronzes that Will told me were very valuable. The sideboard was black walnut like everything else and Edith's elaborate silver service made it look so out-of-date that I put on it instead my own mother's old coffee-pot—the one that used to be so heavy for me—and our old-fashioned silver water pitcher with four high goblets to match. I didn't even unlock my enormous chest of silver. Alec had let me take from the safe at home the forks and darling thin spoons and knives that had always been in our family. It was like sheltering old friends under my roof to care for them again.

Edith would have hated the life I drifted into. She would have called it "a mere existence" or "worse than the frontier." From September to February, I didn't go to a single luncheon, tea, or bridge! People had called—members of the faculty, I suppose, I'm sure I don't know, for the cards were mere names to me and I was always out when they were left. You see one evening I had run across something in a pamphlet of Will's on our living-room table that set me to thinking. The pamphlet was a sort of bulletin of lectures given by different professors in the college. There was a star after several of the announcements and at the bottom of the page it said, "Open to the Public." I hadn't a notion whether it was the right thing for me to go to them or not, but one rainy afternoon I hunted up Tyler Hall and Room twenty-one on the second floor and slunk into one of the back chairs at five minutes to three, very much frightened and wondering if I would be turned out. The lecture was the second or third of a series given by a Dr. Van Breeze on something in philosophy. I didn't understand more than about two sentences, but no one seemed to question my right to sit there, and I felt ten times more comfortable than I ever had at bridge parties in Hilton.

You see I have never been to college. Although I hated boarding-school with all my heart and soul, I have always had a sneaking idea I might have done better at college. I always liked to study and when I became aware of the fact that Juliet—who, though the best and staunchest girl in the world, was never very brainy—was soaring above me in knowledge, I used to be a little envious. It may seem odd to you for a married woman to be trotting across a campus every other day to attend lectures in class-rooms, as if she were an undergraduate, but after my first plunge into that discourse on philosophy by Dr. Van Breeze I never missed a single lecture in the series. I went the next week and the next and the next; and also bolted bravely into a series of French lectures every Monday afternoon. I liked just to sit and breathe the air of those class-rooms. I liked the long line of blackboards covered with unintelligible words that belonged to a previous lecture, the row of felt erasers, the smell of dry chalk-dust. I liked sitting in those studious-looking chairs with a big arm on one side. It was as strange and foreign as a new country in those class-rooms, with the bare maple-tree branches grazing the window-pane, and in my ears the music of the French language which I hadn't heard since I left high school. I was a thousand, thousand miles away from the atmosphere of limousines and Edith, five hundred and two wedding presents, and a wedding-dress that cost two hundred dollars. It was like a distant echo from another world when I received an invitation for a bridge one day from a Mrs. Percival. It had completely escaped my mind that she was one of the individuals who had given me a dozen Dresden plates. Even if I had recollected I shouldn't have accepted the invitation. Why should I put handcuffs on myself again, now I was once free from a bondage that I loathed? I sent a very proper note of regret to Mrs. Percival, pleading a previous engagement. It was true. An old white-haired gentleman whom I often met at Dr. Van Breeze's lectures had asked me to sit beside him that particular afternoon at three o'clock in Tyler Hall.

I didn't tell Will about the lectures. He was usually busy at the medical school daytimes, and I was always at home when he arrived at six. I was ashamed to confess to Will that I, who never studied a science in my life, was presuming to attend lectures on the Geology of Fuels and Fluxes (for I took in everything that was starred), the Influence of Science upon Religion, and something about the Law of Falling Spheres. I hated to have him laugh at me, so I kept absolutely quiet on the subject of my ridiculous search for knowledge. I didn't even tell him about my new acquaintances.

The white-haired old gentleman and I developed quite a friendship. Every Thursday we used to walk home together as far as the Library, and he would explain things in the lecture that I didn't understand. He called me Pandora in fun because I was so inquisitive and couldn't bear to let things unknown to me alone. Once in a while a queer little man in a frock coat and a soft artist's tie would join us, and a woman—a Miss Avery in an ugly brown suit and a stiff linen collar like a man's. They used to think that my questions were the drollest things they had ever heard in their lives; but I couldn't help but feel that the sweet old man took quite a fancy to me. He gave me a book once on philosophy, by a famous scholar, and another time he asked me to come to his house to meet his wife. Naturally I didn't go, for I wouldn't have let any one guess I was Mrs. William Ford Maynard for all the wives in creation. It was a funny existence to drift into, wasn't it—cake and snow-pudding in the morning (I loved to mess about in the kitchen); economics, geology, philosophy and French in the afternoon; and evenings our open fire and cribbage with dear old Will, by the light of our big bronze lamp? It was a happy existence too.

I found something in those lectures of Dr. Van Breeze's which I had lost a long time ago. It was a precious thing and at first I didn't recognise it. You see every once in a while Dr. Van Breeze would say something that was better than anything I had ever heard in any church. I wasn't sure that I quite understood him, so I asked the old gentleman. It was a great eye-opener to me when I learned that such a great thinker as Dr. Van Breeze had a religion.

"Why, even *I* don't believe anything," I told my white-haired friend.

His little eyes twinkled at that. "And proud of it too, I'll wager," he laughed.

I blushed, for I think I did feel rather superior, just as I had felt wise when I knew there was no Santa Claus. Juliet and I had talked quite a good deal about religion. She took a course in "Bible" at college, which seemed to knock all the inspiration and the miracles out of it for her; and when it came to her course in philosophy, well—she said that she thought that ministers were a very credulous lot of men. She said you couldn't argue with them because they always wanted to prove things by quoting the Bible, while there existed simply dozens of other worthy reference books. She said that she preferred to rely on great scholars and philosophers for truth, rather than on men who only looked in *one* book for information. Naturally I didn't want to keep on believing in a fallacy, simply because I had never been to college. Childish as it may seem at first, I used to feel awfully unanchored not to say my prayers at night; but of course such a custom was silly, if I really was an unbeliever. I told my white-haired old friend in defence of my shocking statement (which by the way didn't shock him at all) that he might laugh, but anyhow I was backed up by scholars and philosophers, who since the year one had all been busy trying to prove that there wasn't anything in religion to believe.

"Why, my dear mistaken Pandora," smiled my friend. "On the contrary, philosophers have all been trying to prove there *is* something to believe, of some nature or other."

"Really?" I exclaimed. "It would be a big relief to me—but are you sure?"

"Did you ever hear of Benedict Graham?" he replied. Of course I had—every one has. He's at the head of the philosophy department at this university. The next week my friend presented me with Benedict Graham's "Introduction to Philosophy." I thought such a book would be way beyond my understanding, but it wasn't. I used to read a chapter or two by myself and then talk it over with my friend afterward. He made everything very simple to me and seemed besides to be an awfully well-informed old gentleman. I didn't think even Juliet could scoff at him, though he did *believe* a lot of things. After a week or two I felt rather ashamed at having so loftily pronounced myself an Unbeliever. I am no such thing! I can't tell you exactly what I am. I really don't know. But so long as minds ten times bigger and greater than mine (like Dr. Van Breeze and Benedict Graham, and lots of those learned old Greeks and Germans) so long as such intellects entertain the idea that there is *something* of *some* nature to believe in, I tell you, I'm going to believe in it with all my might and main.

CHAPTER XVII

EDITH didn't remain in Europe as long as she expected. She dropped down upon us one night, with Ruth trailing on behind, as unexpectedly as a falling star. I had just had a letter that said that she and Ruth and Alec—my brother had since joined them—were all installed in a fashionable hotel in Paris for six weeks. You can imagine my surprise when Edith and Ruth appeared at my front door.

Will and I were playing cribbage. He had laid down his big book; I had put aside my sewing; and the four little pegs on the cribbage-board had already run the course twice. We always play five games of cribbage every night before we go upstairs to bed. We call it our sleeping-powder. Will had just dealt the cards—it was almost nine o'clock—when the door-bell rang. Old Delia had creaked up to bed ages ago, so Will went to the door himself. I didn't bother even to uncurl my feet—I was sitting Turkish fashion—for I thought it must be the expressman. I yawned and waited.

I heard Will say, "Hello! hello! Well, well, of all—When did you—Where—" and a moment later, resplendent in a long sealskin coat, a sealskin hat, a perfectly enormous muff and a gold chain purse, Edith pushed into our hall, eyes simply sparkling and cheeks aglow.

"Hello, Turtle-doves!" she exclaimed. "Hello, Brother Will! Hello, Mrs. Bobbikins!"

I started up.

"Of all things!" I ejaculated.

Edith kissed me through a prickly veil. Ruth kissed me too. Ruth was simply overwhelming in a huge blue hat with not less than six blue ostrich plumes. They both kissed Will. We all began to laugh.

"We *knew* you'd be surprised," said Ruth.

"But I thought—" I began.

"Where's Alec?" asked Will.

"Why in the world—" I tucked in.

"Listen! Wait!" commanded Edith. "*I'll* explain. We thought," she said, gurgling with mirth, "it would be great fun to surprise you, so—"

"Alec got a cable last week—" put in Ruth.

"From my dad," Edith went on. "Business! Wasn't it disgusting when we weren't planning to sail for six weeks? Al had to go right on to Chicago—and The Homestead—"

"We had the bridal suite on the *Mauretania!*" I heard Ruth exclaim to Will.

"—isn't open," finished Edith. "The servants are scattered to the four winds. I've written to them, but of course they haven't had a chance to open things up yet. So we thought it would be fun to—"

"To pop in on you!" giggled Ruth.

"Can you put us up?" snapped Edith.

"Of course! How nice!" I tried to say cordially, with the image of my cold, unused, north guest-room dancing before my eyes, the floor covered with newspapers, two cut-glass punch-bowls, thirteen berry dishes and seven vases. "*Of course* I can put you up. Take off your things."

Will produced two dining-room chairs and Edith and Ruth buried them in no time beneath a stack of coats, hats and muffs. Edith was gowned—slick as a black suede glove—in a tight-fitting, broadcloth, one-piece dress, Irish lace at neck and wrists. Ruth's new Parisian hair was simply glorious. They strutted into our comfortable living-room like two peacocks, Edith surveying the walls and ceilings as if she were examining the dome of the Boston Statehouse.

"So this is where you coo!" she said in her horrid patronising manner. Imagine Dr. William Maynard of the medical department of one of the biggest universities in the country cooing! I blushed for Will. He pushed up a chair. It chanced to be one of Father's old morocco leather armchairs I had found in the storeroom at home. Edith made opera-glasses of her two hands, and pretended to gaze intently at the poor old piece of furniture.

"Hello, old friend!" she said, and made a mock salute. "You look familiar. Back into service again, hey? 'Comfy' anyhow!" she finished and settled into it.

"What sort of a passage was it?" asked Will, and for the next half-hour we listened to an account of a perfectly disgusting customs officer in New York, who made Edith pay one hundred and ninety-five dollars on a half-dozen mere gowns that already were simply worn to shreds.

It was when Will had gone to the kitchen for some water that Edith leaned forward and said to me:

"How'd you happen to take *this* house, my dear? And don't you dress for dinner, Lucy?"

"Oh," I said, "this? It's short and I can hook it up myself."

"I just *knew*," chimed in my own sister Ruth, "that Lucy would be one of those to get slack after she was once married. Now I've always said that *I*——"

"I didn't know," broke in Edith in a sudden burst of laughter, "that there were any houses left nowadays that had those funny old-fashioned storm-doors that you hook on every winter."

"Trust Lucy to pick out the oldest shack in the town," tucked in Ruth, touching the surface of her perfect coiffure with light fingers, and glancing sideways at herself in an old gilt-framed mirror on the wall.

"By the way, Lucy," Edith added, piling it on, I thought, a bit too thick, "people aren't using doilies under ornaments any more. Where are all those stunning plateaus?"

"Dear me," I laughed, bound to be good-natured, "I'd completely forgotten the plateaus. They must be in one of the barrels we haven't opened."

"Haven't opened! I *never* saw any one like you. Haven't opened! It certainly is a good thing that I've come home."

It was with a sinking heart that I took Edith and Ruth up to the guest-room in which I had put one of Will's black walnut bedroom sets.

"If I'd only known you were coming!" I began going up the stairs trying to explain. "The bureau is chuck-full of silver things—we ought to have a safe. And the closet—all my good dresses are there. We have so little closet-room in this house. In the morning I'll clear it out. I know you'd like separate beds too, but when Will's things were all unpacked there wasn't room for much new furniture. And I'm sorry, Edith, that you haven't a bath connected. We have only one bathroom in the entire house and even that—"

Edith wouldn't let me finish. We were in the guest-room now. Her eyes were on the cut-glass in the corner.

"I ought never to have gone to Europe," she announced. "Never in this world!"

I wished she had never come home, and when I kissed her good-night, all the old rancour and rebellion, dormant for so long, was raging in my heart. I stole downstairs after I was undressed, pulled out Edith's silver service from underneath the stairs and put it on the sideboard; I unlocked Edith's chest of silver, and began laying the breakfast table with the horns-of-plenty; I dragged out some elaborate breakfast napkins; I hauled down from the top shelf of the pantry a Coalport breakfast-set. At one A. M., when I was crawling back stealthily to our room, I had to pass the guest-chamber door. I heard voices, and stopped a moment.

"It's human nature for a man, single or married, to prefer a woman in pretty clothes, whoever she is," said Edith.

"Of course," Ruth agreed. "When she came in to say good-night did you see the horrid old red worsted bedroom slippers she had on?"

"And moreover," Edith went on, "a man likes an attractive house—pretty pictures, pretty ornaments, a place where he is proud to bring his friends."

"Naturally."

"A man likes to be proud of his wife too," went on the sage, "proud of her friends, of her place in society. Now Lucy—absolutely *no* social-sense—not a spark. No doubt, if she's made any friends at all, they're the grocery-man and the seamstress, or the woman who washes her hair."

Ruth giggled.

"Now *you*, Ruth," Edith pursued, "are a girl after my own heart. *You* are the kind to be the wife of a famous man. *You* could be Mrs. William Maynard with the right sort of go."

I had to smile at the thought of Ruth and Will. Will hates false things—puffs and brilliantine; he hates fluffy negligees, and silly, high-heeled unwalkable shoes; he hates fuss and feathers. I passed on down the hall.

"It will take more than Edith Campbell and my young sister Ruth to disturb me, I guess," I said to myself as I turned out several flaring gas-jets in the hall and bathroom, left by those two extravagant creatures to burn all night.

Edith awoke the next morning armoured for battle. I could see it in her eyes and feel it in her manner. I knew it was to be no slight skirmish, but a well-thought-out and carefully-planned campaign. I knew it was to be a serious engagement because neither she nor Ruth criticised a single thing for the next two days. If they were shocked and surprised, I knew it only by raised eyebrows, critical smiles or covert glances. I hated their silence. I felt as if the entire foundation of my life was stealthily being honeycombed with tunnels, laid with bombs and dynamite, and I wondered a little uncomfortably when Edith would light the fuse. Edith is wonderful in some ways, as you know. At a hotel or on a steamer she catches on to the right people to know within the first twenty-four hours, and by the third day she's playing bridge with them. As soon as ever her half-dozen pieces of baggage had arrived, she donned a Paquin three-piece velvet suit and set out to call on Mrs. Percival. That night the explosion took place.

"I called on Mrs. Percival this afternoon," she began after dinner. "She says, Lucy, that you never returned her call."

Will had gone to a lecture that evening. Ruth was playing solitaire in front of the fire.

"Has Mrs. Percival called on me? I didn't realise it," I replied.

"Not only has Mrs. Percival called, but every one else who should. That impossible servant of yours said that all these people had called." Edith took down the brass jardinière where I deposit all my visiting-cards. "She said that you were never in afternoons and had not seen *one* of them. Where under the heavens were you, Lucy?"

I felt ashamed to tell Edith about the lectures, so I said instead:

"Oh, anywhere—walking, shopping—*anywhere*. I never stay in afternoons. I can't bear to."

"How many of those calls have you returned?" cross-examined my sister-in-law.

"Well—I am *going* to return them all," I began. "They're such strangers to me that I've been putting it off. You know how I hate making calls anyway. But of course—"

Edith interrupted me.

"*The* people in this town are the ones connected with the university. I have always heard that. You've had every opportunity to know them. They've all called on account of Will. You've simply thrown away chance upon chance. Here are the Philemon Omsteds' cards. Mrs. Percival says that Dr. Omsted is awfully queer—kind of a socialist—but that Mrs. Omsted's musicales are the selectest things given. Here are Mrs. Daniel Haynes McClellan's cards, the Bernkapps, Madame Gauthier. I found out from Mrs. Percival, indirectly of course, that all these people are *in* things. Mrs. Benedict Graham—even *she* has called on you. And Mrs. Percival says that *she* was a Granville—daughter of President Emeritus Granville. Dr. Graham is an awfully prominent man himself. Surely you've heard of Benedict Graham, Lucy. Surely—"

"Of course!" I interrupted. "Every one has, Edith, and I'm reading his book, but I'd be frightened to death to go up and pull the Benedict Grahams' bell. I couldn't!"

"You ought to be married to a clerk or a barber, and then you wouldn't need to. I should hate to think I had married a man whom I couldn't live up to. Every one has heard of Will. He has been talked about all over the country. But what about his wife? Who is she?" Edith's words were beginning to cut now and I bit my lip. "There was a tea this very afternoon to which Mrs. William Maynard ought to have been invited. Were you?"

I shook my head.

"Of course you weren't, nor last week to a musicale that Mrs. Omsted gave, and I'll bet you had nothing whatsoever to do with the Charity Bazaar that the younger women in the university set get up every Christmas. Do you think a man wants to be married to a person who is not received—absolutely ignored, as if something was the matter with her? Whom in the world do you know here, anyway? Any one at all?"

Pictures of the little man with the soft tie, the dear white-haired old gentleman whose name I did not even know, and Miss Avery, all impossible I knew to Edith, flashed before my eyes. So I shook my head and Edith went on.

"And the house—it's simply impossible! Such a location! Why, no one lives in this part of town. You would think that Will couldn't afford anything better, but he can. You ought to have two maids. And why under the heavens all this old furniture? People don't use black walnut any more, and that old narrow, square dining-room table is simply beyond words!"

"And you have no butler's pantry nor back stairs," put in Ruth.

"And you ought to make your maid wear black afternoons."

"And turn down the beds," added Ruth.

"It's *my* house," I began. "If you don't like it—" I got up quickly and started to leave the room.

"Oh, come, Bobbikins," Edith said in her persistently cheerful way. "Don't get cross. I was only trying to be helpful." Then she went on: "I found this on the floor, by your desk. I couldn't help but see it. It's an invitation for dinner from Mrs. Benedict Graham. I can't understand why she invites you if you've never returned her call, but of course it's on account of Will. I can't imagine your not accepting this invitation and yet I heard you say that next Thursday, the sixth, the very evening of this dinner, you and Will had tickets for the theatre."

"Yes, we've been planning to go on that particular night for three weeks. It's a little secret anniversary of ours," I said sullenly; "and we're going too. Why should you, Edith, come here and try to upset the whole universe? We're happy. Will is satisfied. He loves things simple. I wish you'd leave us alone. Will doesn't care a scrap about society, and I hate it, hate it, hate it!" I was on the verge of bursting into tears.

"Well, if there's going to be a scene, excuse *me*, please," said Ruth, and started to leave the room.

"If you're through with that card-table, please fold it up and put it in the closet," I said to Ruth with my eyes full of fire. "I haven't got six servants."

"Whew!" whistled Ruth and began gathering up her cards.

"I should think," calmly went on Edith like a repeating alarm-clock, "you'd like your husband to be *proud* of you."

"Oh, please—please—" I fired back, and then suddenly, too full to speak, I turned abruptly and fled up the stairs to my room.

The sweet darkness enveloped me. I drew a chair to the window. *Will* would ask her to mind her own affairs; *Will* would talk to her; *Will* would tell her how he hated her mean ambitions, how he abhorred her contemptible snobbishness; *Will* would defend and stand up for me; *Will* would fix her! "Just wait for *Will*," I said, and listened for his step on the sidewalk outside and the sound of his key in the latch. I heard him come in about half past ten. It was almost twelve when he came up to me.

"Not in bed?" he asked gently and leaned down and kissed me. "Edith was downstairs when I came in and we've been talking. I don't know but what we ought to keep two maids, Bobbie dear," Will said, and I felt as if I had been struck. Will went over and lit the gas. "I guess we might as well postpone our theatre party for next Thursday," he went on. "I think, after all, we'd better go to the Grahams' dinner. By the way," he broke off, "didn't you get an invitation to the Omsteds' affair last week?"

"No, Will, I didn't," I said dully.

"Perhaps you'll find time to pay back a few of those calls some time pretty soon, Bobbie dear," he said to me. And that morning about four A. M. I cried myself to sleep.

Edith went to the dinner too. She had Will telephone and fix it up someway. I don't know how nor I didn't ask. I was very miserable, very unhappy. My heart was heavier than it had been for a whole year. "Will wasn't satisfied, Will wasn't proud, Will was ashamed of me," rang in my ears from morning till night. During the few days that still must be lived before Thursday the sixth at seven o'clock, Edith exhibited the usual kindness and gentle consideration of any victor over the vanquished. I didn't make another plea. I was as resigned as a fatalist, and as unmurmuring as a stoic. I wrote my acceptance at Edith's dictation without a word, and silently fought the tears that came to my eyes, as I sealed the envelope.

"O Bobbie," said Will gently, "don't worry so about it, dear. You weren't so frightened about your own wedding."

"Exactly," said Edith. "And I've had dinners at The Homestead just as grand as this. You're simply out of training. People won't notice you so much as you think anyhow. Just act slowly, and don't try to talk. That's all. *I'll* be there and you can 'lean on me, grandpa.' *You'll* be all right," she assured me grandly.

I couldn't explain to Will and Edith how I felt about that dinner at the Grahams'. They wouldn't understand. Of course I had been to Edith's parties at The Homestead, but then I was simply Lucy Vars; and now I was Mrs. William Ford Maynard. Everybody in Hilton had accepted Lucy Vars long ago as a queer, quiet sort of shy little mouse, and treated her as such. She was used to it. But here, no one had as yet discovered Mrs. William Ford Maynard. She had been living for six, beautiful, unmolested months in idyllic secretion. But she had been run down at last, she must give herself up like a hunted convict, and by Thursday at midnight all of Dr. Maynard's learned associates would know just what sort of insignificant little person he had married. Oh, if only for Will's sake I had been born clever and brilliant; if only I had possessed a little of Edith's style; Ruth's *savoir faire*. Do you wonder then, that I trembled in anticipation of this occasion? Ruth's coming-out party, my wedding, a dozen dinners of Edith's, were as doll's tea-parties as compared to this, when Mrs. William Ford Maynard must come forth from her hiding-place and meet this test of a searching inspection.

I shall never forget the faint, sickening feeling inside of me as we stood waiting for admittance before the big colonial house. We must have been the last ones to arrive. A babble of voices in the drawing-room at the left greeted us as we entered. We walked up the old colonial stairway, and into a big bedroom at the top with a black walnut bedroom set. I noticed that even in my fright.

"Mercy, child, don't take off your gloves," whispered Edith to me.

"I *hate* them," I said, and ripped my arms bare. I wore a light blue silk dress with a Dutch neck, in spite of Edith in her low-cut ball-gown plastered over with glittering black spangles. My hair was done in its usual everyday knot at the back of my neck, bobbed up in the last five minutes after Ruth's sixth attempt at dressing it in the "new way." Edith looked like a fashion-plate: she had a perfect figure; her neck is marvellous; she wore diamonds and a string of pearls.

I followed her down the stairs very carefully, lest I trip in my little French-heeled satin slippers or lose the silly things altogether. My heart was in my mouth. "What shall I say when I am introduced? What shall I say? What shall I say?" I kept thinking in a panic and watched Edith sweep across the hall in her most impressive manner. I waited an instant. A minute more and Will was announcing, "And this is my wife, Mrs. Graham." My heart fluttered as it used to at parties at home.

The grand lady smiled upon me. She took my hand.

"So this is *Mrs.* William Maynard," she said. "I'm glad you could come. We all know Dr. Maynard so well—we're so proud to have him one of us—that I am glad to meet *you*." Was she thinking how funny and young I looked? Was she saying "What a strange little insignificant bit of thing indeed for such a man as William Maynard!" I wished, after all, I had had my hair marcelled.

"I want Dr. Graham to meet you," my hostess continued and, leaning over, touched the great philosopher on the shoulder with her fan. He was talking to Edith. "Benedict, my dear." He turned. "Mrs. Maynard!"

I trembled in my shoes and raised my eyes.

"You!" I gasped and stepped back. Dr. Benedict Graham—*the* Dr. Benedict Graham—was no other than my dear sweet old white-haired gentleman of the philosophical lectures! His hands went out to me—both of them—and gathered my ten cold trembling fingers in his warm grasp.

"You?" he repeated with the sweet light of recognition in his eyes. "You! *Pandora!* Julia," he said to Mrs. Graham, "Mrs. Maynard is Pandora of whom I have told you, my little friend who takes a walk with me every week. Well—well," he chuckled. "Well—well." Then to astonished Will he exclaimed, "Your wife and I are old friends," and oh, I could have kissed him!

The colour rushed back into my cheeks. My hand was in Mrs. Graham's again, and when I looked around the room I found I stood in a little circle—every one's eyes, like the lights, upon me. It was like a surprise-party, or a fairy story, or some trick worked by a skilful magician. First my eyes fell upon Dr. Van Breeze; and then, in a flash, on Monsieur Gauthier, who gave the French lectures; and suddenly coming toward me was the funny little man with the soft wide tie. He wore it even to-night. He took my hand cordially and Will exclaimed, "Do you know her too, Mr. Omsted?"

It all happened in a minute. I can't tell it quickly enough. "She has read one of my books from cover to cover," I heard Dr. Graham laugh, eyes twinkling into mine; and I think it was just after that remark of Dr. Graham's that Monsieur Gauthier stepped forward and bowing before me in the dearest, Frenchiest manner in the world, said in his own language with every one listening, "I have never been presented to Mrs. Maynard, but if I am not mistaken I think I have observed her face at my Monday afternoon lectures. Is it not so? Always the same chair—third from the back, two removed from the aisle—always the same. It has been a pleasure to see you there each week."

I understood every word. I didn't lose a phrase. The warmth, the light, those words in French, everybody's eyes upon me acted like just enough champagne.

"*Merci, Monsieur*," I dared to say and swept him a little bow. I can hear now my voice and those two little French words falling upon the silence of that room like a noise on a still night. I don't know how I ever presumed to speak in French. I would have thought it affected in any one else, but at that exultant moment I could have mimicked Chinese. Two words in a foreign language I know should not be very amazing (any one could do it) but I could feel a little murmur pass among the people after I had spoken that was something—a little—like the applause at the theatre. A moment later the talking began again; I was being introduced at left and right; my own voice and laughter mingled with the general babble. It was exactly as though I had taken my plunge, come safely to the surface and now was swimming along with long even strokes with the others for the shore. Edith looked at me astonished. Will observed me as though I were a stranger. Easy words came to my lips, my cheeks burned, and every one was so kind—so good to me, that I forgot my dress, my hair and my French-heeled shoes.

I don't mean to imply that I was the belle of the evening. Of course I wasn't. It would be absurd for a mere slip of a girl, married though she was, to come among learned men and sages and have them all turning their attention and thought upon her. Even if she had been pretty, and skilful in the art of smiles and glances, which I am not, such an event would be amazing. I only mean to say that I didn't feel awkward nor wonder where to put my hands between the courses. I was placed at the left of Dr. Graham and felt as easy as if I were sitting beside my own father. The dinner, it seemed, was in honour of Dr. Van Breeze on account of his book about to be published, consisting of the very lectures he had been delivering in Tyler Hall. The talk centred about the book a good deal and though I didn't contribute a single idea to the conversation I understood perfectly what was being discussed. But I do not think Edith enjoyed herself. She was over-jewelled, in the first place, and kept running on to Dr. Omsted, who, you know, is a kind of socialist, about the gorgeous bridal suite on the *Mauretania*, the one hundred and ninety-two dollars duty she had to pay, and of how she smuggled in a thousand-dollar pearl necklace, until I was embarrassed.

We went home about ten-thirty. Just at the door as we were going out Mrs. Philemon Omsted stopped me. Will had me by the arm. Edith was just in front.

"Mrs. Maynard," she said to me, "just a moment, please. I have been very glad to meet you. And, by the way, Easter Monday I am giving a small musicale. Mrs. Graham is to pour for me. I should be delighted if you will assist."

I thanked her quietly (but oh, in my heart I could have crowned her with flowers) and passed out to our hired carriage.

I sat in the middle between Edith and Will. We drove away in silence, my heart singing, and my cheeks warm with excitement. Will pressed my arm with his bare hand hidden underneath the folds of my party-coat. I could feel his joy. It was Edith who spoke first.

"What a miserable stuffy little carriage," she said; then after a moment, "Those people may have brains, but I don't think I ever saw such a lot of frumpily dressed women in my life."

Will leaned forward then, and said playfully, but with a queer little sure sound in his voice, "What was your impression of Mrs. William Maynard?"

"Of Bobbie?" Edith asked raising her eyebrows, disgusted with Will's little streak of fun.

"Of Mrs. William Maynard," he corrected; then in a low voice he added, "Of Mrs. William Maynard, of whom I am so proud!" and I had to draw away my hand to wipe away two silly tears.

CHAPTER XVIII

IT used to be a source of great anxiety to Father that none of his children was married. He had a notion that the only way to make a family name a strong one was by increase. When Tom and Alec were scarcely out of college and the twins were still in short trousers, Father announced that he was going to present to the first grandson bearing the name of Vars, a check for three thousand dollars. We treated it a good deal as a joke then and used to poke a lot of fun at the boys about it. That was a long time ago—before Father died—and when we found the same offer written out in plain black and white in Father's will we were a little surprised and a little touched too, realising how dreadfully in earnest the poor dear man must have been about it, and how disappointed. According to his instructions, however, the three thousand dollars was put away at interest to await the coming of the first Vars heir.

At the beginning of this chapter three of us were married—though of course I didn't count, being a girl—and still the three thousand dollars remained unclaimed. Poor unlucky Elise had had four girls, and Edith hadn't had a baby of any kind. However, we all knew if ever such an event should take place in Edith's career it would be the most important occasion in the entire annals of the family. And we weren't mistaken. Edith had been married several years when the wonderful preparations were begun. One would have thought she was the Queen of Holland. Everybody in Hilton seemed to vie one with another in embroidering tiny martingales, knitting worsted blankets, or scalloping flannel shawls for Edith Vars' baby. The nursery that she had had built on the sunny side of Father's house four years before fairly bloomed into pink and white equipment. You had only to spend a half-hour there to discover what a popular person Edith was and what a select place in society she had at last attained. She was more than accommodating about telling from whom each little gift had come. For instance the superb baby-dress with Irish insertion Mrs. Alfred Sturtevant brought over herself yesterday; the elaborate hand-embroidered bassinette sheets were from Mrs. Barlow—*the* Mrs. Barlow, you understand; the silk puffs, silk socks, silk caps from Beatrice, Phyllis and Bernice. A hand-made, finely-worked Christening dress of Alec's, proving the family's prosperity thirty-five years ago (Edith herself had risen from the sod, you know; you may be sure *her* Christening dress wasn't on exhibition) had been rooted out of an old trunk in the storeroom. The most expensive "Specialist" within reach had been engaged, and a nurse from Boston was to remain for four months at the rate of twenty-five a week. You could trust Edith to do the thing up in the proper style; you could trust her also to carry away that three thousand dollars premium in Father's will. She felt cock-sure of it herself. Things had always come her way, hadn't they?

She never did the ignominious thing, did she? Poor Elise and her four little girls she had always held in the lowest esteem. Fate simply wouldn't allow Edith Vars' baby to be a girl. Every one said so. Even I was convinced.

Alec treated Edith as if she were the centre of the universe. When the shocking news about Oliver reached us, Alec's chief concern was in regard to the effect of the news upon poor Edith. It was two years after that first dinner of ours at Dr. Graham's that the knowledge of my brother Oliver's latest escapade reached me one morning in early April.

I was diligently dusting the black walnut bookcases in our sunny living-room. I sat down in the nearest chair at hand, perfectly stunned for a moment, my jaw hanging open, no doubt, and read through the letter containing the fatal news at least three times before I had the strength to get up. The first thing I did was to hang up the square piece of hem-stitched cheese-cloth at the head of the cellar stairs; then I went and hunted up a time-table. There was a train due to leave for Hilton at eleven-ten. Will had left early that morning, for he had a nine o'clock recitation, so he wasn't at home when Alec's letter came. But I knew that nothing less than a death in the family could drag him away from his precious clinic the next day, so I hurried off for the train alone. I stuck a note of explanation into the dish of ferns on the middle of the dining-room table:

"*Dear Will,*

"I've had a letter from Alec. Oliver was married to a Madge Tompkins in February! He's bringing her to Hilton to-night. This is all I know about it. Will try to be back before Sunday.

"BOBBIE."

During the last half-year Oliver had been superintending a gang of granite workers in a little town in Vermont. City life hadn't seemed to agree with Oliver's purse very well, and the diversions of the several middle-western cities, in each of which Oliver had made a great hit with all the nicest girls and their mothers, had interfered with his business hours. It was after he had tried six or seven positions, starting with banking in Pittsburg, and ending up with shipping automobile tires in Akron, Ohio, that Tom and Alec deposited Oliver, with scarcely a cent to his name, in Glennings Falls, Vermont, where the possibilities for spending money were rather limited.

Poor Oliver! I felt awfully sorry for him. He's such a brilliant-appearing fellow! It seemed to me as if he had struck an awfully hard run of luck since he graduated from college. He really is a civil engineer, but fate has swerved him into other lines, which I think is the cause of his checkered career. He always loved to build bridges and dams and toy railroads even as a small boy. After he finally succeeded in squeezing through college he conceived a foolish notion—foolish according to Tom—to take a course in Civil Engineering at Cornell. Of course he didn't have anything else to study—no bugbears like English Composition, Latin or Greek, so perhaps that is why he did so well in the Engineering. Anyhow he passed the examinations with some kind of an honour—the only one, poor boy, that he had ever been able to boast of in his life. Tom, who had pooh-poohed the idea of Oliver's wasting a year at Cornell, finally gave up his plan of putting the boy to work in his lumber camps, and Oliver started forth, hopes high and spirits aglow, to accept an engineering job in Arizona. On the way out, at Pittsburg, he stopped off to visit an old college friend for a fortnight, and at the end of the first week he wrote that he had struck a "gold mine." His friend's father was prominently connected with half a dozen banks in Pittsburg and had offered him a position. I could have told the friend's father that Oliver would never make a banker, but he found it out himself in a little while.

After Oliver left Pittsburg everything went wrong with him. No civil engineering jobs presented themselves, no more friends' fathers, no more "gold mines" seemed to be available. After that Oliver became a regular rolling-stone. He couldn't seem to keep any of his positions, or he wouldn't, I don't know which. He tried everything. It was manufacturing automobile parts in Toledo; selling motorcycles in Buffalo; making out orders for plumbers' supplies in Cleveland. He fizzled miserably each time. He never had any money. He was forever sending to Tom or Alec for a check for fifty until his salary was due. He was forever running down to New York or over to Chicago for a class reunion or a dance. He was forever writing to me vivid descriptions of new "queens" he had met.

It was when Tom and Alec had to pay fourteen hundred and fifty dollars for a "swell" little last season's roadster that Oliver had secured at a wonderful bargain from a friend of his in Akron (this was when he was a shipping clerk in a tire factory) and in which he had been sporting about through the streets of the place at a speed of thirty an hour, that he was summoned to the court of his older brothers, and after due consultation was sent up to Glennings Falls, like a convict, to work in the mines. His roadster was sold at a terrible sacrifice, he said, and that fact seemed at the time to be his greatest regret.

I could have cried for Oliver. There would be no "queens" in Glennings Falls; there would be no Sunday-night Lobster-Newbergs over a chafing-dish; there would be no stunning "visiting girls" whom he met at Class-Day or in Pittsburg when he was there, or in Toledo, Cleveland or Buffalo, for him to call on until eleven P.M.

When I arrived in Hilton, Alec was at the station in the automobile to meet me (I had had just time to 'phone him that I was coming) and Tom who had come flying on from the West the minute Alec's shocking telegram had reached him was there too. Malcolm had caught the midnight from New York and was waiting on the veranda when we ran up under the porte-cochère. It was really a family reunion, but all the joy of seeing each other again was buried beneath the horror and consternation in our hearts. Oliver's act was astounding. We're not an erratic family. We never figure in accidents or tragedies of any kind. We hate notoriety.

"And besides all the horrid publicity of a secret marriage," said Ruth, "Edith says the creature is too *common* for anything." Ruth dangled a dainty velvet pump on the tip of her toe as she made this remark. We were gathered in the room that used to be the sitting-room, all of us—Tom, Malcolm, Edith, Alec, Ruth and I. We had been talking for an hour.

"Common!" took up Edith. "She's absolutely impossible, I tell you! We stopped off to see Oliver for an hour on our way to the Green Mountains," she explained to me, "last fall, in the automobile. He didn't know we were coming. It was Sunday and he had some dreadful little frowzy-headed creature in tow, I'm sure her name was Tompkins—silly, simpering little thing—perfectly enormous pompadour and a cheap Hamburg open-work lingerie waist, over bright pink—oh, horribly cheap! I can't begin to tell you!"

"Well—well—we must try to make the best of it," said Tom lightly.

"Best of it!" scoffed Edith. "Well, if Oliver thinks for one minute that I am going to throw open my house to his precious Madge Tompkins he's greatly mistaken. Ruth is having a large bridge party Thursday—ten tables. This affair has simply got to be kept quiet until after that. Breck Sewall is coming up from New York to spend Sunday. You all know he's paying marked attention to Ruth, and the Sewalls—Heavens!—they're particular to a degree! Oh, we mustn't let a single word of this miserable affair leak out—not a single word! Oh, when I think of it, I just want—"

"Come, come, Edith," interrupted Alec. "Gently, dear. Gently, you know."

"Well, if any of you expect *me*," Edith went on, "to have that common person here, I must tell you that I can't—I simply can't! I'm not in a condition to endure it. I—"

"Now look here, dear," Alec said soothingly, "no one expects you to. Everything will be exactly as you wish."

Oh, he would have stopped the sun from rising if Edith had requested it. I've never witnessed such dog-devotion as Alec shows to Edith. He can't be five minutes late to an appointment with her, without telephoning a plausible excuse, or sending a special messenger. She has him wonderfully trained. You ought to see him run around and put down windows, raise shades, carry chairs or rush upstairs for her work-bag which she forgot and left on her bureau just before dinner.

At about five o'clock that afternoon Malcolm, who had been haunting the station all day in the hope of meeting Oliver and his companion, and hurrying them quietly into a closed carriage as soon as possible, burst in upon us, all excitement.

"What in the world is the matter now?" exclaimed Ruth.

"Have they come?" asked Alec.

"Has any one heard of it?" gasped Edith.

"Heard of it! It's gotten into the papers!" Malcolm announced.

Tom and Alec both got up.

"Very bad?" asked one of them, and Edith sprang forward like a cat and snatched the paper out of Malcolm's hand.

"On the front page," said Malcolm. "Here! There it is. Oh, no one can miss it."

"Heavens!" Edith ejaculated as her eyes fell upon the headlines.

"Read it," commanded Tom.

> "Romantic Love Affair of Oliver Chenery Vars ends in an Elopement. Son of William T. Vars, former President of the Vars & Co. Woollen mills of this City Marries his Landlady's Daughter."

She stopped short.

"Go on," said Tom in a low voice.

"Hadn't *I* better?" suggested Alec.

But Edith continued:

> "The friends of Oliver Chenery Vars will be surprised to learn of his marriage to Miss Madge Tompkins of Glennings Falls, Vermont. For the past year young Vars has been connected with the Glennings Falls Granite Works, and the attachment between himself and Miss Tompkins, daughter of Mrs. Ebenezer Tompkins, a widow with whom he boarded, has been a matter of some concern to the Vars

family. The news of his marriage, which is said to have taken place last February, comes as a total surprise and few particulars are known. However, it has been ascertained that the young lovers have been forgiven and that they will be the guests of the Alexander Vars at The Homestead for the remainder of the week. The new Mrs. Vars is but eighteen and carried off the blue ribbon in the Pretty Girl contest at the Glennings Falls Agricultural Fair last September."

"How perfectly disgusting!" broke in Ruth.

"Rotten!" muttered Malcolm.

Edith couldn't speak. The paper fluttered to the floor and Alec went over and put her gently in a chair. Tom scowled and looked hard out of the window. We sat in silence for a full half-minute, then Tom turned suddenly.

"Look here," he said, "here he comes! Here Oliver comes!"

I leaned forward quickly, picked up the discarded paper and thrust it under my elbow on the table.

Oliver was alone. I shall always remember how he looked on that spring evening as he swung along, overcoat open and flapping in the wind, head held high and brow smooth and cloudless. His step was as sure and firm as when he joined us all after he had received his diploma on his graduation day at college. My heart went out to him—poor Oliver always getting into trouble, gifted and talented in a way (he can sing like an angel) awfully good-looking and lovable (he has friends everywhere), poor Oliver—what would become of him? I heard his step on the veranda, and a minute later he was standing, six feet high, smiling and confident in the door of the library. There is something irresistible about Oliver's smile. If he had only looked at me I should have smiled back, but his eyes rested on Tom.

"Hello, everybody!" he said. "Hello, Tom! Mighty good of *you* to come way on East. Well, well," he glanced swiftly around the room, "all here, aren't you?" Then he added, "Well, what do you think?"

"Seen the paper?" inquired Tom.

"Is it in the paper?" asked Oliver, and Malcolm pulled the horrible thing from beneath my elbow and thrust it into Oliver's hands. I watched Oliver closely. I saw the slow, dark colour spread over his face and across that cloudless brow of his. I saw his eyes travel once through the article and then go back and retrace each painful word of it again. When he had satisfied himself he laid the paper down and looked up.

"Well, it's true," he said, and six pairs of eyes glowered upon him.

"What explanation have you for this—step of yours?" asked Tom.

Oliver's confidence fell away a little. He picked off a bit of lint from the sleeve of his coat.

"Oh, why hash the whole thing over?" he said. "I'm married all right. What's the use—of course I'm sorry it is in the paper."

"Sorry!" sniffed Ruth.

"But *I* didn't let it out. Hang it all," he broke off, "you bury me in a hole like that—she was the only girl worth looking at. *I* didn't want to go to Glennings Falls. It was *your* plan."

"You had had six other positions before we resorted to Glennings Falls," fired Alec.

Oliver flushed.

"Oh, well—if you've all made up your minds to be disagreeable! I left Madge at the station to come up in a carriage," he explained. "She'll be here in five minutes. I hope at least you'll be decent to *her*."

"Decent to *her*, Oliver Vars!" Edith had found her voice, "I guess you better begin and think how *you* can be decent to *us*. Do you know what you've done? You've simply ruined our reputations and just when Breck Sewall—oh, you've disgraced us all! I shall never want to hold up my head again, and Ruth has invitations out for a big bridge. Madge Tompkins! Don't ask *me* to be decent to *her*. She'll never spend a night under *this* roof as long as *I* live. Oh, I've seen her—common little—"

"Be careful," shot back Oliver, flushed and angry now. "Madge's father was a minister, an educated gentleman, when yours at that period of his career was collecting scrap iron and junk from people's back yards!"

Edith grew red. The early life of her iron-king father had always been a sore point with her. I don't know what she would have done; perhaps literally have scratched Oliver's eyes out, if Tom hadn't interrupted.

"Oh, come. None of this," he said. "Oliver, you were hasty in what you said; and, Edith, let us see the young lady before we pass judgment on her. I think she's coming. At least here is a carriage."

It was very touching to me when Oliver went down to the carriage at the curbing and helped out the girl whom of all the hundreds (for Oliver could have had almost any one: Women adored him) he had chosen to honour the most highly. She was short and a little shabby with a sort of cheap flashiness that you could see a hundred yards away. I knew particular, fastidious Oliver must feel a little ashamed of the wrinkled checked suit she wore, the big-figured gaudy lace veil over her hat, the dingy white ostrich plumes. I felt very sorry for Oliver when at the library door she stepped back to let him enter, and he said gently, "*You* first, Madge." She stumbled in smiling and confused. She really was rather impossible: pretty in a way, but oh, miles and miles away from everything that is essential to a good taste and good manners. She wore white kid gloves and patent-leather slippers that pinched her feet. There was a celluloid comb in the back of her hair with rhinestones in it.

"Well, here they are, Madge!" said Oliver heartily.

Her first words jarred us.

"I guess we surprised you some," she laughed.

"Well—it was unexpected," said Tom finally.

She giggled at that; then she asked, trying to appear at ease, "Well, aren't you going to introduce me around, Oliver?"

It was very painful. She gave her fingers to us in a ridiculous fashion. "Pleased to meet you!" she said like a machine after each name, and then after I, the last one, had dropped her hand, in a moment of deep confusion she remarked, glancing around the room, "Oh, my, I think your house is just grand!"

Malcolm coughed; Oliver flushed.

"Did you have a long trip?" I asked.

"Just dreadful," she replied eagerly. "The dirt was something awful. We came up in a parlour-car. I just love parlour-cars! We've been staying at an elegant hotel in New York."

"Sit down, won't you?" said Malcolm kindly. He pushed up a chair and she glanced at him archly.

"Thank you ever so much!" Then she added coyly, and my heart bled for her poor pitiful attempt, "I know *you*. *You're* Malcolm. I was awfully gone on your photo once." She giggled again. Alec took out a large white handkerchief and wiped his brow. Malcolm shifted uneasily to his other foot, and she added confidentially, "It was something awful the way it used to make Oliver jealous."

At that moment Edith swept up before her. "I think I met you once," she began loftily.

"I remember," said Madge. "You came through in a big auto. My, but I thought Oliver had some stylish folks!"

"I'm extremely sorry that our rooms are all filled to-night," went on Edith grandly, "and that it will be impossible for me to ask you to remain."

Madge reddened. "I wouldn't trouble you for anything," she apologised.

"No," said Oliver and his voice shook with scorn, "we wouldn't trouble you. Madge, please wait for me a moment on the veranda." She looked up frightened. "Yes," he said, and she rose and without a word walked out of the room. Oliver closed the door. He was red in the face with indignation.

"Thank you all for your kindness," he said very scathingly; "I'm sure I'm very grateful. If this is what it means to be a member of a family, let me be free of it."

Tom got up. "Well—" he drawled, "if you can get along without us, why we—"

"Very well," retorted Oliver. "Very well, if that's your answer. I've thrown up the charming job at Glennings Falls anyway. I'm not so everlasting dependent as you have an idea. I'm off, and thank heaven! It's too bad if I've interrupted Ruth's bridge party. It's really too bad. I'm through with the whole lot of you. I'm through!" He turned. The door slammed. The room trembled to the very ceiling and a gust of wind snatched a pile of loose papers on the table and whirled them on to the floor. We heard the angry bang of the outer door and Oliver had gone.

That evening I wired to Will: "*Three of us will arrive to-night. Bobbie.*"

CHAPTER XIX

THE minute I heard Oliver explode out of that house of ours, and swing down the street—proud, angry, indignant, with that ridiculous little creature running on behind—I felt that he was headed straight to unhappiness and disaster. I understand Oliver pretty well, and knew that he saw, as plainly as any of us, all the crude rough corners of the little country girl, to whom he had been attracted, and married in some mad impulsive moment. After listening for half an hour to a lot of plagiarisms from Tom and Alec such as, "He must paddle his own canoe," "Experience is the best teacher," etc., I slipped out of the house and down to the station.

I told Will about it late that night.

"I found them sitting on a bench in the waiting-room. They weren't speaking. She had been crying. Oliver was glum and very silent. I think he was feeling awfully sorry that he had married her—I do really—and I don't know whether I felt sorrier for him or for her. So right then and there I decided to bring them home with me. We *must* do something, Will. We *must*. I finally wormed it out of Oliver that he was down to his very last one hundred dollars and not a single thing in sight. I know as well as you that Madge is a difficult proposition, but we've got to have her for a sister-in-law whether we like it or not. I know that our reputations are all tangled up in this thing, but a snarl will never get untangled unless somebody begins to pick it apart. Will, I'm so glad that you have got a mind that is concerned with the ailments of guinea-pigs rather than society and what people think. For you see, dear, I've told Oliver that he and Madge shall stay right here with us until something turns up for Oliver to do."

"But, Bobbie, my dear girl," said Will, "have you forgotten that for Commencement week we have invited Dr. Merrill, who is to receive an honorary degree, and his wife to be our guests?"

"No, Will dear, I haven't forgotten it, nor that I was giving my first really-truly little dinner next Wednesday; but I know that Oliver is my own brother and that I've simply got to stand by him and see him through."

Three days later I received a scathing letter from Edith:

> "I suppose that you are posing as the Good Samaritan. We all think you acted very unwisely and not at all for Oliver's best good. You may be interested to know that the doctor says he wouldn't have allowed me to keep the girl here for one minute. I am still in bed, as it is, from the bad effects of the shock of the whole affair. I made Alec write something for the paper yesterday, denying the report that we were

entertaining the couple here. On the contrary I have let it be known that I do not intend to recognise the new Mrs. Vars at all. It is the only safe policy. If you want to know *my* opinion, *I* think you are extremely foolish to have taken that girl into your house for one night even. You'll simply kill yourself socially. Remember you're a new member in the circle in which you are moving and will be known and judged by the friends and connections you have. It's a shame when you've just got started on the right path to ruin your chances, and Will's too. However, it's your affair. Do as you please."

"Oh, thanks," I said and stuffed the charming epistle into the kitchen stove.

My real difficulty however lay with Madge herself. The poor deluded girl had been brought up to believe that she was irresistibly charming. There hadn't been a prettier girl than she in Glennings Falls. She could boast of more "best young men," as she called them, than any girl I ever knew. Four young aspirants, before Oliver had appeared, had proposed to her, and she was only nineteen. Her father, a man of enough education to be a minister, had died of consumption, when Madge was a baby. Since then, she and her mother had managed to make a living by boarding some of the foremen and superintendents at the quarries. They had always had the distinction of entertaining the owner of the granite works whenever he came to Glennings Falls for a yearly inspection. It was he who had procured a position for Madge "to wait on table" summertimes at one of the big mountain hotels. There she had picked up a great many ideas on style and fashion, and copied them now in cheap exaggerated imitation.

The first evening after her trunk arrived at our house, she appeared decked out in a fearful display of lace and flashy finery, redolent with cologne, and manners that matched her clothes. She talked incessantly. Her lace and perfumery seemed to give her confidence. She discoursed volubly on New York, and aired her newly-acquired knowledge of hotel life in a way that was pitiable. Even Will, quiet and dignified, failed to impress Madge. All the scientific knowledge in the world could not awe the little village coquette into silence. She even dangled her ear-rings at solemn old Will and tried to flirt with him. It was not Madge who appeared ill-at-ease; it was the rest of us who squirmed in our boots, blushed at her mistakes, coughed, gulped down desperate swallows of water to cover our confusion. She was quite unconscious of the horrible burlesque she was playing. As the days went on, the more silent the rest of us became, the more she prattled. The more we failed to appreciate her loveliness and wit, the more toggery she pulled out of her trunk and exhibited for our benefit, the crimpier grew her hair, the higher, if possible, became her pompadour, the noisier her laughter. Once I humbly suggested that she leave off her ear-rings on a certain occasion when we were going shopping. She treated my interference with utter scorn, and appeared half an hour later ready to accompany me to the market, with two large pearls screwed securely into the lobe of each ear. "Every one wears them in New York," she announced.

I didn't know what to do with the child. For two weeks I rose every morning and went downstairs to a painful ordeal at breakfast; for two weeks I saw Oliver flush and try to keep his eyes from meeting mine when Madge opened her mouth to speak; for two weeks I saw a threatening frown hover about Oliver's brow. I began to despair. Then suddenly, one evening, I found my poor brother in the gloomy living-room, brooding over an open fire. His head was in his hand, his elbow on his knee. I hadn't spoken to Oliver directly about Madge. I didn't now. I simply said very gently, "Want me to read aloud to you?"

"She wasn't like this at Glennings Falls," he burst out miserably, not stirring. "I want you to know it, because, well—I suppose you wonder why I ever was attracted to her. I wonder sometimes myself now—" He stopped a moment, then went on, talking straight into the fire. "I used to see a lot of her, you see. Every night and every morning. She used to pack my lunch and bring it up to me to the grove near the works every noon. I used to look forward to having her come—a lot. Glennings Falls is the deadliest hole you ever struck, and well—Madge was bright and full of fun. She isn't herself now. She wasn't like this. She was just as natural and simple. Upon my word," he broke off, "I've seen a lot of girls, one time and another, winners too, but somehow they none of them took such a hold on me as Madge. I thought she'd learn quickly enough, as soon as I got her down into civilisation, and so—anyway, I married her. Since—Well, it's no go, that's all. It's been bully of you to take her in, but I see clearly enough it can't work. Of course I mean to stick to her," he went on. "*Of course*. I suppose I've simply got to find a job out West somewhere, a long way off from everything and every one I know or—care about, and clear out. I mean to do the right thing." Then raising his eyes to mine he said with a queer, forced smile, "I guess *my* fun's all over, Bobbie."

"Oh, no, no, *no*, it isn't." I said fiercely. "Don't say that." I put my hand on his shoulder. "No, it isn't, Oliver," and suddenly, because I couldn't bear to see Oliver unhappy and despairing, because my voice was trembling and there were tears in my eyes, I went quickly out of the room and upstairs.

I was surprised on passing the guest-room to hear muffled sobs. I stopped and listened, and then, quite sure, I abruptly knocked and immediately opened the door. I was amazed to discover Madge face downward on the bed in tears.

"Why, what's the matter?" I exclaimed. I had never seen anything but arch glances in her eyes before.

"I want to go home! I want to go home! They're not ashamed of me at home!" she wailed.

I closed the door and went over to her.

"I just hate it here, I just hate it!" she went on. "Oliver thought I was good enough at home." She was crying all the time and each sentence came brokenly. "Oh, I wish I'd never *heard* of Oliver Vars," she choked. "I've tried and tried to be like his folks but he finds fault with every single thing I do, or wear, or say, or think, and I'm going home. I think his people are all stuck-up, horrid old things anyway and I just hate it, hate it, *hate it here*. Oh, go away, go away!" she cried out at me in a torrent of sobs.

Instead I sat down beside her.

"Look here, Madge," I said sternly. "Stop talking like that. Stop it. You can't go home. Don't you know you're married? Why, it's perfectly absurd!"

The sobbing stopped suddenly and she lay still with her nose buried in the down comforter. I went on talking to the cheap rhinestone comb in the back of her head.

"I've got something to say to you," I said, "and I want you to listen. I've been wanting to talk to you ever since you came to this house, and now I'm going to do it. You say Oliver finds fault with you, and let me tell you I don't blame him a bit. He certainly has reason to. Why, I never have run across a young lady who knew so little about things as you do. You don't know how to do anything properly. Your clothes are atrocious, and your manners—your self-assured manners here in my house are inexcusable. You're only a young girl of nineteen years who never has had any experience nor seen anything of the world. I don't blame you, understand. It isn't your *fault* that everything you do or say or wear makes us all blush with shame; but it does—it does, Madge. Why, I had to give up inviting some people here to dinner because I was afraid of the breaks and the horrible remarks you might make before my friends. Edith wouldn't have you in her house. That's the bald truth of it, my dear. You might as well know how we feel. It may sound cruel and hard, and I wouldn't say these things to Oliver's wife if she had come here modest, unpretentious, and anxious to learn; but she didn't, I should say she didn't! The worst ignorance in the world is that which parades itself up and down thinking itself very grand and elegant while all the lookers-on are laughing up their sleeves. That's what you've been doing, Madge." I stopped a moment to give the poor girl a chance to say something.

"Go away—go away—*go away*!" she burst out at me, turning her head enough to let the words out into the room. "Oh, go away!"

I stood up.

"No, Madge," I replied calmly. "I shan't go away, and neither shall you. You don't seem to know what's best for yourself, so I will tell you. You're going to stay right here with me, and work and study and learn. You are married to Oliver Vars and you're to make a success of it if it kills you; and it won't kill you. You're going to make him and the rest of us all proud of you before you get through and I am going to help you. Do you hear me? We're going to work it out together. You've got it in you. I know you have. I *see* you have," I lied. "You're a fine girl underneath. Don't you remember up there in Glennings Falls how you used to bring Oliver his lunch at noon? He has told me all about it—how nice you were, I mean—and how sure he was that you would learn as soon as you came down here. Well—you're going to begin to-night. Hereafter you'll do exactly as I say."

"Go away!" came again from the depths of the down comforter.

I ignored it entirely.

"Get up now and bathe your eyes," I said cheerfully. "Dinner will be ready in half an hour. I want you to wear the white muslin you had on this morning and no ear-rings. Remember," I added distinctly, going to the door, "remember, absolutely no ear-rings to-night, please."

But Oliver and Will and I had dinner alone that evening. "She won't come down," Oliver had announced gloomily. "She's in an awful state. She's crying. She wants to go home," he said, and my heart sank for I knew I had played my last card and lost.

That night Will had brought home the long-looked-for good news of a position for Oliver. We discussed it quietly at dinner—the three of us with Madge crying upstairs. A friend of Will's, a civil engineer, had said that if Oliver cared to go down into South America to some God-forsaken spot in the Argentine Republic—no place for a woman, by the way—there was an engineering job down there waiting for somebody. The job would take some five or six months; there might or might not be any future—Will's friend couldn't say.

"I'll go. I'll go right off," said Oliver. "Madge is unhappy and wants to go home anyway. I'm sure it's best. It was all a mistake," he admitted sadly to Will, "my taking her away from Glennings Falls. I might have known it wouldn't work." I stared hard at a saltcellar. Will began carving the steak silently. "You can go ahead now and have your people here for

Commencement," observed Oliver; "Madge and I will both be gone in a week. I'm relieved it's settled," he added gravely.

It was during our dessert, after Delia had taken up a tray to Madge, that I was told that Mrs. Vars wanted me in her bedroom. I excused myself and slipped upstairs quietly. Madge was in bed; her hair was parted, braided neatly down her back; her tears were dried; her plain little nightgown buttoned at her throat. I had never seen her look so pretty. Her dinner stood beside her bed untouched.

"You wanted me?" I asked.

"Yes," she replied. "I'm not going home. I'll do anything you tell me," she said.

And she didn't go home. We packed Oliver off alone for South America, the next week, and as I rode back from the station in the open car with his slip of a wife beside me, on my hands for the next half year, I drew my first long free breath. Oliver, I recognised, had been more of a responsibility on my mind than Madge. My way was clear now. Lessons could begin any day, and no one will ever know what earnestness and determination went into the task that I had undertaken. From the beginning I took it absolutely for granted that since our stormy talk that evening in the guest-room our relations thereafter would be those of scholar and teacher; my authority would be unquestioned.

I overhauled the child's entire wardrobe with the freedom and cruelty of a customs officer. The cheap lace things I sent to the Salvation Army. The rhinestone comb I dropped into the stove before her very eyes. Ear-rings, jingling bracelets, glass beads, enameled brooches, I put in a box in the storeroom. A much-treasured parasol made out of cheap Hamburg embroidery I presented to Delia. Even Madge's toilet accessories were somehow done away with. Her elaborate hand-mirror with decorated porcelain back and hair-brush to match were replaced by a set of plain white celluloid that could be scrubbed with safety every week. The perfumery was poured down the bathroom sink. As soon as I was able, I purchased for Madge a few plain white shirt-waists with tailored collars, and a "three-fifty" stiff sailor hat made of black straw. When the crimp had all been soaked out of her hair, a wire pompadour supporter, three side-combs, eighteen hairpins, a net, a switch that didn't match, two puffs and a velvet bow had been extracted from her coiffure, I parted the little hair that remained and rolled it into a bun about as big as a doughnut in the back of her neck. She looked as shorn as a young sheep that has just been clipped. Her eyes fairly stared out of her head. I discovered that they were large and blue, with long lashes. Her features, unframed by the dreadful halo of hair, were flawless—small and finely cut. After I had gotten all the dreadful veneer off of the child she reminded me of a lovely old piece of mahogany discovered in some old attic or other, after the several coats of common crude paint have been scraped off and the natural grain finally appears perfect and unharmed.

She looked on at her metamorphosis, and at the cruel ravage of her treasures, passive and apparently indifferent. After her surrender to me she had no spirit left. She accepted my rule with a meekness I couldn't understand. After that night in the guest-room she became a different creature. She dropped her little airs and affectations as abruptly as if they were a garment that she could hang up and leave behind her in the closet. She became dumb at our table, and with Will actually shy and frightened. I thought her sudden change was due to ill-temper, and I bullied the poor beaten little creature terribly. I domineered, tyrannised, scorned and mocked. I didn't dare be tender, for I was convinced that success lay only in complete submission. Poor little "alone" thing—I did feel sorry for her at times! Her eyes were often red from crying. She didn't eat very much and her cheeks grew pale before my sight. She used to sit sometimes for an hour at a time without saying a word, until I longed to put comforting arms about her. When she accompanied me to the market several weeks after Oliver had gone away—quiet, silent, subdued, Glennings Falls would never in the world have recognised their gay sparkling little village coquette who had had a word, a nod, and a smile ready for every one who passed.

Oliver had been gone about six weeks when Madge told me her astounding news. I didn't know what to say to her for a moment. I was awfully surprised. She seemed such a baby, and I suppose it always comes with a jolt when you first realise your younger brother is actually a man. I was amazed too that such an apparently weak little thing as Madge had so pluckily kept her big secret to herself for so many weeks. She had known of it before Oliver had gone away, but she hadn't liked to tell him, she confessed. He had left her without as much as a premonition of the truth, and it was because of what was waiting for her in the future that she had been frightened into staying with me. She hadn't known what else to do. I stared at her open-eyed. It was when I saw her under lip tremble like a little child's and two tears fall splash upon her wrist, that I put out my hand and drew her down beside me on the couch. She leaned against me and began to cry in earnest then.

"Oh, don't, don't cry, Madge," I pleaded quietly. "Please! I'm just as glad as I can be, dear," I said. "Everything will be all right. Don't be afraid." But still she sobbed. "Listen; I've been wanting to tell you for days how well you're doing—even Will remarks on it. Please, please don't cry, Madge. Why, I hadn't an idea of *this*. I didn't dream of it. But we'll see you safely through.

Oh, Madge, don't cry so hard. Listen, my dear girl, you can go home tomorrow if you want to."

Suddenly she turned and buried her head on my shoulder. Her hand sought mine and held it tight. She clung to me as if she needed me very much.

"I don't want to go home. I'd rather stay right here with you," she sobbed.

My arms went around her. Remember I have never had many friendships with girls. Staunch, true, loyal Juliet would nurse me through the smallpox if necessary, but she doesn't like to be kissed. Years ago when we stayed all night at each other's houses we slept on the extreme opposite edges of the bed and if one of my elbows as much as grazed Juliet's shoulder-blade, I was vigorously poked in the ribs and told to get over to my side. My younger sister Ruth had not sought one of my hands since she was able to walk alone. She would rather cry into a pillow than on my shoulder. If there had ever been any doubt about my loving this little helpless creature, who turned to me now in her hour of fear and dread, it was entirely dispelled during that half-hour on the couch in our living-room.

It was after that day that our best work began. I continued stern and severe with Madge, but there was unmistakable affection underneath. I resorted to every device in the world for my little protegée's education. I laugh as I look back to some of the drills and tests I put her through. Fridays, for instance, were our shopping days in Boston. Department stores are regular educational institutions. It wasn't a month before Madge was able to detect machine embroidery from hand-work; imitation Irish crochet from real; coarse linen from fine. We spent hours at "window-gazing." In that old, popular childhood game of "Choosing," Madge became quite an adept. I used to make her pick out the suit, or the hat, or the piece of dress-goods in a window display which was the most conservative, and verify her choice by my selection. Conservatism I preached to her from morning till night, and she got so she could recognise it a block away. Homeward-bound from those Friday shopping days, I would indicate an individual opposite to us in the car, and that evening a vivisection of her toilet would take place in our library. I have often felt sorry for the poor mortals whose oversupply of imitation fillet, high-heeled ill-kept pumps, or spotted veil we so severely criticised; for the young girls—gay, unconscious creatures—who laughed too freely, talked too loudly for our fastidious requirements.

Madge's table-manners had been shocking. She mashed her food with the prongs of her fork and poured gravy over her bread; she ate enough butter for three men. We used to have written examinations on table-manners. After she had progressed so that she could eat a poached egg without daubing the entire plate, and a half-orange with a spoon without sprinkling the front of her waist with drops of yellow juice, I advanced her to my place at the table. For a month she sat opposite Will and played at hostess. She offered the bread; she inquired if any one would have more of the dessert; she learned to address Delia with consideration. I left it to my pupil to suggest that we adjourn to the living-room at the close of our meals. I made her pour the coffee into our tiny best china cups.

The effect of all this training upon myself was as miraculous as upon Madge. You don't know what confidence in a subject it gives you to teach it. I honestly believe Madge did Will and me about as much good as we did her. Our meal-times became regular little models of perfection—quiet voices, good conversation, and manners fit for a queen. I began to dress every evening for the ceremony, as an example for Madge, and it was then that Will who entered into the game beautifully began changing every night into a dinner coat. The fussy little frills—candlelight and coffee served in the living-room, which I had spurned after leaving Edith—I returned to for Madge's sake. For her (for I discovered that my pupil considered me as a model of all that is proper and correct) I dressed myself with greatest care—spotless white kid-gloves, carefully adjusted veil, neat and well-kept boots—and sallied forth to pay some calls. As an example to Madge I invariably inquired what time Will would return in the evening and made a point of arriving at the house at least a half-hour before him, so that he might find me calm, quiet and freshly attired, like a lady leisurely awaiting her lord, in an apartment as neat and well-kept as the library of his Club. I didn't allow myself to slump awkwardly into a comfortable chair in his presence, nor yawn and stretch my arms. I even tucked away the horrid, red worsted bedroom slippers and from my supply of unused negligees drew forth a blue china-silk kimono. There was a pink one like it which I gave to Madge. Her eyes sparkled as they fell upon it. "Save it till Oliver comes," I said, and I, who had scoffed in my heart at Ruth's and Edith's conversation which took place in that same guest-room of mine eight months before, repeated their very words, as if they had left them printed on the walls. "You mustn't be the kind to grow careless before your husband. A man likes a woman to be dainty whether he is married to her or not. A man likes to be proud of his wife," I repeated parrot-like. Oh, you see, there was more than one conversion taking place that spring in the ugly brown house in the unfashionable street, and the greater of these was not, in my estimation, that of the little country girl from Glennings Falls, Vermont.

CHAPTER XX

WILL and I used to run up to Hilton for over Sunday very often. But when Edith found out that Oliver had gone to South America and Madge had remained with us, she wrote to me immediately and warned me never to attempt "to cram the girl down her throat." She had no idea of *ever* recognising Oliver's wife as any connection of *hers*. If Will and I came up to Hilton she must ask us to leave our preposterous protegée behind.

I didn't see that it would hurt Edith any to be formally courteous to Madge. She needn't have become intimate. I didn't expect Madge to be invited everywhere I went. I didn't take her anywhere with me in my social life at the university. But I did think that Edith was neglecting her duty as a woman to ignore Alec's own brother's wife, whoever she was. It was almost inevitable to avoid the growth of a feeling of hostility between Edith and me; but I did want to escape an open break. I didn't want to quarrel about Madge, so whenever I saw Edith I tried to overlook the existence of any bone of contention between us. I made a point of running up to Hilton very often for the day, and tried to refer to Madge in a natural, open, frank sort of manner that made little of the seriousness of the situation. I didn't go to Hilton to court trouble, I assure you. I made my fortnightly trips for the express purpose of promoting family peace and harmony.

The arrival of Edith's baby was only about a month off when I went up to carry her a little afghan I had crocheted. I found her unpacking some baby scales and the most elaborate weighing basket I ever saw. It was all beruffled and trimmed with artificial rosebuds around the edge. It was when I stood off and admired it that I remarked with a sigh, and in the most offhand way in the world, that I guessed Madge's baby would have to be weighed on the kitchen scales if at all. I meant it as a kind of tribute to Edith's basket. Besides I thought it a good idea to refer to Madge's expectations. It seemed more friendly to the family to take them into my confidence in such a matter.

You would have thought a bomb had gone off in the room.

"That creature going to have a baby!" Edith exclaimed.

"Yes," I said. "Just think of it! Oliver with a little son or daughter!"

Edith turned suddenly upon me.

"Oh, I see!" she flashed. "I see! A son indeed! So that's the story! I suppose the girl has her eyes on that three thousand, without doubt. Designing little minx!"

"Why, your baby comes first, Edith," I replied. "Of course if you shouldn't get the prize, I think Madge could make pretty good use of three thousand dollars. She probably needs it more than you."

"Oh! So you hope I won't have a boy! That's it. Very well. We'll see. You hope—"

"Why, Edith," I interrupted, "I don't hope anything of the sort. I—"

"We'll see if this girl of Oliver's has any right to that money," Edith went on excitedly. "We'll see about that. When is her precious baby expected? Too soon for decency's sake, I suppose—horrid, common little—"

I flushed. "Edith Vars," I fired, "don't you imply anything like that about Madge. Don't you *dare*!"

I was angry now and Edith knew it. She seemed to glory in it, for she prodded me again with another false accusation against Madge, and before I could stop it we were quarrelling dreadfully. I don't remember all we said to each other that morning in Edith's room, but I know our words came thick and fast; I know our voices shook with our fury, and that we glared at each other across the expanse of the snowy bed with actual hatred in our eyes. It all ended by Edith's suddenly flinging herself face down upon the pillows, and bursting into awful sobs. Not until then did I realise that my sister-in-law was not well, nor quite herself these days—I had never seen her cry before in my life—and frightened I went out of the room to call for help.

That noon Alec sent for a doctor, and half an hour later it was announced that Edith had a temperature. A trained nurse appeared at four o'clock and Alec called me into the library.

He was dreadfully concerned about the consequences of my news in regard to Madge; I shouldn't have mentioned it, it seems; it might be the cause of the most dreadful results—he couldn't tell. Edith was very excitable just now. I ought to have known better. He blamed me wholly. I had been careless, inconsiderate and cruel. I had better leave for home as soon as possible. The thought of me in the house annoyed and disturbed Edith even now; she had inquired three times if I had gone. Alec had ordered the automobile; I could catch the five-thirty if I hurried. He wished I hadn't come to see Edith at all; she had been so well; everything had appeared very favourable before my arrival; Alec couldn't understand my attitude toward Edith anyway; she had done everything for Ruth and me (had I forgotten my wedding?) and I paid her back with gratitude like this!

I didn't reply to my brother. Alec and I had travelled too many miles in opposite directions to understand each other now. A bitter antagonism arose in my heart against Edith. I should have quarrelled with Alec too had I opened my mouth to speak. I went out and got into the automobile without a retort, and as I whisked out of the driveway and looked back at Edith's curtained windows, a wicked wish was born in my heart. I said to myself, "I hope it *will* be a girl. 'Twould serve her exactly right."

It was, however, a pretty discouraged ambassador of peace who crawled back to her little brown refuge that night about eight o'clock. Will was sitting by the fire reading a big book, his hair all ruffled up as it always is when he reads. Madge had gone upstairs to bed. The comfortable lamp-light, the dear, homely black walnut furniture, Will's quiet sympathy, never seemed more precious to me than that night.

"O Will," I said tearfully when he kissed me, "I've quarrelled with Edith and Alec. And, oh, dear, it was the last thing in the world I meant to do."

"Tell me about it," he said and laid aside his big book. I took its place on the arm of his chair, and told him my story. After he had rung up Edith's doctor by telephone and found that there wasn't cause for alarm, he came back to me and called me "young wildcat" which sweet words were music to my ears. I knew at the sound of them that Will didn't consider the quarrel serious. "It will all blow over in a week. You see!" he laughed, and I went to sleep comforted.

But it didn't blow over. That fateful visit of mine marked the beginning of an understood family war. Clouds of trouble grew thicker instead of blowing away. The very next evening I received a brief note from Alec asking that I postpone any more visits to Hilton until after Edith's illness. Ruth wrote she couldn't understand me in the least; she thought it was dreadful that Madge was going to have a child anyway, but if she got Father's three thousand dollars it would be the unjustest thing that ever happened! Tom—even fair-minded Tom from out West—told me to remember that Oliver's marriage had been rather out-of-order, and asked me if I was championing a cause I could call worthy. When Ruth ran across me one day in town a fortnight later she treated me like a bare acquaintance. Alec went so far as to cancel a Saturday golf engagement with Will. Long distance telephone calls between our houses came to an abrupt end. Malcolm from New York bluntly referred to the "family row."

I didn't tell Madge about the trouble brewing in our family. I never even imparted to her the knowledge of the premium to be paid for the first Vars grandson. Silently I sat with her sewing by the hour on her meagre little outfit of five nainsook slips, three flannel Gertrudes, two bands, two shirts, and three flannellette night-gowns, with never a word of my eager thoughts. I became very loyal to the cause I had chosen to defend. It didn't trouble me that our little baby-clothes were so much plainer than Edith's, for night and day, day and night, I was hoping against hope, wishing against chance, willing and frantically demanding that Madge's splendour might lie in her victory.

You can imagine the ecstatic state of excitement I was thrown into when the news of the arrival of Edith's nine-pound daughter reached me some six weeks after my last visit to Hilton.

I must have felt a good deal like the supporters of a weaker foot-ball team when their side makes the first touchdown. I could have thrown up my hat with joy; I could have shouted myself hoarse. Madge had an opportunity! Madge had a chance! It seemed too good to be true, and I longed to share with Madge the triumph so nearly hers. But Will was afraid she might worry and fret about it,—there was, of course, the possibility of disappointment,— so I followed his advice and kept on building my air-castles in secret.

It was on November twenty-first that Madge's little child was born. We had written to Oliver in June and he had started on his homeward journey as soon as Madge's belated letter reached him, some time in August. He had tramped a hundred miles down a tropical river, had lain sick for five weeks with a fever in a native camp, had dragged himself in a weakened condition twenty miles farther on to the coast, and finally had caught a slow-travelling freight-boat bound for Spain. Blown out of its course, becalmed, disabled by a terrific storm, Oliver never saw the coast of Europe until well into November. His mite of a child was two weeks old before he reached home.

Oliver had done well down there in South America. Reports of his ability had reached the Boston office months before Oliver himself appeared. It seems that Oliver's chief had written a long letter telling all about the ingenuity which young Vars had shown in working out some technical problem connected with a suspension bridge down there. I told you Oliver's line was civil engineering. The Boston office informed Will they had offered Vars a good position right here at home with a salary that he could live on. I was delighted, and as soon as we learned that he had started for God's country, I began to hunt up apartments.

I wanted Oliver to see for himself and *by* himself what a perfect little housekeeper—what a lovely little creature, simple as she was, he had chanced to pick out up there in the mountains of Vermont. I honestly began to fear Oliver wouldn't appreciate half of the delicate points that Madge had developed. I wished I could give my brother a course of training too. He is the kind to be rather impolite inside the walls of his own domain. I selected for Madge and Oliver a suburb where the rents were not high, about half an hour by trolley from Boston. I planned to have Madge well established in her own five sunny little rooms before the arrival of either her husband or child.

From my safe-full of silver and attic-full of Will's furniture, which I couldn't use, I could easily have set up two brides at housekeeping. I sent over a whole load of things from our house to Madge's and we spent days afterward settling the darling little rooms. On November twenty-first I went over to the apartment alone. Madge had complained of not feeling very well and I didn't want her to get all tired out before she actually moved the following week. The kitchen utensils were waiting to be washed and set in rows on the cupboard shelves, so I started out straight after breakfast and spent the whole day "playing house" there alone. I didn't get back until after seven o'clock at night. Will must have been watching for me, for he met me at the door. The instant I entered the house I knew something unexpected had happened. There was a white pillow on the couch in the living-room. I smelled ether.

"Will," I said all weak in my knees, "where's Madge? What's happened?"

He closed the living-room door and turned up the gas.

"She's all right, dear. We didn't send for you, because there was nothing you could do. I was here all the time."

"You mean—" I began. "Will," I said, and then my mind leaped over a league of details to one question, and after I had asked it Will took my hands and replied gently:

"No, dear, a sweet little girl."

I couldn't answer at first. I crumpled down in a heap in Will's big chair.

"It was the only thing I ever really, really wanted," I said brokenly. "Oh, Will, I can't believe fate would be so unkind! Tell me again—did you say a girl—really a *girl*?"

"Yes, dear, a fine, perfect, lovely little girl."

I stared straight in front of me.

"Isn't it too bad, too bad, too bad," I said. "Oh, Will!" I broke out, and began to cry.

Will came over and put his arms around me.

"Why, Bobbie dear," he said sadly, "I should think the little kiddie was yours."

I couldn't have been more disappointed if it had been. All the victorious telegrams, all the confident, buoyant notes to the different members of the family were more than useless now. The poor little mite of humanity wrapped up in a piece of flannel upstairs in the sewing-room in the clothes-basket, which Madge and I had lined with muslin, had shattered all my plans—had frustrated its poor little mother's only chance for glory.

It was all I could do to muster up a smile for poor, broken, beaten Madge herself, when the nurse ushered me into her bedroom the next day. I was glad when I saw her smiling up at me from the pillows that I had not confided my eager hopes to her.

"Oh, Lucy," she said to me, "it's a girl! I knew you hoped it would be a little girl, because you were so happy when Edith's baby came. And I—"

"Are you glad?" I asked tremblingly, feeling like a hypocrite before an angel.

"I—oh, I *prayed* for a girl. I wouldn't know what to do with a boy. My dolls were always girls."

It wasn't until I ran across Edith, most unexpectedly, several days later in town, that I woke up to the fact that that little girl of Madge's was a blessing in disguise. Edith's daughter was then about three months old and she was flitting about again as gay as ever, feathered and furred, stepping like a horse who has just had a good rub-down. I had seen her several times in the last month. She does all her shopping in Boston and I am often there myself. Of course we had spoken, even chatted on impersonal subjects as we chanced to meet here and there. On this particular day we happened to find ourselves in the drapery department of a large department store both waiting for the elevator to take us to the street.

"Oh, how do you do?" she said to me loftily. "Gorgeous day, isn't it?"

"Fine," I replied.

And then she asked evasively, her curiosity getting the better of her. "How's everything at your establishment?"

"Oh, all right. I have a note already written to you. There's a new member in our family, you know."

I saw the colour rush to Edith's face.

"No!" she exclaimed. "Really?" Then arming herself against a dreaded blow she gasped, "Which is it?"

"A girl," I hated to announce; "born Thursday."

"A girl! Did you say a girl?" Edith's voice broke into a nervous laugh. "Lucy Vars, has Oliver's wife a little girl? Is she dreadfully disappointed? How is she? When was it? How much does it weigh? A girl! Well, well, is it *possible*?" Her eyes were fairly glowing now.

I followed her into the elevator.

"You mean it? You aren't fooling? This isn't a joke?" she exclaimed as we dropped a floor.

"No," I assured her.

"Poor thing! Poor thing!" she ejaculated with sparkling eyes. "A girl. A girl!" She found my hand and gave it an eager little squeeze. "Won't Oliver be just too cute with a daughter?" she bubbled.

By the time we reached the ground floor, she had slipped her arm through mine.

"You've got to come and have lunch with me, Bobbie Vars," she said. "Let's let bygones be bygones. I hate fights. I'm tired to death putting myself out to be disagreeable. Heavens! I can hardly wait to tell Alec. A little girl!" She led me out into the street. "I'm starved," she ran on. "We'll blow ourselves to the best luncheon in this town. I want to know *all* the details—every one. Do you know I felt in my bones she would have a daughter, and I simply never make a mistake; and by the way, way down in my boots, *I* wanted a girl myself. I *said* I preferred a boy, but that was talk. You can dress girls up in such darling clothes. That's what I'm telling people anyhow," she confided frankly. "Remember, should any one ask."

In spite of the many things about Edith I do not like, she has some splendid qualities. "Look here," she ejaculated abruptly, "I believe I'll send that poor little creature of Oliver's some flowers. I don't suppose she has many. Come on in here, Bobbie, and help me pick out something stunning!"

Next Wednesday Ruth 'phoned from town. Friday she came out for dinner, and not very long afterward, the expressman left a lovely embroidered baby's coat and cap "for the dear little daughter," it said on Edith's visiting-card in her bold unmistakable handwriting.

It was Oliver himself, who had been at home about two days, who opened the package. He and I were alone in the living-room. He flushed when his eyes fell upon the card.

"So Edith—" he began.

"Yes," I assured him; "and the roses on Madge's bureau are from Edith too."

He flung the card down on the table and came over and stood before me.

"Look here, Bobbie," he said. "I must have been completely run down or something, before I went away. I don't know what ailed me. Everything bothered me horribly and to think I took it out so on poor little Madge. Why, Madge—Say, Bobbie, isn't Madge—" He stopped. "Pshaw!" he went on,

- 164 -

"I've known a lot of girls in my day but not one to come up to Madge. Did I ever tell you how she can cook? Like a streak! You ought to see her arrange flowers in the middle of the table. Looks as if they were growing! Madge is worth twenty society girls. Could Ruth run a vegetable garden, do you think? Could her boarding-school friends go into the village store and run the accounts when the regular girl's off on a vacation? Madge can! I knew she would learn city ways and manners quickly enough once she was here. I *knew* it. And say—isn't she pretty? Isn't she simply—lovely with the kid? Humph—" he broke off, picking up Edith's card and tossing it down again. "I knew the family couldn't help but like Madge once they knew her, and I'm mighty glad!"

"So am I, Oliver. She's got the loveliest, sweetest disposition! Sometimes I've been afraid that *you* would be the one not to appreciate it. She's thinking a lot how to make you happy, Oliver. Her head is full of schemes and little devices to please and satisfy you; and I've been wondering if you've been thinking up little ways to please her. Sometimes married people take it for granted that schemes and methods and contrivances for happiness are superfluous, if they love each other; but *I* believe that new love needs just about as much care and tending as that little helpless baby in there. I hope you think so too, Oliver."

"I don't know as I'd thought much about it. I'm not much of a philosopher on such subjects. Things come to me in flashes, and they stick too. I remember the last time I ever had a real good old time with the college crowd was at Ruth's party, two or three years ago. I drank more than was good for me that night and when I came to go upstairs about four A. M., right there on the landing waiting for me was Father. Somebody had left his picture lighted up, you know, and it was absolutely gruesome how he stared down at me out of his frame—like a ghost or something. I never forgot it. I tried to get the fellows to put out the light, but they couldn't find the switch. It was horrible to struggle up in front of Father in my condition—I can't explain it; but from that day to this I've never been able to enjoy that sort of a time since. I've never taken more than I should since that night, and I never shall again. I'm sure of myself now."

"Isn't it splendid to live on in the way Father does?" I remarked quietly.

"Well," went on Oliver, "the first sight of Madge in there with the baby was like that lighted picture of Father. Do you know what I mean? It flashed over me, 'Heavens, I've got to amount to something now *anyhow*,' and those flashes stick, as I said. I *shall* amount to something. See if I don't!" He stopped a moment, embarrassed. "I don't know as you understand at all about that picture of Father, and Madge in bed in there, as if they had any connection. They haven't, only—"

"I do understand, Oliver," I said; "I do perfectly. And I'm so glad and happy and proud! I always felt you had it in you!"

About a week later Edith called me up from Boston.

"Hello," she said. "You, Bobbie? It's Edith. Ruth and I are in town. We've just had lunch. I've got to go to the tailor's at two, but we thought later we might come out and see the baby." ("It's Edith," I whispered excitedly to Will with my hand over the receiver.) "Will it be all right?"

"Surely," I called back. "Come right ahead."

"Is Madge able to see people yet?" ("She wants to see Madge," I told Will.) "Oh, yes! She comes downstairs every afternoon now. We'll expect you—good-bye."

I hung up the receiver, and went into the butler's pantry to prepare my tea-tray. Ten minutes later I casually remarked to Madge:

"Oh, by the way, Edith and Ruth are coming out this afternoon. I think I shall ask you to pour tea, Madge."

"All right," she replied quietly, like a little stoic. "I understand. I'll do my very best, Lucy."

I felt something of the same tremulous pride of a mother listening to her daughter deliver a valedictory at a high school graduation, as I watched Madge at the tea-table that afternoon. Her parted hair, simply knotted behind, pale cheeks tinged with a little colour, her frail hands among the tea-cups, her shy timid manner, were all lovely to behold. Oliver, from the piano-stool, glowed with pride; Edith and Ruth, from the couch, could not fail to appreciate the careful, calm, and correct collection of napkin, plate, tea-cup and spoon. Edith has a great faculty for observation. I knew she was sizing up Madge out of the corner of her eye, even as she rattled on to me on the wonders of the little niece in Hilton whom I had never seen.

She and Ruth stayed until just time to connect with the six-thirty train for Hilton. It was closeted in my room that Edith said to me in her erratic way, "My dear, I never saw such a change in any living *mortal*. Do you realise that having that baby has simply made that girl over? It's wonderful—put refinement into her. Why, really, one wouldn't guess the child's origin *now*. Listen to me. I've decided to invite the whole family bunch, as usual, for Christmas (one may as well be forgiving in this short life, I've concluded); so I came to have a look at Madge. She isn't half bad, you know. I had a nice little chat alone with her when you were showing Ruth the baby. She says she was simply crazy for a girl, and I think she means it. She isn't as impossible as I feared—not half. All she needs are some clothes and I've gotten it into my head to take her to my own dressmaker in town. One may as well be generous, Lucy. Besides, if the girl comes to the house at Christmas she must dress decently. I've a good mind to take the little thing in hand myself and polish her up a little. She's pretty enough. You see," Edith broke off, "Breck Sewall will probably be around Christmas-time—won't it be wonderful if he should marry Ruth?—and I simply had to have a look at Madge before inviting her. However, I really think she'll do."

The instant the door had closed on Edith I rushed back to Madge. I threw my arms about her.

"You've passed your preliminaries, dear child!" I said and kissed her hard.

CHAPTER XXI

DID you ever attempt to buy a lot of fifteen thousand feet at fifty cents a foot, and build a house on it of twelve rooms, three baths, a shower, a sleeping-porch and a small unpretentious garage for fourteen thousand dollars? This isn't an example in mental arithmetic, but it was a problem Will and I laboured over every March and April for three successive springs, before deciding each year to stay on for another twelve months in our old rented brown box, gas-lighted and tin-tubbed. I am not going to explain how such a problem can be solved, because frankly I don't know.

Will is a regular miracle-performer in some lines. He'll work for hours over some knotty proposition in his laboratory, and come home from the hospital simply glowing with enthusiasm over the successful onslaught of a squad of his well-trained microbes upon an unruly lot of beasts who were making life miserable for a poor man almost dying with carbuncles. The medical journals describe Dr. William Ford Maynard's accomplishments as miraculous. However, I can vouch that he is utterly unable to perform any feats with wood and plaster and plumbers' supplies. Two hours working over our house-plans used to exhaust Will more than four days solid in his laboratory. He said there was more hope in discovering the haunts of the wary meningitis microbe than in finding a contractor who would build us a house at our price.

Will and I adored our first little home, of course, but then there were disadvantages. Every time it rained I had to put a basin in the middle of my bed—in case the roof leaked—and the fireplaces did smoke when you first lit them, and the kitchen stove did need a new lining. The owner was awfully disagreeable about repairs, and after we had been vainly pleading for three months solid for a new brick or two in a disabled chimney, which threatened to burn down the house, we began to consider moving. We didn't intend to build. We thought it would cost too much. We didn't even intend to buy. We simply wanted to find something better to rent.

Rummaging about among second-hand houses is very depressing, I can tell you. Some of the same old arks that had been on the market when we were first married, were still without a master, like certain wrecks of servants who haunt intelligence-offices. Dilapidated run-down old things—I hate the very thought of them! They have a musty, dead-rat sort of odour that's far from welcoming when you enter their darkened halls. You always wonder if it's the plumbing and ask why the last people left. And oh, the closets in those houses—little, black horrid holes! I used to pull open their doors, and time and again find some sort of human paraphernalia left behind on one of the hooks—a man's battered straw hat, or once, I remember, a solitary pair of discarded corsets. Spattered places in the bedrooms, paths worn on the hardwood floors, ink spots, grease spots, and on the walls an accurate pattern of the arrangement of the last family's pictures, actually offended me. I've heard that robins will never take possession of a last year's birds' nest. I know exactly how they feel about them. Oh, it isn't inspiring to hunt for a home among other people's cast-offs. Will and I were awfully discouraged after we had inspected the fifteenth impossibility—a dreadful affair with high ceilings, elaborately stencilled, and in the corners of each room little arched plaster grooves designed for statuary. For six months Will and I searched in vain for the sweet, clean little ready-made cottage of our dreams, shining in a fresh coat of white paint, its perennial garden in full-bloom, waiting for two nice home-loving people like ourselves to open its gate, stroll up its flag-stoned walk, and claim it for our own.

On our way home from impossibility the fifteenth, we took a street that had just been cut through some new land where little brand new houses were springing up like mushrooms. There was one, a tiny plaster house trimmed with light green blinds with half-moons cut in them, that I thought was simply adorable. It wasn't completed; I could see the workmen through the open windows. The temporary pine door stood open.

"Let's go in, for fun," I suggested, and Will helped me up the inclined plank that led to the little front stoop.

We stayed for a whole hour in that house! It was like gazing on sweet sixteen; it was simply refreshing; we didn't know anything so lovely existed. There was a darling little bathroom with open plumbing, and a shining porcelain tub. There was a marble slab for mixing in the pantry. The bedrooms were painted white. The closets, tiny though they were, smelled of fresh plaster. Will got into conversation with the contractor while I amused myself by planning which room I would choose for ours. But the house wasn't for rent. A man who ran a fish-market was building it. I saw Will get out an old letter and begin figuring on the back of the envelope. That place, lot and all, wasn't going to cost that fish man but ten thousand dollars—Will told me that night that we could own a house that cost fourteen thousand and still save money on our rent. I was excited. We didn't look at another house to hire. We dropped them as if they were infected. The very next Saturday afternoon we set out to search for lots.

We weren't very particular at first. Any little square of ground that we looked at with the idea of possible ownership seemed perfectly lovely to me; anything with a tiny glimpse of horizon, and a place in the back for a garden, was like a little piece of heaven. We were both awfully easily pleased the first month. There were so many pretty places to build on, we simply didn't know which one to choose. Then one day the agent sent us up to look at some land that had just been put on the market at sixty cents a foot. Of course it was more than we could pay, and we went to inspect it simply out of idle curiosity. The result was that the next day among that whole townful of open spaces and green fields, there was only one solitary spot that Will and I wanted for our own. You see after we had once climbed up on to that expensive little hilltop and looked off and seen the view—a round bowl of a lake with a clump of pines beside it, and beyond, a hill with a long ribbon of road leading up to a real New England white farmhouse with a splash of red barn beside it, we couldn't think kindly of any other spot in town. After we had sat down on the stone wall that ran right square through the back of the lot, and watched a glorious sunset reflected in the lake below, Will said, "By Jove, we'll have this!" There were six old apple-trees on the lot, a wild cherry and a dear little waif of a pine-tree. Will and I made a solemn vow to each other that we would build a cheap house, and get along a while longer with one maid for the sake of that lovely sunset every night when we ate supper. I said I'd as soon live in a lean-to. Will said we'd live just where we were for another year until we could afford to put up even a lean-to. We bought the darling of our hearts seven days later. It used up over two-thirds of our fourteen-thousand-dollar house fund.

We ate picnic suppers on our stone wall, and winter-times drank hot coffee there boiled over a tiny bon-fire built in the rocks, for three solid years before we began to dig the cellar of our lean-to. I had hollyhocks and a whole row of Canterbury-bells flowering in our garden for two springs before there was a door and some steps to lead out to it. It's all very well to vow you'll build a cheap house, but it's another thing to do it. Of course we had to have plumbing and heat; electric light fixtures seemed a necessity too, as well as a few doors here and there.

Will and I literally laboured over those plans. They had to undergo a dreadful series of operations. Every spring when it seemed to us as if we couldn't endure another summer cooped up in our noisy, stone-paved, double-electric-car-tracked street, I'd haul down the architect's blue-prints and stretch them out on a card-table. We amputated so much from those plans I wondered they held together. Of course the shower-baths and the garage, oak floors, and a superfluous bathroom came off as easily as fingers; but when we began cutting out partitions here and there, a treasured fireplace or two, two closets, and even the back stairs, I tell you it was ticklish! Even when we'd shaved off two feet from the length of the living-room, four from the dining-room, and squeezed our hall so that it was only nine feet wide, even then we couldn't find a generous-hearted builder who would even try to be reasonable in his charges.

Our house wasn't, by the way, anything like the fish man's. It wasn't a plaster house with light green blinds, with half-moons cut in them. It seemed to our architect (and to me too, as soon as he suggested it) that the most New

England type of house possible—flat-faced, clapboarded, painted white, a hall in the centre and a room on each side, would fit in with those apple-trees better than anything quaint or original. Oh, ours was just the housiest house possible, with nothing odd about it like oriel windows, or diamond trellises, or unexpected bays and swells.

The first day the plans arrived I did some measuring, and cut out of cardboard on the same scale as the plans, patterns of our furniture. That night Will and I moved into our paper house, shoving the furniture around the rooms with lightning speed, shifting hall-clocks, davenports, and grand pianos from parlour to bedroom with surprising little effort. Why, I rearranged my rooms time and time again before I ever stepped foot in them. If you'll believe me, I made a complete new bedroom set for the nursery, and a little crib which I placed between the windows, when the real room was only a square block of air above the apple-trees.

You can imagine how excited we were when at the end of three years we finally signed the contract with McManus & Mann, Contractors and Builders. We were simply house-crazy by that time. I wanted to celebrate the important occasion somehow, so I went down to Mr. McManus's office and ordered several bundles of six-foot-length laths, such as are used in plastering a room, to be sent up to our lot on Saturday morning. Will and I always spend Saturday afternoons together, and, provided with the roll of plans, a yard-stick, a hatchet and my lunch-basket packed with tea and sandwiches, we started out about two P. M. to lay out our house, life size, with the laths on the very spot where it was so soon now to stand. By five o'clock I was serving tea before the fireplace in the living-room, and apple-blossom petals were blowing through the kitchen and hall partitions into the very cream-pitcher by my side.

It was just when the water over my alcohol stove had begun to boil that our first guests arrived. Dr. Van Breeze is married now, and his wife, Alice, and I are very good friends. For the three years that Will and I had been working on house-plans she had followed the changes in them as if they were hers. So I 'phoned her that I should be delighted if she and George (George is Dr. Van Breeze) would take tea with us Saturday afternoon at four-thirty in our new house. When they appeared in their touring-car at the foot of our hill, I saw that dear Dr. Graham and Mrs. Graham were in the back seat, and I dashed through the living-room wall and down to the road to meet them. Ten minutes later the Omsteds arrived strolling up the hill from their house which is the nearest one to ours. Will had already arranged boulders for chairs around the fireplace, and my dainty little sandwiches and tiny cream puffs were laid out neatly on plates covered with fresh napkins. The tea was hot and strong and fragrant; the decorations of six trees full of apple-blossoms, lovely to behold; the illumination of a pink and blue sunset, reflected in the lake below, more beautiful than a hundred electric lights.

After we had drank tea and eaten the last cream puff, I invited my guests to inspect the house. Every one entered into my little game. Dr. Omsted made us all respect the partitions as if they existed; George Van Breeze insisted on walking up the front stairs; and dear Dr. Graham found a grasshopper somewhere and exclaimed chuckling, "Oh, my dear Pandora" (he still calls me that silly name), "what of your housekeeping? I saw dozens of these in your pantry!"

Oh, it was just the nicest house-warming in the world. I like every one of Will's friends; they may be awfully learned, but they seem just plain natural and unpretentious to me. They stayed until nearly six o'clock. We waved them good-bye from our front door. When they all had disappeared over the brow of the hill, Will drew me into our hall and kissed me, just as if there had really been walls. Then he came into the living-room and helped me clear up.

I haven't mentioned yet the thorn I keep hidden in my heart and carry everywhere I go. I don't like to talk of it because Will doesn't like to have me, but it robs every joy I have of completeness. As Will and I strolled home that night perhaps we ought to have been very happy. We had the best and pleasantest friends in the world—I granted it; ground for our dream-house was to be broken on Monday morning; we had been married four years, and loved each other more than ever.

"Oh, Will, four years—four long years," I exclaimed, and sighed.

"Pshaw," he replied, and changed the subject.

Ever since Madge's little baby was born, I've wanted one of my own. I didn't care before that, but when I held the warm little thing in my arms for minutes at a time, dressed it, cared for it when the nurse was out, and listened to its poor pitiful little cry in the middle of the night, something seemed to spring open in me that I can't close.

I want a little daughter-companion of my very own! I want to wash her, and dress her and take her out with me. I want her to sit with me rainy afternoons in her little rocking-chair and play while I sew. I want her to tell me all her secrets, and I want to give her all the love, all the good times and pretty things a little girl wants. When Madge brings over her Marjorie, and I see her clinging to her mother's knee when I come into the room, I'd give anything in the world to have some little girl cling to *me* like that! Will has always loved children; he has wanted them even longer than I, though he never told me. Will affects indifference on the subject, but he doesn't deceive me in the least. I know the lurking hunger is always in his heart as it is in mine.

Why I was so especially down-hearted to-night as we walked home from our tea-party on the hilltop was on account of a remark of Alice Van Breeze's thrown off in her quick, careless fashion. I think Will kissed me in the hall to soothe a little of the hurt of Alice's unconscious words. People who have babies of their own don't guess how many times they stab those who haven't.

"What an ideal place this is for children!" Alice had exclaimed. "Such air! Such sunshine! If you don't mind, Lucy," she had caught herself up, "I shall bring Junior up here often to get some tan in your adorable garden."

"Do," I had said, looking away.

"How is the little chap?" Will had asked her kindly. Will can't even talk about a child without a little note of tenderness in his tone.

"Oh, he's perfect!" Alice had laughed. "The very world revolves about him. Why, we're prouder of that little bundle of bones and flesh than of his father's latest book!"

I didn't look at Will and Will didn't look at me. We're so filled with pity for each other at such moments (and there are many of them) that we can't bear to gaze upon the hurt look in the other's face.

Our whole sad little story can be traced in our house-plans. When we first decided to build, we talked bravely *then* about the nursery on the sunny side; it looked out towards the south and east; it was large and airy, with four big windows, and a fireplace for chilly nights. When the first sketches arrived the room was plainly labelled in printed letters, and I remember that the mere word gave me a queer thrill of joy. I had, as you know, immediately made patterns of the nursery furniture, placed the paper crib in position, and estimated the number of steps from my bed to the baby's. I had had it beautifully planned for contagious diseases: Will could move into the guest-room, and I and the sick children could be absolutely isolated from the rest of the house, in two lovely rooms with a bathroom of our own. But I needn't have planned on children's contagious diseases. There will never be any little children with measles, or chicken-pox, or whooping-cough in our house, to take care of. I am sure of it now. On the last roll of plans which our architect submitted to us the word printed across the face of the southeast room had been changed from Nursery to Chamber! I think Will must have requested it and I knew then with awful finality that even Will had given up hope. I never asked how or why the room's name had been changed. I simply understood without asking and cried it out by myself in my room. The next day I burned the nursery paper furniture—the crib, the folding yard, the toy-case like Edith's—in the kitchen stove, with a pang as big as if they had been real.

After that I called the southeast chamber, "Ruth's room." I had always secretly hoped that Ruth would live with me if ever I had a house of my own.

I had hoped it ever since Alec had married Edith. It hadn't come to pass—it never would. Ruth is so fastidious. But she has spent a night with me very often so I decided to make over the room that no little child seemed to want to occupy, for my only sister. It really was easier to refer to the room as Ruth's. I was glad, after the first shock, that Will had made the change. The evident question and pity in people's eyes when we had called it by its old name had become unpleasant for both Will and me.

I grew very philosophical about my disappointment as time went on. I didn't mean to allow it to shadow my whole life. There was lots else to be thankful for. But that night after our little tea-party my philosophy seemed to leave me. It always does when I'm a little tired and need it most. I couldn't keep up any kind of conversation at dinner that night. I tried, but I couldn't. My thoughts got to travelling the wellworn path that they will stray away to every once in a while in spite of me, and it's always Will who comes to my rescue and pulls them back on to safe sure ground, before they lose themselves in utter dejection.

"Let's play some cribbage!" he suggested lightly after dinner.

I laid down my useless embroidery and listlessly drew up to the table. We played three games without an interruption. I won them all. Then just as Will was dealing for a fourth game I had to get out my handkerchief and wipe my eyes.

"Oh, my dear girl!" said Will accusingly.

"I know it, but I can't help it!" I replied. "It seems *too* cruel! I simply can't bear not to use the room we built the house around. I wish we could find a little child somewhere that we could—borrow. You see, Will, a woman, to be really happy, seems to require a family to take care of, unless she's a genius—an artist or a poet, or something like that, which I'm not. Why, Will," I broke out, "I'm getting so I don't like to hear about other people's children—or see them or want them around. When Alice spoke about bringing her baby into my garden it seemed as if I'd simply have to find *somewhere* a little creature of our own to play with the flowers I've planted. Don't I *know* it's a perfect place for children? Don't I know it? And does she think we also wouldn't be prouder of a little child than of your discoveries? Oh, Will, I know how disappointed you are. You won't say it but I know it's awfully hard for you too."

"Nonsense," Will scoffed. "What's hard about it? I've got you, haven't I? You and I are the two best children at playing games in a garden that *I* ever saw. *I'm* perfectly satisfied. Come ahead, cut the cards. I'm about to beat you now at five games of crib."

I shook my head and looked away.

"You're mistaken," Will went on, "if you think *I'm* envying anybody anything. I've yet to meet two people happier than we. Children are pleasant enough incidents in life," Will went on, "but don't you draw any wrong conclusions that happiness is dependent on them. It isn't. Look at Dr. and Mrs. Graham. They never had any, and two more congenial, more contented, happier people never existed—except perhaps ourselves. Dr. Graham has too much sound thought to allow the denial of any *one* of the supposed blessings of life to disturb his peace. And so have we, Bobbie, don't you think? Some of the very best people in the world, some of those who have accomplished the most effective work, never had children. It isn't the first question we ask about a great man or a good woman. I might have reason to complain if I didn't have my health or a good sound mind, or if after these few precious years together, I lost *you*. But as it is—well, please don't ever say again, young lady, that our present conditions are hard for me. Hard—Nonsense!"

Dear Will! I'd heard this same little speech of his dozens of times before. When he tries so hard to cheer me it seems too bad not to respond; so I smiled now.

"Will Maynard," I said, "you don't deceive me for one minute by all this talk! Don't think you do! *I* know—*I* understand. But I'll say this—and I've said it a hundred times before—you certainly *are* the kindest man I ever knew."

"Bosh!" he laughed.

"Yes, you are—yes, you are. And I guess if I've got you I'd better not complain." I put away my handkerchief. "It's all over now," I announced, "and I'm ready to beat you at those five games of crib."

He dealt the cards and for five minutes we played in earnest; then suddenly Will reached across and took my hand.

"Who says you and I aren't perfectly happy?" he asked.

CHAPTER XXII

IT wasn't a week after that Sunday afternoon of ours on our darling hilltop that I received a letter from Ruth announcing her intention of paying me a visit. I was amazed.

Ruth usually prefers to visit at houses where she can stay in bed until ten o'clock in the morning and sink luxuriously into an upholstered limousine fitted up with plum-coloured cushions and a bunch of fresh flowers, every time she goes out of doors. She isn't the type who likes making her own bed and helping with the dishes—not that I require such toll from a guest; but you know our house has only one bathroom and Ruth says a tin tub always looks greasy. She says that black walnut furniture has a depressing effect on her, and assures me that she doesn't dare turn over in my guest-room bed for fear the head of the thing—a big towering mass of black walnut blocks and turrets—will fall down on top of her in the night. Ruth suffered the hardships of my establishment only when it was necessary. Whenever a taxicab did draw up to my door and deposit my dressy sister for the night, I knew that it was because she had an early appointment with her tailor the next morning, or had missed the last Hilton Express. I didn't remember that Ruth had ever spent a single night under my roof for the mere friendliness or sisterly love of sleeping between my embroidered sheets. Ruth has a very sensitive temperament—so sensitive that certain combinations of colour will affect her spirits. My guest-room has mustard-coloured walls with reddish fleur-de-lis.

Ruth is an extraordinary girl. She doesn't seem a bit like a Vars. We're such a conventional and just-what-you-would-expect kind of family. Ruth contrives somehow to shroud herself in a veil of mystery and create an impression everywhere she goes. I guess she's the most discussed girl in all Hilton. She affects heliotrope shades in her clothes, combining several tones in one gown, and wears large, round, floppy hats. She always manages to select big stagy chairs to sit in, that set her off as if she were a portrait. I have to pinch myself every once in a while to make sure she isn't a foreign adventuress of some kind with an exciting past, instead of just my common ordinary little sister Ruthie. She has the queerest ideas on life and love that I ever heard talked outside of a book, and she preaches them too. I don't know how she dares; but somehow a little wickedness, a little cynicism, from so very pretty a girl seems simply to add to her piquancy and charm. Ruth dabbles in every artistic line that exists—sings with the finish of a prima-donna and loves to improvise by the hour on the big drawing-room piano at home, while some love-lorn suitor sits in silence in the half-dark and worships. She's clever at drawing—has designed book-plates for all her friends, besides having modelled in bas-relief several of their portraits in clay. She writes poetry too.

She never read any of it to *me*; I suppose I'm not sympathetic enough for it; but I got hold of some of her papers once and spent a whole hour with them. I never knew till then what deep ideas Ruth really has! I copied several of the verses and Bob Jennings, who is an instructor in English at the university down here, said they were "full of promise."

When Ruth's letter arrived announcing her proposed visit, my only sorrow lay in the fact that her room in the new house wasn't ready. I was going to have it papered in lavender chambray and had already selected a wisteria design in cretonne for the hangings. It was going to be the most artistic room in the house. I wasn't going to hang a single picture on the walls (no pictures is Ruth's latest fad) and the furniture was going to be plain colonial mahogany. It's queer how all the family pay homage to Ruth. She's younger than I, by three years, but I've always longed for her approval. I used to criticise her extravagance, and tell her she was vain and selfish, but down in the bottom of my heart I've always thought Ruth was wonderful. Will makes fun of me for laying out my best linen every time Ruth comes to see us. It *is* foolish, but I don't want Ruth to think that I don't possess any of the fine points of the people she most admires. I began to plan to make her first real visit with me as much of a success as I knew how. Ruth likes to have parties planned ahead for her, so I decided to invite the Van Breezes to dinner one night, and Bob Jennings another.

Bob is a perfectly splendid young man and awfully good-looking. I was sorry that Ruth had to meet him for the first time in the unkind surroundings of our house. Setting, background, atmosphere, influence her so much. If she sees a man for the first time in company with black walnut and marble-topped tables, she is apt to think him as offensively old-fashioned as the furniture. And I did want to prove to Ruth that there existed a decent man with several degrees to his name, who knew how to dress properly for dinner and converse intelligently on the latest opera.

Will and I both met Ruth at the station when she arrived. She kissed me and gave both her hands to Will in her most engaging manner. She presented him later with three trunk checks. I was flattered. I was glad that there happened to be several teas on hand, and a musicale at the Omsted's that week. I would show Ruth that all our friends didn't live in ugly brown French-roofed houses, and that she hadn't brought all her pretty gowns to my house in vain.

But here I was disappointed. After dinner Ruth announced, "Oh, no; I couldn't. Don't make any engagements for me, please. My time won't be my own while I'm here. I didn't mention in my letter that Breck Sewall is coming up from New York to-morrow. He has invited me to several things in town. I thought it would be simpler for me to spend my nights here, than to go back so many times to Hilton."

I didn't say a word, but my heart skipped a beat, I think. I had thought the affair with Breck Sewall had blown over. The Sewalls haven't occupied their summer place near Hilton for three years. It hadn't occurred to me that Ruth's visit could have any possible connection with Breck Sewall. Ruth knew that Will and I disapprove of him; she knew the sound of his very name was unwelcome in our house. I felt like telling Ruth to go upstairs, lock up her precious trunks, and go home. Once I would have spat out something nasty to my sister about accepting attentions from a man she knew was not nice, but now I was too anxious to become her friend to quarrel with her on the first night she arrived. I had learned that the safest course for me to follow was simply not to oppose Ruth in anything.

It was Will, turning from fastening the windows, who blurted out bluntly, "Are you still keeping up your connections with that man?"

Ruth smiled, raising her eyebrows a little, and then folded her hands behind her head, her pretty arms bare to the elbows.

"Don't you approve of him, brother William?" she inquired archly as if she didn't care a straw whether he did or not.

"Do *you*?" asked Will.

Ruth laughed an amused, silvery laugh and replied lightly, "I am engaged to be married to Breck Sewall, I suppose, if that answers you."

Will didn't say a word for a minute. Then, "I am sorry to hear that," he replied shortly.

"Really?" smiled Ruth. "Breck and I shall certainly miss your blessing, William." She always calls him William when she's making fun of him. I don't see how she dares to mock a man so much wiser and older than she, but Ruth would deride the President of the United States if he interfered with her little schemes.

Will replied; "You're too fine a girl to make such a mistake, Ruth."

She rippled into another laugh and my cheeks grew warm with indignation. She leaned forward and selected a chocolate-cream from a box of candy on the table.

"That's a very prettily veiled compliment, William, and I thank you," she said. She nibbled a bit of her candy as she spoke.

She was awfully exasperating, sitting there so gay and unconcerned. Will stepped up to her chair and I could tell from his voice that he was angry.

"I know all about Breck Sewall," he said. "He's not the kind of man for any nice girl to associate with. He spent a year at this university. He was expelled, not only because he could not keep up in his courses, not only because he was brought home time and time again too disgustingly drunk to stand alone, not only because of these things, but because of another and more disreputable affair. I think you ought to know about it before this goes any further. It was an affair with a girl. There was no doubt about it. He acknowledged the whole thing. Why, Ruth, he isn't the kind of man for you even to speak to!" Will said. "Sometime I will tell you the whole story—sometime—if it's necessary."

Ruth took another bite of her chocolate-cream.

"Do *now*," she smiled, "if it amuses you. But it will be no news to *me*. I know all about that college affair of Breck's. He has told me the whole story himself. I know the girl's name and all the particulars. Breck isn't afraid to tell me the truth. Nothing in the world shocks me, you know," she announced with bravado. "Did you think I was so narrow-minded and hemmed in by prejudice not to overlook the follies a man may have committed when he was hardly more than a boy? I don't care what Breck did before he knew me. What other awful news have you to break to me, William?" Ruth inquired sweetly.

Will stared at Ruth as if she were something he never knew existed.

"Nothing else," he said shortly, "if that isn't sufficient."

There was an uncomfortable silence. My sister must have felt a little uneasy under the gaze of Will's astonished eyes; for when she had finished her candy, daintily touched her lips with her bit of a white handkerchief, tucked it away, and spoke again, her manner towards him had changed.

"Will," she said, "I'm so different from any one you ever knew that you can't understand me, can you? Now I know you told me just now about that little unfortunate affair of Breck's because you want me to be happy. And I do appreciate your interest in me—I do really. Of course I have no mother," she put in quite tragically; "I never had. Perhaps that is why I am so different from other girls. I'm not shocked at the things young girls are brought up to be shocked at. I don't tremble at the sound of unadulterated truth and bare facts. I am aware of it. I am not living under the false illusion that the man I am to marry is perfect. I know he isn't, and I am content. Why, the very qualities I require in a man preclude at least a few of the supposed virtues. Perhaps, Will," said Ruth patronisingly, "you do not understand a man of Breck's tempestuous nature. *You're* so scientific. It's easy for you to stay within the narrow path. But you shouldn't be severe on others."

"Do you love Breck Sewall?" asked Will point-blank.

"Oh, *love*!" Ruth shrugged her shoulders. "Love would be the last thing I would marry a man for. I'm not as short-sighted as that. Love may last a year, or two perhaps, but it is not enduring. I marry for sounder reasons than love. You must know that the Sewalls are immensely wealthy. Their position is as established as royalty in England. Oh, you see," laughed Ruth, standing up and walking over toward the bookcase, "how dreadfully worldly and wicked I am! Have you La Rochefoucauld? Let me read you a little saying of his."

"No, not dreadfully worldly—not dreadfully wicked, Ruth," said Will; "only dreadfully young, I think."

Ruth hates to be accused of youth.

"But old enough to marry whom I please, William, perhaps," she flashed.

"Oh," scoffed Will, "that doesn't require much age, nor much wisdom. You are young enough to think it rather clever and smart to scorn virtue, make fun of love, and pretend to marry a man for his wealth and position. It sounds so bookish and so sophisticated!"

Ruth would not have deigned to respond to such an insulting assault as that if I had made it, but to Will she replied, "You're mistaken there. I've thought and read on this subject. I'm not so young as you think." She walked over to the mantel and leaned her back against the white marble, then folding her arms across her chest, like a judging goddess, she continued: "I believe, and several people of reputation agree with me, that the most important thing to consult in considering marriage is one's temperament. Ask yourself what your tastes are and then see if the new life will gratify them. Temperament never changes. If you love music when you are twenty, you will love it when you are forty. Well, I have studied my nature very closely. I know what pleases it. I know what annoys and disturbs it. I'm different from the others in our family. I often wonder from whom I inherit my peculiarities. I love beautiful music, beautiful pictures, soft rugs, fine furniture, delicate lace at the windows. Low, artistic lamp-light, the comings and goings of soft-footed unobtrusive servants, a dinner perfectly served, exquisite china, old silver, exclusive people—all such things give me actual physical pleasure. I enjoy position and influence. My nature grows and expands under recognition. It dries up and dies under slight and disregard. The people I envy most in the world are those who are born in high positions. I can't alter my birth, but I have been invited to become a member of a prominent and influential family, and as one of that family I shall be invited and received everywhere, without any of the humiliating striving. I'm proud, you know. I despise toadying. I don't want to work for social position. I want it placed upon me, like a king his crown. Why, Will, Breck Sewall can supply my nature with everything it demands. Why shouldn't I marry him?"

"Can Breck supply your intellect with what it demands?" asked Will.

Ruth laughed good-naturedly.

"Poor Breck! Poor old maligned Breck! He isn't exactly intellectual, I agree, but don't you worry, Will, I shall find congenial minds enough in his circle. The Sewalls entertain all sorts of interesting professional people—the top-notchers, I mean. My intellect won't suffer. Where is the woman, anyhow, who discusses her soul with her husband? How can a woman read poetry with a man who has just been grumbling at the price of her prettiest gown?" Ruth shuddered. "No, no! Please! I prefer not. But I shan't be lonely. Never fear." She gave Will a meaning look from beneath her eyebrows and added in a sort of bold, daring way, "There will be some one."

I don't know why Ruth loves to preach such wickedness. She doesn't mean half she says. I waited for the walls to fall. Will abhors married women who attempt to flirt with other men. Ruth waited too for the clap of thunder she thought must follow her startling implication. But when Will spoke there wasn't a trace of anger in his voice—just disgust—just plain unflattering disgust. "Come, Lucy," he said to me; "I've had about enough of this. Let's go upstairs to bed."

The Sewalls are the high-muck-a-mucks of the Hilton summer colony. They're New York people and their place, just outside Hilton, reminds me of the castles that give distinction to so many otherwise nondescript little towns in Europe—not in age, for I can remember when the Sewalls' place was rough cow-pasture land, but in its relation to the town and the surrounding country. It's Hilton's show-place. We always point it out to strangers when we take them on their first drive. The wrought-iron gates cost five thousand dollars; the distance around the house and adjoining buildings added together measures half a mile; the big entrance hall, we state (and we're proud of our knowledge too) is hung with old tapestries and furnished in carved English oak.

After Mrs. F. Rockridge Sewall's advent, there was established among the Hilton summer colonists a new law of society. You were either of the elect or of the rejected; you were either entertained by Mrs. F. Rockridge Sewall or you were an ignominious nobody. There existed no self-respecting middle position in Hilton after Mrs. Sewall arrived in mid-July with her retinue of some twenty-odd servants, her four or five automobiles, and half-dozen hunters. Mrs. Sewall was for some time a very disturbing factor in Edith's life. The lights of a ballroom, the sound of dance-music, however lovely they may be, are absolutely irritating to my sister-in-law, if seen and heard from the outside. It took two long discouraging seasons of scheming, manipulating, and rather bold attacking, before Edith gained the proper kind of entrance to the hallowed ground inside those five-thousand-dollar wrought-iron gates. It was really due to Ruth that she was admitted then. Young Breckenridge Sewall had chanced to see a stunning young creature in lavender and grey at a garden-party at Mrs. Leonard Jackson's, one afternoon late in August, during his mother's second season at Grassmere, the name of their place in Hilton. He had only to see Ruth once to beg for an introduction. That is the way it is with every man across whose field of vision my sister steps. I think that Ruth is the loveliest production that Hilton, or Hilton's environs, ever produced; and Breckenridge Sewall thought so too. Three weeks after that introduction at Mrs. Leonard Jackson's Ruth rushed in upon Edith one Friday noon and announced, "I'm invited to a house-party at the Sewalls'! One of the out-of-town guests has disappointed Mrs. Sewall at the last moment and Breck wants me to fill in!" Before the Sewalls went back to New York that fall, Ruth was the most distinguished young lady in all Hilton. She was pointed out everywhere she went as the girl to whom Breck Sewall was paying such marked attention; she burst into notoriety; and Edith's position was at last made secure. Trust Edith to squeeze into the limelight along with Ruth. I don't know how my sister-in-law manages such things but it was clear sailing for her after Breck's discovery.

That man rushed Ruth for two years and a half before there was any word from my sister about an engagement. During the summer he used to call on Ruth about six evenings a week, and as Edith made us all go upstairs (this was before I was married) on the nights that Breck came, by nine o'clock, it got to be a nuisance. At first I remember we were all a little flattered by the young millionaire's attention to our pretty Ruth and even I used to feel a thrill of pride at the thought of such a brilliant match in our quiet midst.

Breck didn't propose to Ruth till after I was married. She came in from a long motor run one Sunday in July, when Will and I happened to be in Hilton, and told us the news before she even took off her hat. I remember it very well for there followed one of our dreadful family discussions. By that time Will and I, and Alec too, had begun to feel a little doubt as to Breck's desirability. We had always heard rumours about his habits, but Edith prized Breck's attentions to Ruth so highly, that Alec had neglected a thorough investigation. He thought that Breck didn't intend to marry Ruth anyway, called it a summer affair and trusted that time would cure them both of their fancy. So when Will came out with a few telling facts detrimental to Breck Sewall's character, Edith was simply furious. She told me that I shouldn't come back meddling after I was married. Ruth loved Breck Sewall—she was sure of it; we might be the cause of wrecking the child's happiness for life if we interfered. Alec looked awfully distressed as we talked but he didn't rise up in indignation, stampede as he should have, and swear that no sister of his should ever marry a man with Breck Sewall's reputation, so long as he lived. Alec is awfully ineffectual when Edith is around.

I don't know how it all would have come out, if Mrs. Sewall hadn't interrupted matters. Suddenly, right in the midst of the thickest of our discussion, three or four days after Ruth's announcement, Mrs. Sewall decided to go abroad. She closed up her summer mansion, mid-season though it was, barred the windows, locked the gates, and sailed away to Europe, Breck and all. She didn't come back for two years, and even then she didn't come back to Hilton. The excitement about Breck and Ruth died down like fire, and about as suddenly. He didn't even write to Ruth after three or four months, and just before Ruth came down to visit me and announced her startling piece of news, I had read that Breckenridge Sewall was reported engaged to his cousin, Miss Gale somebody or other, a débutante of last season.

Ruth's news was an awful shock to me. I knew without being told how jubilant Edith would be, how helpless Alec in the face of what seemed to both the women of his household such a brilliant victory. I didn't know what to do. It didn't seem as if I could stand by and watch my own sister marry the kind of man Will said that Breck Sewall was. I lay awake a long while that night after Ruth's arrival at our house, wondering what under heaven I, whose ideas on life my sister considered so provincial—what there was that *I* might do to swerve her from her purpose.

I could hope for no help from Will. Ruth had thrown him utterly out of sympathy with her. He washed his hands of the whole affair; he told me so that night when we came upstairs to bed, and I knew by his manner to my sister the next morning at breakfast, courteous enough though it was, in what contempt he held her. I told Will I couldn't send Ruth back to Hilton, and, as distasteful as I knew Breck Sewall's coming to our door would be to him, I hoped he would let me keep Ruth with me as long as she would stay. I didn't have any plan, any deep-laid scheme. It simply seemed to me that it must have been an act of heaven that Ruth had been sent to me during such a critical period in her history, and I didn't want to fly in the face of Providence.

I began by being just as nice and kind to her as I knew how. I didn't offer one word of opposition; I didn't advise; I didn't criticise; I appeared even to welcome her suitor when he first arrived to carry my sister in town to dinner and the theatre; I chatted with him pleasantly while she put on her party coat upstairs. I served Ruth breakfasts in bed at eleven A. M.; and admired and praised all her gowns and lovely fol-de-rols as she dressed every afternoon in preparation for her lover.

For five days Ruth blandly carried on her love-affair in our house, going and coming at her own sweet time, accepting our hospitality as a matter of course, while she bestowed her rarest smiles upon a man whom she knew Will considered disreputable and whom therefore I could not approve of. For five days she lunched, motored, and dined with Breck Sewall, and in between times talked with him over the 'phone for twenty-minute periods. I despaired. I didn't see any way out, and as the days went on and the house became more and more perfumed by Breck Sewall's roses and violets and valley-lilies, I began to give up hope.

On the sixth day I received a letter from Edith:

> "Ruth would go down to you. I told her that neither you nor Will liked Breck Sewall and it wouldn't be a bit pleasant. Alec and I are both very much pleased about the engagement, because Ruth really loves Breck Sewall with all her heart, and since his renewed attentions, the dear girl has been simply radiant. I write this because I'm afraid that you'll try to poison Ruth's mind against the man she loves. We all want her to be happy, I'm sure, and I think you would assume a lot of responsibility in trying to stop a girl from marrying the only man she ever has cared for or ever will. She likes to boast that she doesn't love Breck. It's pose. I, who have been with Ruth so intimately for so long, know she is *wild* about Breck Sewall, and loves him madly. Don't meddle with it, Bobbie. I'd hate to be to blame for *my* sister's broken heart."

That letter of Edith's set me to thinking. It hadn't occurred to me that Ruth was simply *pretending* to marry for position. I didn't think that such a repulsive creature as Breck Sewall could inspire anything so divine as love in my sister's heart. And yet, perhaps—how did I know (I understand Ruth so little anyway)—how did I know—perhaps Edith was right. Perhaps, after all, Ruth was simply trying to conceal her love by contempt and scorn of it. It wouldn't have made any difference as to my opposition, but it would have cleared Ruth of unworthy motives, at any rate. I was determined to find out.

She had told me when she left the house at three that afternoon that she and Breck were going to motor to somebody's place on the north shore and would not be back until late in the evening. It was eleven-thirty when I finally heard Breck Sewall fumbling with the lock and a minute later I caught the odour of his cigarette, as I lay waiting for it in bed. I knew then that he and Ruth were established in the living-room for their usual half-hour alone before he bade her good-night. I don't suppose it was a very honourable thing to do, but after about five minutes I got up, put on a wrapper, and crawled quietly down to the landing, stepping over the third step which creaks awfully. It was pitch dark in the corner near the wall; there was no danger of being seen from below; and I stood perfectly still, eavesdropping for all I was worth. Ruth had lit one dim burner by the piano and from my balcony I could plainly see Breck Sewall, low as the light was, ensconced in a corner of our davenport-sofa.

CHAPTER XXIII

HE was making himself entirely at home. He had crossed his feet and had placed them square in the middle of the mahogany seat of my nice little Windsor chair, which he had drawn up in front of him. His toes pointed to the ceiling; his cigarette pointed there too; for he had comfortably pillowed his greasy old head (Breck's hair is jet black and always looks as if it was wet) on the top of the low back of the sofa. The smoke that he blew at times from his nose went straight up like smoke from a chimney on a windless day. I didn't think it was a very pretty attitude for a man to assume in the presence of a young lady. His hands were stuffed in his trousers pockets, and when he spoke the only trouble he went to was to roll his head in Ruth's direction. He's anything but good-looking. He has half-closed eyes like a Chinaman's, and a yellow, unpleasant complexion.

"Come on over here," I heard him say in that kind of guttural voice a man uses when he tries to talk with a cigarette in his mouth, and I saw him shift up one shoulder to motion Ruth to sit down beside him.

I couldn't see my sister but I heard her reply. "I don't feel like it to-night, Breck," she said.

Breck smoked in silence for half a minute, then he asked, removing his cigarette, "Say, what's the matter with you to-night? Are you back again on that old subject which your precious saint of a professor here raised up out of the past? Haven't I explained that to you a dozen times?"

"I wish you wouldn't refer to members of my family in such a way," replied Ruth. "It isn't respectful to me. You're not marrying beneath you, as your manner sometimes seems to imply. My brother-in-law whom you choose to call a saint is a noted man, if you only read enough to know it, Breck. Oh, no, I'm not thinking about that college affair of yours. I'm not a jealous kind of girl. You know that."

"Well, what is it then? It gets *me* what I've done to deserve such treatment. Weren't they the right kind of flowers?"

"Don't be absurd, Breck. As if ornaments or flowers were what I required! I'll tell you what's the matter, if you want to know," said Ruth. "It's simply this: I don't think you're treating your engagement with proper respect. It seems out-of-order to me that I should have told my family about our intentions before you have told yours. It isn't a bit as it should be. I hate even to speak about so delicate a thing—but, Breck, why hasn't your mother written to me? Why hasn't she set a day for me to come and see her? Here *my* family are all recognising *you* as a future member of their group, while your family haven't even as much as made a sign."

"Oh, now, now," replied Breck soothingly. "That's it, is it? Don't you worry, little one. The mater will come around, all right. Give her time. For my part, though, I'd rather step into the Little Church Around the Corner and get it over with in a swoop."

If Ruth was sitting down, I'll wager she stood up now. Her reply came like lightning.

"Breck Sewall," she exclaimed, "that's the third time in a week that you've suggested eloping to me! I wish you'd stop it. It is absolutely insulting!"

Breck looked up surprised.

"Insulting?" he repeated dazed.

"Exactly. Insulting," went on Ruth in hot haste. "I'm not a servant-girl. I require all the proprieties that exist, understand. Why," she added, "until your mother recognises me publicly as your fiancée, I'll never marry you as long as I live!" She stopped suddenly. I knew she was very angry, for Ruth.

Breck chuckled in a horrid insulting sort of way, and lay down his cigarette.

"Say," he broke out, putting his feet down on the floor, leaning forward with his elbows on his knees and rubbing his two hands together, "say, you're simply stunning when you're mad." He was looking at Ruth as if he'd like to gobble her up. "You're glorious! You're great! Most of 'em cry and make sights of themselves, but you—you—" He got up. He strode over to Ruth. I suppose she was simply too stunning, too glorious, too great to resist. I don't know. The portière hid her and I was glad of it. I shouldn't enjoy seeing Breck Sewall as much as lay a finger on my sister. I closed my eyes and waited. I should have been afraid of a man like that, myself, but I suppose Ruth suffered herself to be kissed by him with the indifference that she offers her cheek for the same caress to a girl. When she spoke again her anger seemed to have spent itself.

"You're very silly, Breck," she said.

"And you—you're as cold as a little fish," he replied as tenderly as he knew how. I really think he loved Ruth, though I was convinced that she didn't have an emotion of any kind for him. "But I'll wake you up, you little marble statue," he went on. "I'll make you care for me. Women are all alike. See if I don't."

"It's more important," I heard Ruth reply, "to make your mother care for me. You see, Breck, if we hope to get married in October you had better tell her your news as soon as possible. Why not to-night when you go back to the hotel? She has been here now three days with you and if she wants me to call I can go to-morrow, or the next day, before I go home. You say she came on so as to make arrangements to open Grassmere this year. Certainly the engagement must be announced immediately, so that I shall be received by your mother properly this summer."

"You seem to care more about my mother than about me," objected Ruth's lover.

Ruth laughed prettily.

"Poor abused creature!" she mocked. "Poor sulky boy! If I showed my feelings for you, Breck, all the time, you wouldn't care for me half so much. I understand men. You call me a little fish and that's what I am—always slipping out of your fingers, always evading capture, for I know that once a man gets his fish and puts it in his little basket, the cat can eat it then for all he cares."

"You're a clever little piece," said Breck admiringly. "Half the time I don't know what you're driving at."

Just here I saw Ruth walk over to the table and pick up Breck's gold cigarette box. I don't remember that I have ever been so shocked in my life as when, staring like a cat out of my dark corner, I saw my sister—my own little sister Ruth, over whose bed hung the pure, clean-cut profile of my mother, in whose heart must dwell the memory of the best, the noblest, the finest father a girl ever had—select a cigarette, light it, and actually place it between her lovely lips! I wanted to call out, "Ruth Chenery Vars, what are you doing? Have you lost your mind? Are you crazy?" I saw her sit down on the corner of the sofa that Breck had left empty and lean her head back in much the same luxurious fashion. I saw her blow a fine little ribbon of smoke up to the ceiling. I waited until I saw Breck cross the room to her side, and then, too sick to endure the awful spectacle another instant, I turned and groped my way upstairs to bed.

I couldn't sleep for hours and hours. I turned over at intervals of four to eight minutes, until it began to grow light. I may have dropped off into semi-consciousness. I don't know. Anyhow my dreams were one continuous nightmare of my waking vision. Had it been Ruth whom I had seen with my own eyes smoking a cigarette in my living-room? Had it been my own little sister? Had she done it before? Did she do it often? If I had been anxious to save Ruth from Breck before my horrible discovery, now I was determined. She shouldn't share such a life as his. She shouldn't! She shouldn't! I waited impatiently for the morning light. I was eager to be about my undertaking. I had a disagreeable task before me, and haunted by the dread of it, very much as we are visited by the fear of an operation that must be undergone, I wanted to get it over with and out of the way as soon as possible.

After Will had left for the university and I, as usual, had carried the breakfast-tray to Ruth (lying as sweet and fresh as a carnation in her white sheets—you would never have dreamed she had ever tasted a cigarette) I went upstairs to my room, put on my best eighty-five-dollar Boston tailor-made suit, and grimly set out for town.

It was ten-thirty when I sent up my name to Mrs. F. Rockridge Sewall at the Hotel St. Mary, where I knew Breck had been stopping since his arrival in town. The clerk behind the yellow onyx counter that enclosed the office of this exclusive hotel, had informed me that Mrs. Sewall had just breakfasted and therefore could assure me that she was in. He asked for my card and summoned a bell-boy. I withdrew to the rose-brocade writing-room at the left, and five minutes later into the envelope in which I placed my card I slipped a note that read something like this:

> "*My dear Mrs. Sewall,*
>
> "It occurs to me that you may not remember who I am from my card, or if so, be quite at a loss to know what prompts this call. I have come to consult with you on a matter that concerns your son, and would be greatly obliged if you will see me.
>
> "LUCY MAYNARD."

I must confess my heart acted like a trip-hammer, as I waited for my answer. I experienced a moment of misgiving and apprehension, as I gazed at the pattern of the rose brocade on the walls. I had not confided to Will my intention of a consultation with Mrs. Sewall, and just for a moment as I sat there on the edge of a formal little gilt-trimmed chair, I wondered if my intuitions were leading me into a dreadful social blunder.

"She will see you; suite thirty-three. The boy will show you up," suddenly broke in on my reflections, and in another moment I was silently shooting up the elevator shaft, gazing at a row of brass buttons on the bell-boy's coat and estimating their number, to keep myself calm.

The room into which I was conducted was empty when I entered it—a typical hotel-suite drawing-room, furnished with elaborate and very puffy looking stuffed furniture. I chose the only straight chair in the room, and sat down and waited again. I had met Mrs. Sewall only once in my life, quite formally at a party of some sort at Edith's. We may have exchanged a half dozen words, not more. I had never been invited to her grand house, and most of my knowledge of the lady had come through hearsay, and the social columns in the papers. It was necessary to keep my mind pretty closely fastened on the cigarette spectacle, or else I might have lost courage, and quietly withdrawn before Mrs. Sewall appeared. She kept me waiting in torture for at least fifteen minutes (I can tell you the subject of every one of the engravings on the wall, I am sure) but the queer thing is, that when she finally joined me and I rose to speak, I forgot to be afraid. Will says that such an experience is very common with him in making an after-dinner speech.

"You don't know me, Mrs. Sewall," I began.

"I fear I do not," she replied, smiling formally. She was dressed very plainly, but elegantly too. Her iron-grey hair looked as if it were cut out of marble not a wisp astray; and you simply felt, so perfect was everything about her, that the nail of her little finger was as nicely pointed, polished, and pinked as all the rest.

"But your card," she went on, "your name sounds familiar."

Of course it did—she probably had seen it signed after Will's articles in the magazines, I thought—but I replied simply, "You met me before I was Mrs. William Ford Maynard—in Hilton—several years ago. My name was Lucy Vars."

I was quite prepared for the expression of hostility that crossed Mrs. Sewall's face at this remark.

"Vars," she repeated a little vaguely. "Oh, yes, I remember. There was, I believe, a Ruth Vars. Are you related?" Then as if she had forgotten it up to this time, she suddenly asked, "Won't you sit down?"

I thanked her and did so, she herself sinking into a voluminous tufted armchair opposite.

"I am Ruth Vars' sister," I explained, "and it is about Ruth and your son that I have come to talk with you."

Mrs. Sewall raised her brows.

"Your sister? My son? Really? How extraordinary!"

"Why, yes. You must know," I went on, "that your son is seeing a great deal of Ruth lately."

Mrs. Sewall smiled in a very patronising manner and replied, "It is very difficult for a mother to keep track of all a young man's fancies."

"This is more than a fancy, Mrs. Sewall. Ruth and your son are engaged to be married," I announced calmly.

A slight flush spread over Mrs. Sewall's face to the very roots of her marcel wave, but her voice showed no emotion when she spoke.

"Would it not have been more delicate to have allowed my son to have told me this piece of news," she asked me cuttingly.

"I was not thinking much about the delicacy of my call, I'm afraid."

"Evidently," she agreed.

"I have come simply to find out if you approve of this engagement and, if not, what we can do about it."

Mrs. Sewall looked me up and down deliberately, then:

"You seem to be a very courageous young person," she said, "but I fear this interview cannot alter my opinion. Your sister is no doubt a very charming young girl, but I have other ambitions for my son, Mrs. Maynard."

"I thought so. I guessed it from a conversation I overheard, and that is why I have come this morning. I thought we could work better together than alone."

"I plainly see," said Mrs. Sewall, gazing pityingly upon me, "that it will be necessary to be quite blunt with you. Did you never suspect that I closed Grassmere three years ago, simply to separate my son from your sister? As soon as I learned that my son actually intended to marry Miss Vars I was forced to take him to a different environment. When you consider that I have fought against this attachment for so long, you will see how absurd it is for you to hope to win my approval now, however bold your attempt."

"Oh," I flushed, "it isn't to win your approval that I am here. You have misunderstood me. It is to win, or rather to assure myself of your disapproval. You see I'm not in favour of the marriage either."

"You're not in favour of it?" Mrs. Sewall ejaculated.

"I'm not in favour of it," I repeated. "Ruth doesn't love your son. She's marrying for position—and I want to save her from such unhappiness. I don't want her to marry any one she doesn't love," I hastened to add.

"Well, well," Mrs. Sewall interrupted, "this is a novel experience for me. I wonder," she broke off in a sudden burst of friendliness, sarcasm and patronage gone from her voice, "I wonder I never discovered you in Hilton, Mrs. Maynard." Then she added with an amused twinkle in her eyes, "You are rather unlike your very enterprising sister-in-law, Mrs. Alexander Vars."

"Yes," I smiled, "perhaps a little. I have rather old-fashioned ideas on marriage, I suppose."

"I trust," Mrs. Sewall went on, "that you are sincere in saying you are opposed to this affair between your sister and my son."

"Sincere? Oh, yes, truly. Perfectly sincere." I blushed in spite of myself.

"I believe you—oh, I believe you," Mrs. Sewall reassured me quickly. "I know without your saying so that there may be other grounds why you object to your sister's engagement. You know," she smiled, "there is a different code of morals for every class of society that exists."

"I know," I murmured.

"But we won't go into that. It is sufficient that you *do* object. And now that we discover ourselves to be, instead of enemies, fellow soldiers, fighting together on the same side for the same cause, I am going to be very frank and tell you how low my ammunition is. I am powerless to do anything to influence this affair, I fear. A mother's wishes are of little account these days—my advice, my desires, not worth consideration. There are some things, I am learning, that I cannot control. A determined and hot-tempered young man in love with an ambitious girl, who sees wealth and position in her lover's proposals, is a combination beyond hope of breaking up."

"Oh, no, it isn't," I interrupted.

She shook her head.

"I have opposed and opposed. My son knows my hostile and bitter attitude toward the whole affair. It does not make the slightest dent upon his intentions. I have talked by the hour; I have cajoled; I have threatened; but to no avail. Mrs. Maynard, my son ought to marry a girl with money. His fortune is greatly overestimated, and until he ran across your sister again—oh, by the merest chance three months ago on Fifth Avenue—he was devoted to his cousin, Miss Gale Oliphant, whom you may have read about when she made her brilliant début last season. I heartily approve of such a match—appropriate in every way."

"Of course," I tucked in. "Why, Ruth has barely enough to buy her necessary clothes."

"Exactly," Mrs. Sewall sighed. "Oh, I don't know how it all will work out; I really don't know. At least your sister is a nice girl. My son might have chosen some one who wasn't educated or cultured—he has had so many fancies—and I shall have the satisfaction also, I suppose, of having avoided the notoriety of an elopement. My consent was forced from me, but it seemed the only way."

"Have you consented?" I asked alarmed.

"Reluctantly. Why, I could do nothing else. Breckenridge threatened a month ago that if I didn't consent he would elope with Miss Vars. At least, if the marriage *must* take place, it had better be decently. When he disappeared from home a week ago, I thought the worst had happened. I was so relieved when I placed my son at this hotel and found he was still single, that I decided to accept the inevitable with as much grace as possible now that I had been given a second opportunity. Breckenridge says your sister will marry him at any time if he but says the word, and he assures me he *will* say it unless my note of welcome reaches Miss Vars—to-morrow. So—" She shrugged her shoulders.

"That isn't true!" I replied. "Not a word of it! Ruth wouldn't elope for anything in the world. She's awfully proud, Mrs. Sewall. I ought not to have done it, but I listened to a private conversation between Ruth and your son. I heard Ruth say, when your son suggested a secret marriage, that the idea was absolutely insulting to her. She was awfully angry, and that was only last night at eleven o'clock."

"You heard her say that? Last night? You are sure?"

"Yes," I went on quickly, "and what is more I heard her say she would never marry Breck in this world till you accepted her publicly as his fiancée. It was when I heard that, that I decided to come and talk with you."

"Breckenridge has been misrepresenting the situation," Mrs. Sewall remarked.

"Ruth *is* ambitious," I went on. "Ruth *is* fond of wealth and position, but she's the proudest girl I ever knew. I thought if you understood how important a part *you* and your attitude played in the engagement, you could act accordingly. Ruth would break it off herself, if—it sounds awfully disloyal to her—but if you made the situation uncomfortable enough for her. I'm sure of it."

Mrs. Sewall got up and walked over to the little mahogany desk.

"I was afraid the maid had already mailed it," she exclaimed, holding up the little square envelope with Ruth's name and my address upon it. "It was a note of—" she smiled wryly—"of welcome to your sister. How fortunate," she added, "that you called just when you did. It throws a different light on the matter."

I remained with Mrs. Sewall until nearly twelve o'clock. We talked the situation threadbare before I left. I told her all I knew of Ruth's hopes and visions of the future. I repeated my sister's speech to Will of the peculiar demands of her temperament. I discussed her as freely as if she were a patient with important symptoms, and Mrs. Sewall the physician. I explained the situation in Hilton, Edith's influence upon Ruth, at what a high value my sister-in-law placed Mrs. Sewall's recognition, how persistently she preached the advantage of a connection by marriage. In the face of the force of Edith's influence, I pointed out Ruth's saving traits of pride and self-esteem. Ruth was as haughty as the highest. I enlarged on the absolute impossibility of an elopement as far as my high-spirited sister was concerned. Oh, I urged Ruth's humiliation as the only hope for success!

Before I left I had the satisfaction of seeing Mrs. Sewall tear up my sister's card of introduction to the Sewall family, and deposit the remains in the waste-basket. As I rose to go Mrs. Sewall took my hand in both of hers. Edith, I am sure, would have been surprised if she could have witnessed such intimacy between grand Mrs. F. Rockridge Sewall and Bobbikins.

"I am so glad you came," she said. "I owe you so much. I haven't entirely decided on my exact course, but if you later hear of my opening Grassmere, do not be surprised. There may be method in my madness."

"I'll leave it all with you," I reassured her. "Only I hope you won't make it any worse for Ruth than necessary."

"I won't, my dear; and by the way, sometime when you are in Hilton, will you let me know? Or by any chance in New York? After this we surely must be friends."

"Instead of connections?" I asked.

"You would be delightful as both," she laughed, and I bade her good-bye.

I felt like a traitor that night at dinner. Ruth never seemed sweeter. She had explained as she sat down to our evening meal that she was going to visit with Will and me alone that night. She was returning to Hilton in two days and she had told Breck that one evening at least, she intended to devote to her sister. I felt dreadfully guilty. But for me, her long-looked-for, much-coveted note of welcome from Mrs. Sewall would now be on its way to her; but for me, her bright visions of a social position being placed upon her head like a crown would have become a reality. I wished she wouldn't keep on piling coals of fire upon my head. She started in on her appreciation of my hospitality right after dinner. She said she would always remember her nice little breakfasts that I had served her in bed, whatever her future life might be (and she implied that it promised to be rather grand); she remarked she hoped I didn't believe all that she said to Will the first night she was with us; she assured me that my quiet and gracious acceptance of Breck had made an impression that she would never forget. She kissed me good-night of her own accord.

I told Will about my call on Mrs. Sewall as soon as we were safely in our room. I wanted to get the secret knowledge of it off my mind. I was beginning to feel a little apprehensive and doubtful. I really don't know what right I have to snatch Ruth's life away from her and treat it as if it were mine. But Will always reassures me.

"Well," he said, "if you do succeed in breaking off this disreputable affair, Lucy, I'll take off my hat to you, and so will Ruth—some day."

"Oh, do you think she will?" I asked relieved.

"Know it. My, but what a girl I did marry! You *do* take the bull by the horns. If you had had a son what a staver he would have been."

I forgot Ruth and her affairs in a twinkling.

I wilted like a flower plucked from its stem.

"You used to say that in the simple future, and now it's past subjunctive," I trembled.

Will laughed at me. "Don't like my tenses! What a particular person! Well, how's this? Here's a sentence in the simple present. It always has been present tense, always will be present." He leaned and whispered something in my ear.

"Pooh!" I scoffed, smiling for his sake. "That's too easy. It's the first tense of the first verb given in every grammar of every language in the world!"

CHAPTER XXIV

IT was five months later, sometime during the last of September, that I again heard directly from Ruth and her love-affair with Breckenridge Sewall.

Miss Kavenaugh, the dollar-and-a-half-a-day university seamstress, had come to help me with my muslin curtains. Miss Kavenaugh is a very much-sought-after lady, and when I am able to secure her for a day, I give up everything else, sit down and sew with her. She plans, cuts and bastes, and I run the chain-stitch machine like mad. We had been working since eight A. M. in my darling new bedroom that looks out on my row of late dahlias. I could hardly keep my eyes on the machine-needle because of the distracting flame of several maple-trees against some dark green cedars across the lake. Will and I had been in our new house about two weeks and we adored it! I was perched on the step-ladder at the particular moment the telephone bell rang, hanging the last muslin curtain in the room we called Ruth's. Miss Kavenaugh was puttering with the cretonne overhangings, pulling and patting them as tenderly as if they had been dainty dresses hung up on forms.

It was Ruth on the telephone calling me from town.

"I'm in here shopping," she said. "Can you possibly come in and have lunch? Do, if you can. I want to see you."

Now whenever Ruth did honour me with an invitation to luncheon it was in quite a different manner. To-day she actually asked me to set the hour and seemed inclined to adapt her plans to mine. I didn't want to leave Miss Kavenaugh in the least (she couldn't give me another day for a week), but if Ruth was as anxious to see me as all that, I decided I had better meet her if it broke a bone. I told her I would be at the appointed place at one-thirty.

Since June, Will and I had been buried in a little out-of-the-way spot in Newfoundland. The few letters that I had received had scarcely mentioned Ruth's affairs. Only one from my sister herself early in July had given me any inkling that Mrs. Sewall was acting on my suggestion. In that letter Ruth had briefly said that her engagement to Breck would probably not be announced till fall, and asked me to say nothing about the matter to any one. I was delighted not to.

Ruth was looking as pretty as ever, when I finally found myself sitting opposite to her at one of the side tables in the dining-room of the only hotel in town where she will condescend to eat. If she had anything of importance on her mind she certainly exhibited no outward agitation. She was dressed in a scant, tailor-made white serge suit, and had on a big, floppy, soft, fur-felt hat, which no other woman I know would have attempted to wear. It was lavender in shade and the brim drooped as if it had lost all its stiffening.

Around the crushed crown was tied a piece of hemp rope. I never saw a hat like it in any shop. Ruth is always discovering odd, outlandish "shapes" in the millinery line and trimming them up with things no one ever thought of putting on a hat before. This particular creation looked as if it had been blown on to Ruth's head, but I must say it had landed at just the right angle to reveal a bit of her pretty hair, and to frame her face in a halo of soft mauve.

"What shall we eat?" asked Ruth in a bored little way, and tossed me a menu. After we had decided on mock-turtle soup, sweet-breads a-la-something, little peas, and Waldorf salad (Ruth isn't the kind to pick up a ham-sandwich and cup of coffee at a lunch-counter, I can tell you) and the superior-looking waiter had departed, Ruth opened her shopping bag and tossed two dress samples down upon the white cloth.

"What do you think of these?" she asked nonchalantly.

I wondered if Ruth had dragged me all the way in town, occupied and busy as I had been at home, to show me dress samples. Always the psychological moment to share a confidence, or to announce a startling piece of news, is after the waiter has departed with your order. But Ruth took her own time.

"I'm trying a new tailor," she went on. "I've ordered the black-and-white stripe. It's very good in the piece. By the way, don't you prefer butter without salt? Waiter!" Ruth is very imperious when she is in a hotel. Clerks and maids and bell-boys simply fly to obey when Ruth gives an order. We were supplied with crescents, corn-muffins and slim brown-bread sandwiches, fresh butter, ice-water and two napkins apiece, before a man lunching alone at the next table could get his glass refilled.

It wasn't until we were well started on our elaborate menu, that Ruth thought best to gratify my curiosity. It was while she was pouring the tea, and after I had given up hope that she had anything thrilling to announce to me after all, that she asked, "Sugar, I believe?" and then as she dropped one little crystal cube into the cup added, "Oh, by the way, I've broken my engagement to Breck Sewall."

I didn't show a trace of wonder or surprise.

"Is that so?" I said, as if I didn't much care if she had, and then after I had taken a swallow of tea I asked, "How did that happen?"

"Oh, I simply decided to," Ruth replied shortly; and as if the subject were closed, she inquired, "How's the new house?"

I was simply aching to ask a few questions, but I didn't allow myself even one.

"Oh, it's very nice," I replied; "we've been in it two weeks now."

"How did the lavender room turn out?" asked Ruth, travelling away as fast as possible from the subject of her engagement.

"*Your* room, Ruth, you mean," I replied patiently. "Very well, I think."

"Is it finished yet? I mean could any one sleep in it—to-night?"

"Will you come home with me, Ruth?" I asked eagerly.

"I thought I might—possibly, if you'd like to have me, and if you have an empty bed. At least," she added, "I'm not going back to The Homestead."

"Oh, you're not!" I replied, vaguely wondering if it were the tailor who was keeping her or the manicurist. "Well, I can lend you a nightgown and you can buy a tooth-brush."

"Oh, my trunk is at the station," said Ruth. "I was determined to go somewhere. You see things are not very pleasant for me just now in Hilton. Besides, Edith and I have quarrelled."

It wasn't very charitable to rejoice at such an announcement; it wasn't very noble of me, I suppose, to delight that conditions at Hilton were too disagreeable for Ruth to remain there; but remember I had always wanted to shelter my sister—remember I had always been jealous of her loyalty and devotion to Edith, and remember, also, ever since the plans of our house had been put on paper, I had hoped and almost prayed that *some one* would wish to sleep in the southeast chamber.

I reached for a biscuit to help conceal my feelings.

"Well," I said steadily, "your room is ready, and you're free to use it or not, as you wish."

"It won't be for very long," apologised Ruth, "and perhaps I can help you settle. You mustn't let me be the least bother. I haven't forgotten, you know," she said smiling, "how to wipe dishes."

"Didn't there used to be a lot of them in the old days at home," I remarked.

"And wasn't I horrid?" she followed up in a sudden burst of generosity. "Wasn't I horrid about helping? I was never very nice to you, I'm afraid, Lucy."

"Of course you were!" I scoffed.

"Oh, I know I wasn't, but you used to be awfully rabid. It seems to me you've improved a great deal in that respect since you were married. I noticed it when I visited you last spring." She stopped a moment. Then, "I want to tell you," she went on, "that I think you were awfully decent about Breck Sewall.

You may not have liked him, but I appreciated your not trying to urge and influence me, the way Will did. If you had mixed yourself up in the affair too much I wouldn't feel like coming to you now."

I lowered my eyes as a hypocrite should.

"Of course not," I murmured ashamed.

Suddenly Ruth shoved her tea-cup to one side, her plate to the other, and folding her hands on the table in front, abruptly launched out into the midst of the details of her broken engagement.

"Edith," she began, "is willing to humiliate herself to any degree for the sake of a promotion in the social world. Now I'm too proud to stoop to some things. Edith actually advised me to marry Breck without Mrs. Sewall's approval. She said Mrs. Sewall would be sure to come around once the affair was settled. Could you imagine me in such a position?"

"Oh," I said, "didn't Mrs. Sewall approve?"

"Haven't you heard?" asked Ruth. "Every one else has. It has been anything but pleasant. When I wrote you that my engagement wouldn't be announced till fall it was simply because I hadn't heard from Mrs. Sewall. Breck said he hadn't told his mother and I believed him. She was ill or something, and I was willing to wait until it seemed wise to break the news to her. I was willing to meet her half-way, you see. I meant to be patient with Mrs. Sewall. Of course I realise I have no money nor position; but I won't be insulted by any one! She opened Grassmere in August, and brought along with her a young niece of hers, a Miss Oliphant—a silly creature, I thought; and she set in entertaining for her as she's never entertained before. Hilton has never been so gay, and everyone who was within the range of possibility was invited to Grassmere—everybody except Edith and me. Think of it! Think of the insult! It was the most pointed thing you ever saw. Edith is simply furious. Mrs. Sewall avoids her everywhere she sees her, and me too for that matter. *I* don't mind so much. It is Edith whom it stings so. *I* simply long for a chance to cut Mrs. Sewall. That's *my* attitude. However I don't enjoy being gossiped about, and all Hilton is buzzing. Oh, it's horrid!"

"I should say so," I murmured, stunned by the disaster I had caused.

"Well, during it all Breck has kept right on coming to see me—late every night after his social engagements at Grassmere. That was the feature I hated most, and the one that Edith, on the other hand, clung to as our only hope of salvation. But I'm not the kind to become the secret fancy of any man, even if he is the King of England. If I'm not good enough for his mother to recognise, then I don't want anything of him. Anyhow I consider myself, from the point of view of culture and education, superior to the Sewalls!"

"Of course," I agreed.

"The whole thing has made me sick and tired of the social game," ejaculated Ruth. "I don't believe there's any such thing as pure, unadulterated friendship between people who are socially ambitious. Why, some of the girls, who I thought were my best friends, have been acting very cool and offish since they've observed Mrs. Sewall's attitude towards me. And both Edith and I are omitted from lots of other people's parties besides the Sewalls, simply because Mrs. Sewall and Miss Oliphant are often the guests of honour. Oh, I think that all women are vain and selfish and insincere, and, if sometimes they *appear* thoughtful or sacrificing, it's simply because such an attitude toward someone will help them up another rung on the ladder. I'd like to get away from society for a while. It almost seems," Ruth added vehemently, "as if I'd like to enter a convent!"

"Oh, I'm awfully sorry, Ruth," I began.

"There's nothing for *you* to be sorry about. You couldn't help it. If I only had more money," Ruth went on, "I'd travel. I'd escape this sort of life. But what can any one do on my income? Eight hundred dollars! And I won't take any more from Edith."

"Did you quarrel very badly?" I dared to ask.

"Oh, quite. She went into an awful passion when I told her that I'd broken the engagement. She called me a short-sighted little fool! Breck, you see, wanted me to marry him in spite of his mother. Imagine me eloping! I wouldn't do such a vulgar thing. Edith said that her mother had run off with her father (imagine comparing me to that impossible Mrs. Campbell!) and that if I didn't marry Breck everybody would think *he* had gotten tired of *me*—cast me off, and all that sort of thing. I don't get angry often, but I gave Edith a piece of my mind that I guess she'll remember for a long time, and Alec didn't like it a bit. So this morning I just decided to decamp."

"But of course Breck will follow you," I suggested cheerfully.

"Oh, no, he won't. I've quarrelled with him too." Ruth smiled. "I seem to have quarrelled with everybody. But Breck threatened, and threats never have the least effect on me. He really did want to marry me, in spite of what people said about his marked attentions to this Oliphant girl. He was crazy to marry me. Things got to an awful pitch of excitement and one night three days ago, he said that if I wouldn't run off with him in the dark like some common girl in a newspaper story, and get married by a country parson along the road somewhere, he wasn't going to spend any more of his time waiting around. He said that Gale—that's Miss Oliphant—would marry him, mother or no mother; she had some heart and feeling in her. I told him that *I* on the other hand wouldn't lower my self-respect one iota, for love, or position, or any other reason. And so ... well, here I am, with all my bridges burned. By the way," Ruth broke off, "please don't ask me to discuss this matter with Will. He was too intolerant last spring for me to care to talk it over with him now."

"You needn't mention it to him," I assured her.

"You can imagine," said Ruth, "that I'm not feeling very much like talking about it to any one."

"I understand, and we won't refer to it at all. I know how hard it is, Ruth,—but time—"

"Oh, time!" replied my sophisticated sister. "There's no scar on my heart for time to heal. You see now, don't you, how safe it is to keep such affairs strictly in the region of one's head."

Two or three weeks later I received a letter from Mrs. Sewall. I didn't know her writing but I saw Grassmere engraved on the envelope, so I suspected before I broke the seal.

"*My dear Mrs. Maynard,*

"You will be interested to know that the engagement of Miss Gale Oliphant to my son is to be publicly announced on Wednesday next. But for you I am afraid this very happy alliance might not have been arranged. Relying absolutely on what you told me I could expect from your sister I have acted on your suggestion, with these results. I was sorry to treat so lovely a girl as your sister seems to be in so cruel a manner, but such an object-lesson seemed to me the most effectual way of showing what a future relation with me might prove to be. Let me say I think she is a very fine-principled and high-minded girl, and another season when I shall return to Grassmere with my son and his bride I trust I may see a great deal of her. Another season I hope I may set everything right with Mrs. Alexander Vars also, whom it seemed necessary to sacrifice for a little while to our cause, if, in fact, I cannot do something toward reparation this year in the few weeks left before I return to New York. Let me add with all heartiness that I am particularly anticipating the pleasure of entertaining, sometime soon, an old fellow-soldier of mine.

"Sincerely,
"FRANCES ROCKRIDGE SEWALL."

"Take off your hat," I said to my husband late that night. "You promised you would. The engagement is broken. Breck Sewall is going to marry his cousin, and Ruth is in bed in the southeast chamber."

During the weeks immediately following Ruth's decision in regard to Breck Sewall, she became an absorbingly interesting proposition, to herself. For the first month she wouldn't show any interest in anything outside her own problem. Ruth has admirers where-ever she goes and under any circumstances; and as soon as it was learned that she was staying with me the telephone began to ring every day—the door-bell every night or so with would-be suitors. But Ruth wouldn't see any of her callers or accept any invitations. She assumed such a blasé and indifferent attitude toward life that it worried me. She used to take long walks alone over the hills and improvise by the hour by firelight in our living-room. Evenings after dinner she spent in her own room reading Marcus Aurelius, Omar Khayyam, Oscar Wilde and Marie Bashkirtseff. I used to find the books missing from the book-shelves, and discover them on the couch in Ruth's room later. A drop-light arranged on a small table by the head of the couch, a soft down quilt wrapped around a china-silk negligee, and Ruth nestled down inside of all that, was the picture to which Will and I always sang out good-night when we closed our door at ten P.M. She used to devote several hours a day to writing, but whether it was a novel or an epic poem that she was so busy about, I didn't know. She kept her papers safely locked away in her trunk and I didn't like to intrude on her intimacy. I think Ruth rather enjoyed herself during these first days after the settlement of her affair with Breck. Her newly-won independence, her freedom, brought about entirely by her own will and volition, filled her with a little self-admiration. She appealed to herself as rather an unique and remarkable young person, bearing the interesting distinction of a broken engagement. She was young and fresh and lovely, and belonged to no one; her future lay in her own hands; she didn't know what she should do with it, but it was hers—hers alone, and full of all sorts of exciting possibilities.

"I don't want to see anything more of men for a long time," she would say. "I haven't decided yet what I'm going to go into, but I want to *do* something. I want to see all sides of life. I have had enough of society and bridge and silly girls who only want to get married. I'm seriously considering settlement work in New York. Sometime I'd like to go to Paris and study sculpture."

At the end of Ruth's third week with us—one Saturday night, I believe it was—the door-bell rang about eight o'clock. The maid answered it and when she came upstairs and passed by the door of Will's study (which is a little room over the front door and where we sit evenings) I said with a sigh of relief, "Thank goodness, it's for Ruth. I did want to finish this ruffle." And a moment later I added, "I wonder what excuse she'll send down to-night."

I was surprised five minutes later by Ruth's appearance in the doorway. She had put on a favourite gown of hers—crow-black meteor satin, so plain it had kind of a naked appearance, with a V-shaped neck that showed a bit of Ruth's throat. There wasn't a scrap of any kind of trimming on it.

"Will you hook this up please?" she asked, and when I had finished, "Thanks," she said, and with no explanation went downstairs.

"I wonder who it can be!" I exclaimed after she had departed. "It's the first one she has seen."

Will looked up and smiled.

"Oh, it's just a *man*. Rest assured that this pose of Ruth's can't last much longer. Three weeks of a diet that excludes all forms of masculine admiration is a long fast for Ruth. They'll be calling here thick and fast now."

But it wasn't just a man! About nine-thirty I stole down the back stairs to get two pieces of chocolate cake and two glasses of milk for Will and me. I peeked into the front hall before crawling back again.

"Will," I said two minutes later, "leaning up against the Chippendale chair in the hall is a man's walking-stick and it has got a plain silver top like Bob Jennings'. I introduced Bob to Ruth last week at a Faculty Tea and he walked home with her, before I was ready to leave. It does seem odd that he didn't send cards up to us too, doesn't it?"

It was almost eleven o'clock before I heard the front door close and Ruth snapping off the lights in the living-room. Will was staying up late to-night, and I had put on a soft wrapper and curled up in the Morris-chair with a magazine. The door was slightly ajar, and as Ruth passed it on her way to bed she stopped just outside, and asked softly:

"Are you both still up?"

"Surely," I replied. "Come in."

She came over and stood by the table where Will was working.

"Can you be torn away from your precious books for a while, Will?" she asked sweetly.

"Of course I can," he replied.

"Because," Ruth went on, "I want to tell you something." She paused.

"Yes?" encouraged Will. "Fire away."

"I suppose," Ruth continued, "you two are wondering when I am going home. I've been here nearly a month now and I ought to decide what I am going to do. I'd like your advice if you're not too busy."

"Certainly I'm not," Will responded heartily.

Ruth can be very complimentary and deferential when she chooses. She chose so to be now. Will closed his books. Ruth was standing by the table; her tapering finger-tips just reached the mahogany surface, she leaned lightly on them; her face was in the shadow, for the only light was Will's low reading-lamp, and her arms suddenly appearing out of the dark were startlingly white and pretty.

"It was Mr. Jennings who called to-night," she went on. "I saw him because he rather interested me last week when I met him at one of your Faculty Teas. I was talking with him to-night a little about my life. It came in after I had read him a few of my verses, which he said he would be kind enough to give me his opinion about, when I told him last week that I wrote a little. He suggested a plan that rather appealed to me. I don't know what you think of it, but he says that there are a lot of girls who take special courses here at Shirley (Shirley is the girls' college connected with the university) and that, even though I'm not a college girl, he thinks he could arrange for me to take a course or two in poetry and literature. He wants me to develop my talent. Oh, I'd love to do it!" Ruth exclaimed, suddenly enthusiastic. "Mr. Jennings is *so* encouraging! He thinks I really might write something worth while some day. I've always thought that poetry was the very highest form of expression. Mr. Jennings thinks so too. He says, Lucy, that you attend certain courses connected with the university that would be excellent for me. He says that I could go to some of those afternoons with you perhaps. He's going to get the Shirley catalogue and lay out a course of study for me. Do you suppose, Will, that you could find a place for me to room somewhere around here?"

"To room, Ruth? Why, we should want you to stay right here with us," I exploded.

"Oh, of course," Ruth scoffed, "I couldn't break in on you and Will that way."

"But, Ruth," I began.

"Oh, no, Lucy, I wouldn't do that. I've been fifth wheel at The Homestead for years, but I don't intend to be here."

"Nonsense," said Will; "we'd like to have you. Lucy spent a lot of time preparing that room you're in and—"

"No. Please. I shan't listen. Why, you haven't even talked it over. Wait till morning anyway. I simply came in to ask your advice on my turning into a 'blue-stocking.' Do you think it absolutely ridiculous?"

We thought it was splendid—both Will and I. We talked and planned and built air-castles with Ruth till after midnight. She even read us some of her pretty verses and before she went to bed at one A. M. she had already become a poetess of renown with contributions appearing frequently in the most exclusive magazines.

A new-found genius slept in the southeast chamber that night, and at seven A. M. when the sun and I crawled into her room together we found her fast asleep with one hand tucked cosily under her cheek. Her hair, which is neither blonde nor brown but kind of a dull mouse-colour and almost mauve when she wears the right shade, was braided and flung up back over the pillow. Upon the pillow beside her lay her left hand upturned and free from jewellery of any kind. That upturned hand had kind of an appealing, wistful expression about it that made me want to cry. Somehow the sight of Ruth's bare unpromised hand making the only dent on the surface of the pillow by her side filled me with a wave of thanksgiving. She breathed softly, regularly, her violet-tinted eyelids quivering a little, a half-smile lingering in the corners of her mouth. A fly lit on Ruth's chin and, unmolested, walked audaciously up along the flushed, velvety surface of her cheek. It stopped just beneath her long-curved eyelashes. She didn't stir—just kept on with her even, measured breathing and her steady sleep. I frightened that bold creature away with a wave of my hand. I honestly believe that Breck Sewall hadn't disturbed my sister any more than the fly on her cheek. She seemed to me the most superbly virginal creature I had ever gazed upon.

I sat down and touched her shoulder softly.

"It's morning," I said, and when she was entirely awake I continued, "It's morning, and you wanted us to wait till morning. We've talked it all over together alone and we both still want you to stay with us as long as you possibly can. Why, Ruth, we built this room for *you*—especially for *you*—and I do hope you'll like it well enough to stay."

"It's prettier than my room at Edith's," replied Ruth. Then suddenly she put out her hand and touched my knee. "Lucy," she said, "I'm *crazy* to stay. I'd *hate* a stuffy boarding-house."

"Of course you would!"

"This is so adorably fresh and clean and simple. Have you and Will really talked it all over? I think I ought not to stay, but I'll promise not to be the least bother in the world."

"Bother!" I exclaimed.

"I'll be busy with my studies daytimes and keep out of the way evenings. Really," she asked, "do you want me?"

"We really do," I said solemnly.

She turned and suddenly sat up beside me on the edge of the bed. She was a lovely creature with her long thick hair, her white arms, and her pretty, soft, beribboned nightgown falling off one shoulder. She seemed too lovely to be my sister. She flung one arm around my shoulders.

"Lucy," she exclaimed, "from this time on, I'm going to be nice to you."

I don't remember that Ruth had ever before put her arm around me of her own accord. A lump came in my throat. Tears blinded me. I got up hastily and began putting down the windows.

CHAPTER XXV

IF you want to know what became of Ruth I'll tell you—I'll tell you right off. She fell in love with Bob Jennings. She fell awfully in love with him—absorbingly, overwhelmingly in love. Ruth, the lofty, the high, the pedestalled! Ruth who prided herself on her coolness and her circumspection, Ruth who boasted that fate had foreordained a brilliant marriage, lost her head over a young college instructor who taught English composition to freshmen and sophomores, at a salary something less than three thousand a year. It simply proves that the eternal feminine will crop out, however much it has been choked and blighted, just like a dry bulb that's been kept in a damp dark cellar all winter. Once you put it in the sun and warmth, and give it a little water, it just can't help but grow up bright and green—brilliant rank green, full of juicy stalks and buds. Why, Ruth got to be such a normal sort of girl that she blushed every time Bob's name was mentioned. Ruth the invulnerable! She even lost her appetite—of all ordinary things—and great circles appeared under her eyes. The most astounding feature to me was that Ruth fell in love before she was asked to. Imagine that if you can. Ruth the haughty! The bulb began to send out shoots like a common onion or potato, before invited by the sun. Things came to such a pass that Will finally touched on the delicate subject with Bob. We thought the man must be blind, crazy or heartless, not to have seen the tell-tale symptoms in Ruth's manner long before circles began to appear. But Will found that Bob was simply penniless. This university pays salaries about large enough to keep two canaries alive, and Bob told Will that though he had loved Ruth ever since the day he first saw her, he couldn't say a word to her about it, because he already had a mother quite alone and dependent living with him, besides a sister he was trying to put through college, and he knew Ruth was a girl who had been used to luxuries.

Bob is a kind of dreamy sort of man. He says the simplest things in a way that thrills you. His letters, even his notes accepting dinner invitations (and such are the only kind I have ever received) have a kind of "way" with them—exclamation points here and there, single words, capitalised and perioded, to express a whole sentence. Oh, Bob is awfully individual; but he'll never be rich. He's a teacher, in the first place; and in the second, he hasn't a father with a fortune. When I realised that Ruth loved Bob Jennings, I was worried about those demands of that temperament of hers—the soft-footed, unobtrusive servants, the exquisite china, the fine lace, the dinners perfectly served, all those expensive things that Bob couldn't supply in a lifetime. If only Bob had had Breck's fortune, or Breck had had Bob's poetic soul, everything would have been all right; for I am sure Ruth would have eloped with Bob Jennings the first time he asked her.

I realised that Ruth was thinking seriously about Bob Jennings when she began inquiring of Will about the salaries of instructors at the university. Later she asked me how much rents were, in this section of the country. She was perfectly aware from the very beginning that Bob earned just about enough to afford an apartment the size of Oliver's and Madge's, which she had formerly pronounced "cunning" but "impossible." If Ruth, as she boasted, confined matrimonial questions to the region of her head she ought to have sent Bob on his way the very instant that she learned these salient facts about him. But she didn't. She kept right on seeing him, night after night, as if he were a millionaire who could supply her every desire by merely dashing off his signature. She kept on reading her poetry with him, discussing art and literature by the hour, and quoting him to me all the next day as if he were an authority. Ruth simply lost her equilibrium over Bob. I don't believe she had ever seen a man like him before. He certainly is different from Breck Sewall, packed with sentiment, full impressions and delicate sensibilities. I overheard him talking with Ruth about women smoking once. He said you might as well deface a beautiful picture by painting cigarettes in the angels' mouths. I suppose it might have been the fact of being classed with the angels that "took" Ruth so. Anyhow she wanted Bob for her own, salary or no salary; she wanted him so badly that we couldn't even joke on the subject in her presence. By Christmas-time the situation was tragic.

The quarrel with Edith, as all quarrels with Edith are sure to be, had been of short duration. The fact that Mrs. Sewall had invited her to assist at a tea before her final departure from Hilton had assuaged her grievances somewhat in that quarter. Moreover a startling piece of news in the New York papers in early December, ten days before the Oliphant-Sewall wedding was to take place, had vindicated Ruth's course of action even in Edith's eyes, beyond a shadow of doubt. It seems that there was already a Mrs. Breckenridge Sewall. Breck had, after all, been more decent than Will thought. He had married the girl whom he had known in college, and it was she who was now bringing suit against the groom-to-be. So as there existed nothing but kindly feelings between Edith and Ruth now, there was no reason why Ruth should not have spent the holidays in Hilton, but she simply wouldn't give up a single hour with Bob Jennings. He always came Tuesdays, Thursdays, Saturdays and Sundays. Our electric-light bill, dim as Ruth prefers the room to be, was a dollar extra a month, after Bob began to call.

I was glad to have Ruth with me during the Christmas vacation. Otherwise I should have been all alone. Early in December Will had gone to a medical conference of some kind in Chicago, and just as he was about to start for home, some big physician out there called him in, in consultation, on the case of a little boy, who had some awful thing the matter with his spine. He was the son of a millionaire, and experts and specialists from all over the country had given up hope of recovery. The father was just about crazy and when Will suggested some radical treatment of his own which he had tried out successfully on one of our little guinea-pigs, he wrote that that father simply clung to him bodily, got hold of him with his hands and told him he could have every cent of money that he possessed in the world if he'd only give him back his son. So Will stayed. He would have stayed if the man had been a pauper, if he'd loved his little boy like that. You see it is just the way Will would feel about *his* son. He understood. I wanted him to stay too. I was only sorry that, after all the long nights he had to sit up by the little chap's bed (for first there was an operation before Will began his treatment; and Will wouldn't leave much to the nurses), after the weary nights, the doubtful dawns, the long uncertain journey to the day of the crisis, I was only sorry that Will couldn't bring the little boy he saved home with him (if he saved him) for ours to keep and love. He fought for the life of that child. He wanted it to live awfully; and I, hundreds of miles away, would wake often in the night during the long struggle—at three, at four, at seven when it grows light—and wonder, and hope, and, I suppose you'd call it, pray.

It was just before Christmas that my dread and fear about that little boy's life in Chicago became intermingled with a thrilling hope that was very much nearer home. My startling realisation came so unexpectedly to me after all the waiting, so undreamed, so miraculously a gift of heaven, that I couldn't believe at first that there was any real substantial fact about it. I couldn't, or I wouldn't, I don't know which. I dreaded disappointment. But oh, the mere possibility of such a joy being mine at last, made me so happy that I couldn't help but show a jubilant spirit in my letters. I wrote to Will that somehow, suddenly, I felt that that little boy out there was going to get well; I'd been as doubtful as he last week, but now, unaccountably, I was sure that the dear little fellow was going to live to grow up. I didn't tell Will *why* I felt so (it was such a silly woman's reason) but I kept on writing it over and over again, every day, as I woke each morning with the reassurance that the thing I wanted more than anything in the world was coming true.

I never thought I was superstitious, but you know how over-particular and over-careful you are about anything that's awfully important. Your anxiety borders on superstition before you know it, and when somebody accuses you, you simply don't care, you're so eager to have everything propitious. Well, I somehow got to believing that that child's life in Chicago that Will was striving so hard to save and the life of my hidden joy had something to do with each other. The idea obsessed me; I couldn't get it out of my head, fanatical and ridiculous as I knew a sensible person would call it, and I kept writing to Will as if that millionaire's son were mine. Will said it was a good thing that he wasn't a practising physician if I took his cases so much to heart as all that; but, just the same, he told me that my letters did fill him with hope and courage.

All during this period, while Ruth was eating out her soul for Bob, and Will was eating out his soul for the little sick boy, and I was eating out my soul for a gift I'd have died to possess for a day, no one would have guessed from Ruth's and my pleasant good-mornings, our casual calm and undisturbed conversations at meal-time, and Will's cheerful paragraphs, that we were all living through crises. Ruth and I with our anxieties grew very near to each other at this time. She was a lot of comfort to me and I tried to appreciate the feelings of a proud girl in love with a man who has not spoken. During the evenings that Bob called I sat up alone in Will's study, embroidering a centrepiece for the dining-room table. Evening after evening my fingers fairly ached to get out the rustling tissue paper patterns that Madge had left. But I wouldn't let myself—I wasn't going to be heart-broken—I wouldn't let myself put a needle to a single bit of nainsook.

It was on Saturday, January fifteenth, at ten o'clock at night, that Will's special delivery letter came. My fingers trembled as they tore at the envelope. I closed the study door to be alone. "If the little boy has died," I said out loud, "I mustn't be superstitious. I simply mustn't." But oh, he hadn't died! He hadn't died! Will's letter was one triumphant song from beginning to end. The little boy had passed the crisis; he was going to live; and live strong and well and normal. The miracle had been performed; the serum had done its magic part; there had been just the response that Will had dared to rely on; everything had been gloriously successful; and he was coming home in five days!

I let myself be just as superstitious then as I wanted. I had said if that little sick boy lived, so would my hopes, and I believed it. I lit a candle and went up into the unfinished part of our attic where there is a lot of old furniture packed away. It's rather a spooky place in the dark, and cold too, but I didn't notice it to-night. 'Way over in the corner stood the little old-fashioned cradle that belonged to Will's mother—one of those low, wooden-hooded ones with rockers, that you can rock with one foot. I had always planned to use that. It's so quaint and dear and old-fashioned. In the cradle in a green pasteboard box was a whole bundle of Will's baby-clothes—the queerest, finest little hand-made muslin shirts, and dresses with a lot of stiff embroidery and ruffles.

I had no idea what time it was when later I heard Ruth calling me from below.

"Lucy, Lucy! Are you up there?"

"Yes," I answered. "What time is it?"

"Why, it's after midnight! *What* are you doing?"

"Oh, looking up some old stuff. I'll be right down."

I met her on the stairs. I felt guilty. I was afraid that joy was written all over my face. I might as well have just left the arms of a lover.

"Oh, Ruth," I exclaimed, "isn't it *fine*? That little boy in Chicago is going to live! I've had a special delivery from Will. Isn't it *great*? He's going to get well!"

"That's splendid," said Ruth, and then, eyes sparkling, voice trembling, she exploded, "Oh, Lucy, Bob has just gone! We're engaged!"

I blew out the candle for safety's sake, and put my arms about my sister.

"Really, Ruth?" I exclaimed, and we sat down side by side on the dark stairs.

"He's cared for me all along, *all* the fall—*all this time*! Of course we both couldn't help but know it! But Bob—he's just that honourable he wouldn't say a word till he told me all about his circumstances and—everything. Circumstances! Oh, dear, I—What do you think of Bob, Lucy?" she broke off.

"I've always said that, next to Will, I'd rather marry Bob than any man I've known," I replied heartily.

"And does Will like him?" quivered Ruth.

"Will calls Bob the salt of the earth. *Everybody* likes Bob Jennings, Ruth!"

"I know they do. I know it. I don't see how I ever got him. You know all the men in his classes simply adore him! His courses are awfully popular. He's going to have juniors and seniors next year. The President stopped Bob the other day in the street and complimented him on his work. Oh, Bob is going to go right to the top! And he isn't a bit spoiled. His dear old silver-haired mother worships him just like everybody else. Do you know, Bob was afraid I wouldn't want her to live with us—she's the loveliest old lady—of course I do! And he thought, besides, I'd hate an apartment and one maid. But he didn't know me. My nature isn't the kind that requires 'Things.' If it didn't have sympathy and understanding and inspiration, it's the kind that would simply shrivel up and die. But Bob, he responds in just the right way, to every side of my temperament. It's wonderful!"

"Isn't it?" I agreed. "Why, we're all happy to-night! Will because of the little boy, and you because of Bob, and I because—" I hesitated just a moment, and then in the pitch-dark of the back stairs I confided to Ruth, "because the southeast chamber has a waiting-list."

"A waiting-list?" queried Ruth.

"Yes, I was upstairs when you called, seeing if Will's little old-fashioned mahogany cradle would do."

"Oh, really!" said Ruth not very much impressed after all. "Of course. My room *was* meant to be the nursery. I remember now. Well, I suppose you're glad, and there'll be a vacancy all right for some one to fill in June. We're going to be married right after Commencement. We've got it all planned. Isn't it exciting?" she exclaimed, eager on the trail of her own happiness. "We're not going to Europe, or anything grand like that. We're going to begin by saving. With my eight hundred a year and Bob's salary, and a little he has besides, our income will be about four thousand. We're going to have a lovely honeymoon! Bob likes the word 'honeymoon' though no one uses it now. Bob's so funny! We're going to camp out all alone for a whole month on a little lake we know about in the Adirondacks and I'm going to cook while he cuts wood. Bob didn't know I could cook. Why, he was awfully surprised when he discovered how practical I am, and that I trim all my own hats even now. Lucy, don't you think that Bob's *awfully* nice-looking?" she asked and pressed my hand.

"Yes I do. I've always told Will that Bob was the best-looking man on the faculty," I replied and pressed back.

An hour later we groped down the stairs together. It was two o'clock in the morning. The light in the study was still going and I went in and turned it off.

At my door Ruth begged, "Come on into my bed, Lucy. I shall never be able to get to sleep to-night."

"All right. In five minutes," I agreed.

When I went into Ruth's room she was sitting by the window ready for bed, her long hair braided, and a knitted worsted shawl wrapped around her white shoulders.

"Well, Ruth, it's half-past two," I said.

"Bob's coming at nine o'clock, before his first recitation," remarked Ruth dreamily. "That's six hours, isn't it?"

"And a half," I smiled.

"Oh, Lucy," suddenly exclaimed Ruth, standing up before me, "I'm terribly happy!"

"Are you? Well, so am I!" I replied.

"It just seems as if I'd have to open a window and let off steam somehow!" said Ruth.

"Well, let's!" said I.

THE END

CPSIA information can be obtained
at www.ICGtesting.com
Printed in the USA
LVHW050004031121
702257LV00007B/541